BROTHERS
WE ARE NOT
PROFESSIONALS
A PLEA TO PASTORS FOR RADICAL MINISTRY
JOHN PIPER

MENTOR

Unless otherwise indicated, all Scripture quotations are from *The Holy Bible, English Standard Version*, copyright © 2001 by Crossway Bibles, a division of Good News Publishers. Used by permission. All rights reserved.

Others translations are indicated by acronym as follows: KJV, *King James Version*. NASB, the *New American Standard Bible*, © the Lockman Foundation, 1960, 1962, 1963, 1968, 1971, 1972, 1973, 1975, 1977; used by permission. NIV, *New International Version*, © copyright 1973, 1978, 1984. RSV, *Revised Standard Version* of the Bible, copyrighted 1946, 1952, © 1971, 1973. Quotations indicated JP are the author's own translations. Italic in Biblical text is added by the author for emphasis.

© John Piper
ISBN 978-1-85792-893-8

Published in 2003,
reprinted in 2004, 2008 & 2011
in the
Mentor Imprint
by
Christian Focus Publications Ltd,
Geanies House, Fearn,
Ross-shire, IV20 1TW,
Great Britain
by permission of
Broadman & Holman Publishers,
Nashville, Tennessee

www.christianfocus.com

Cover design by Alister MacInnes

Printed by Bell & Bain, Glasgow

FSC
www.fsc.org

MIX
Paper from
responsible sources
FSC® C007785

BROTHERS
WE ARE NOT
PROFESSIONALS

JOHN PIPER

DEDICATION

———————————■———————————

To
George Verwer
and
Greg Livingstone

whose passion and perseverance in the pursuit
of the unreached peoples of the world
have pushed me toward radical commitment
to the global purposes of Jesus Christ
on the other side of
pastoral professionalism

CONTENTS

PREFACE

SOMETIMES MASSIVE suffering comes so close to home that for a brief season the fog of our foolish security clears, and we can see the sheer precipice of eternity one step away. The cold wobble passes through our thighs, and for a moment everything in the universe looks different. Those are good times for pastoral realism. Oh, how hollow much of our lives and ministry seem in those moments! The last thing we regret then is being less professional.

The beginning of the twenty-first century is a good time to be a pastor, a time full of uncertainty and danger. The political and religious atmosphere of the world pushes us—if we have ears to hear—relentlessly toward the unprofessional center of faith and ministry: the brutal, bloody, hideous, heaving, crucified God-Man Jesus Christ. We are driven more and more in these years to say with the apostle Paul, "I decided to know nothing among you except Jesus Christ and him crucified. . . . Far be it from me to boast except in the cross of our Lord Jesus Christ, by which the world has been crucified to me, and I to the world" (1 Cor. 2:2; Gal. 6:14).

Insulated Western Christianity is waking from the dreamworld that being a Christian is normal or safe. More and more, true Christianity is becoming what it was at the beginning: foolish and dangerous. "We preach Christ crucified, a stumbling block to Jews and folly to Gentiles" (1 Cor. 1:23). "The hour is coming when whoever kills you will think he is offering service to God" (John 16:2).

The rise of radical Islam simply intensifies the ever-present truth: preaching Christ crucified ruins professional pastoral politeness and wakens us to the wreckage of relativistic pluralism.

Professional harmony shatters on the rocks of Golgotha. Professional peacekeepers rush to the podium to announce the common ground of monotheism and everybody's high regard for the prophet Jesus. But "they have healed the wound of my people lightly, saying, 'Peace, peace,' when there is no peace" (Jer. 6:14). Real pastors know differently and love their people better. They do not nullify the grace of God by minimizing the centrality of the cross. The all-important, and pervasively rejected, truth is this: "[He] was delivered up [to death] for our trespasses and raised for our justification" (Rom. 4:25).

This is precisely what Islam denies. Thus one Sunni Muslim says, "Muslims believe that Allah saved the Messiah from the ignominy of crucifixion much as Allah saved the Seal of the Prophets from ignominy following *Hijra*."[1] And another adds, "We honor him [Jesus] more than you do. . . . Do we not honor him more than you do when we refuse to believe that God would permit him to suffer death on the cross? Rather, we believe that God took him to heaven."[2] The issue is *not* whether Islam is monotheistic. The issue is *not* whether Islam tries to honor Jesus. The issue is: Does Islam— or any other faith besides Christianity—cherish the crucifixion of the God-Man, Jesus Christ, as the only ground of our acceptance with God? The answer is no. Only Christians "follow the Lamb"

1. Badru D. Kateregga and David W. Shenk, *Islam and Christianity: A Muslim and a Christian in Dialogue* (Nairobi: Usima Press, 1980), 141. *Hijra* refers to the flight of Muhammad from Mecca in A.D. 622. It is derived from Arabic *hijrah*, literally, flight. The portion of the Koran that provides the basis for this denial of the crucifixion and resurrection says, "And for their [the Jews'] saying: 'We slew the Messiah, Jesus son of Mary, the Messenger of God'—yet they did not slay him, neither crucified him, only a likeness of that [*shubiha lahum*] was shown to them. Those regarding him; they have no knowledge of him, except the following of surmise; and they slew him not of a certainty—no indeed; God raised him up to Him; God is All-mighty, All-wise" (4:157/156–57). Quoted from, J. Dudley Woodberry, editor, *Muslims and Christians on the Emmaus Road* (Monrovia, Calif.: MARC, 1989), 165.

2. Quoted from a 1951 article in *The Muslim World* in J. Dudley Woodberry, ed., *Muslims and Christians on the Emmaus Road*, 164. Similar things were being said by Muslim clerics in the early years of this century as well, "We believe in Jesus; more than you do, in fact."

who was "slain" as the one and only Redeemer who sits on the "throne" of God (Rev. 14:4; 5:6; 7:17).

In other words, the center of Christianity and the center of pastoral life is the dishonorable, foolish, gruesome, and utterly glorious reality of the tortured God-Man, Jesus Christ. More and more, He must become the issue. Not a vague, comfortable, pleasant Jesus that everybody likes but the one who is a "stumbling block" to Jews and "foolishness" to Gentiles. The closer you get to what makes Christianity ghastly, the closer you get to what makes it glorious. "I do not nullify the grace of God, for if justification were through the law, then Christ died for no purpose" (Gal. 2:21). No gore, no grace, no glory. All religions that deny the cross nullify the grace of God and lead people to perpetual ruin. Preaching that truth ill-fits today's professionalism.

Beware of replacing real truth-based tolerance with spurious professional tolerance. Once upon a time tolerance was the power that kept lovers of competing faiths from killing each other. It was the principle that put freedom above forced conversion. It was rooted in the truth that coerced conviction is no conviction. That is true tolerance. But now the new professional tolerance denies that there *are* any competing faiths; they only complement each other. It denounces not only the effort to *force* conversions but also the idea that any conversion may be necessary. It holds the conviction that no religious conviction should claim superiority over another. In this way, peaceful parity among professionals can remain intact, and none need be persecuted for the stumbling block of the cross (Gal. 5:11).[3]

The aim of this book is to spread a radical, pastoral passion for the supremacy and centrality of the crucified and risen God-Man, Jesus Christ, in every sphere of life and ministry and culture. Increasingly, a

3. This paragraph is adapted from John Piper, "Hate and Tolerance: Obstacles to the Eternal Life of Muslims," *World Magazine*, 27 October 2001, 65.

ministry under the banner of Christ's supremacy will be offensive to the impulses of professional clergy who like to be quoted respectably by the local newspaper. The title of this book is meant to shake us loose from the pressure to fit in to the cultural expectations of professionalism. It is meant to sound an alarm against the pride of station and against the expectation of parity in pay and against the borrowing of paradigms from the professional world. Oh for radically Bible-saturated, God-centered, Christ-exalting, self-sacrificing, mission-mobilizing, soul-saving, culture-confronting pastors! Let the chips fall where they will: palm branches one day, persecution the next.

I know some folks will quickly point out that there are sick shepherds who, in the name of countercultural ministry, need to offend people and can't flourish without a fight. Other critics will instruct us that incompetence is not a virtue. Others will remark that finding favor in the guild is not all bad. And, of course, there will be many rankled by the word *brothers*. To all these I say, yes, you have a point. I receive it. If you believe that such things are the crying need of our age, then say them. But that is not my assessment of things.

For every sick shepherd who offends unnecessarily, a hundred are so frightened to offend that the sword of the Spirit has become rubber in their mouths and the mighty Biblical mingling of severity and kindness has vanished from their ministry. For every incompetent pastor who justifies himself with spiritual coverings, a hundred incompetent pastors are desperately doubling their spiritual incompetence by seeking remedies in Babylon. For every pastor who enjoys respect in the guild in spite of prophetic faithfulness to the cross, a hundred pastors enjoy that respect because the cross has been compromised. And to those who want me to write for "brothers *and* sisters," I say, let everyone be fully convinced in his own mind. As for me, the Biblical teaching is clear: God calls spiritual, humble, Christlike men to lead the family as husbands and to lead the church as elders (Eph. 5:20–33; 1 Tim. 2:12–13).[4] I believe, and I have experienced for twenty years, that godly, gifted, articulate, intelligent, ministering women flourish in such families and churches.

My vision of the pastoral ministry is full of joy. Flying over our embattled labor is the banner of Hebrews 13:17, "Let them do this with joy and not with groaning, for that would be of no advantage to you." And the apostolic trumpets resound: "Shepherd the flock of God . . . not under compulsion but willingly, . . . not for shameful gain, but eagerly" (1 Pet. 5:2). There are many tears, to be sure. But, as Paul said, we are "sorrowful, yet *always* rejoicing" (2 Cor. 6:10). In fact the tears deepen and intensify the joy of our hope (James 1:2–4; Rom. 5:3; 2 Cor. 4:17).

There are not only tears; there are antagonists. "A wide door for effective work has opened to me, and there are *many adversaries*" (1 Cor. 16:9). We could wish for peace. And we should labor for unity in the truth. But in this fallen world the gospel is always the aroma of life for some and the aroma of death for others (2 Cor. 2:15–16). So ours is a besieged joy but will always be undaunted because of the triumph of Christ. And ours is a tearful joy, but our tears are the tears of God-centered joy impeded in the extension of itself to others. The peace and satisfaction of our aching souls—and our hungry churches and the waiting nations—flow not from the perks of professional excellence but from the pleasures of spiritual communion with the crucified and risen Christ. I am jealous to spread this joy to (and through) my fellow pastors, which is why I say, "Brothers, we are not professionals."

4. See John Piper and Wayne Grudem, *Recovering Biblical Manhood and Womanhood: A Response to Evangelical Feminism* (Wheaton, Ill.: Crossway Books, 1991).

A WORD OF THANKS

FIRST, I THANK Jesus Christ who called me to the ministry of the Word during a three-week sickness with mononucleosis at Wheaton College when I was twenty years old and then focused that call onto the pastorate in 1979 when I was thirty-three.

I thank the people of Bethlehem Baptist Church in Minneapolis for making Hebrews 13:17 a reality for me since the summer of 1980. "Let [pastors keep watch over your souls] with joy and not with groaning, for that would be of no advantage to you."

I thank Justin Taylor and Vicki Anderson who assist me in so many ways that a hundred burdens are lifted that would otherwise make projects like this impossible. Justin also took on the subject index and added one more way the book might be useful.

I thank my wife Noël for thirty-three years of faithfulness. In everything I do I lean on her.

I thank Eileen Anderson who devoted her excellent skills to preparing the person and text indexes.

I thank Don Anderson, the former editor of *The Standard,* the denominational magazine of the Baptist General Conference, for stirring me up to write twenty of these chapters for that magazine.

And I thank Len Goss at Broadman & Holman for his eagerness and support in shepherding this book through the publishing process.

God has been kind to me, and I pray that, while I have breath, I may be a good steward of His grace in spreading a passion for His supremacy in all things for the joy of all peoples through Jesus Christ my Lord.

God, deliver us from the professionalizers! Deliver us from the "low, managing, contriving, maneuvering temper of mind among us."[2] God, give us tears for our sins. Forgive us for being so shallow in prayer, so thin in our grasp of holy verities, so content amid perishing neighbors, so empty of passion and earnestness in all our conversation. Restore to us the childlike joy of our salvation. Frighten us with the awesome holiness and power of Him who can cast both soul and body into hell (Matt. 10:28). Cause us to hold to the cross with fear and trembling as our hope-filled and offensive tree of life. Grant us nothing, absolutely nothing, the way the world views it. May Christ be all in all (Col. 3:11).

Banish professionalism from our midst, Oh God, and in its place put passionate prayer, poverty of spirit, hunger for God, rigorous study of holy things, white-hot devotion to Jesus Christ, utter indifference to all material gain, and unremitting labor to rescue the perishing, perfect the saints, and glorify our sovereign Lord.

Humble us, O God, under Your mighty hand, and let us rise, not as professionals, but as witnesses and partakers of the sufferings of Christ. In His awesome name. Amen.

---

2. Richard Cecil quoted in E. M. Bounds, *Power through Prayer* (Grand Rapids, Mich.: Baker Book House, 1972), 59.

> For my name's sake I defer my anger,
> for the sake of my praise I restrain it for you,
> that I may not cut you off. . . .
> For my own sake, for my own sake, I do it,
> for how should my name be profaned?
> My glory I will not give to another.
>
> Isaiah 48:9, 11

> God's chief end
> is to glorify God
> and enjoy His glory forever.
>
> John Piper

> God loves His glory more than He loves us,
> and this is the foundation of His love for us.
>
> John Piper

2

BROTHERS, GOD LOVES HIS GLORY

I GREW UP in a home where 1 Corinthians 10:31 was almost as basic to our family as John 3:16. "Whether, then, you eat or drink or whatever you do, do all to the glory of God" (NASB). But not till I was twenty-two years old did I hear anyone say that God's first commitment is to His own glory and that this is the basis for ours. I had never heard anyone say that God does everything for His glory, too, and that is why we should. I had never heard anyone explain that the role of the Holy Spirit is to burn in me what He has been burning with for all eternity: God's love for God. Or more precisely, God the Father's delight in the panorama of His own perfections reflected as a perfect image in His Son.

No one had ever asked me, "Who is the most God-centered Person in the universe?" And then answered, "God is." Or, "Is God an idolater?" And then answered, "No, He has no other gods before Him." Or, "What is the chief end of God?" And then answered, "God's chief end is to glorify God and enjoy His glory forever." So I was never confronted forcefully with the God-centeredness of God until I sat under the teaching of Daniel Fuller and was directed by him to the writings of Jonathan Edwards.

Since those explosive days of discovery in the late sixties, I have labored to understand the implications of God's passion for His glory. That is now the title of a book I wrote as a tribute to Jonathan Edwards, half of which is a reproduction of his book, *The End for Which God Created the World.* Edwards' thesis in that book is this:

> [God] had respect to *himself,* as his last and highest
> end, in this work; because he is *worthy* in himself to be
> so, being infinitely the greatest and best of beings. All
> things else, with regard to worthiness, importance, and ex-
> cellence, are perfectly as nothing in comparison of him.
> . . . All that is ever spoken of in the Scripture as an ulti-
> mate end of God's works is included in that one phrase,
> *the glory of God.*[1]

Why is it important to be stunned by the God-centeredness of God? Because many people are willing to be God-centered as long as they feel that God is man-centered. It is a subtle danger. We may

1. Jonathan Edwards, *The End for Which God Created the World,* in John Piper, *God's Passion for His Glory: Living the Vision of Jonathan Edwards* (Wheaton, Ill.: Crossway Books, 1998), 140, 242.

think we are centering our lives on God, when we are really making Him a means to self-esteem. Over against this danger I urge you to ponder the implications, brothers, that God loves His glory more than He loves us and that this is the foundation of His love for us.

"Stop regarding man in whose nostrils is breath, for of what account is he?" (Isa. 2:22). "Put not your trust in princes, in a son of man, in whom there is no salvation" (Ps. 146:3). "Cursed is the man who trusts in man and makes flesh his strength" (Jer. 17:5). "Behold, the nations are like a drop from a bucket, and are accounted as the dust on the scales. . . . All the nations are as nothing before him, they are accounted by him as less than nothing and emptiness" (Isa. 40:15, 17).

God's ultimate commitment is to Himself and not to us. And therein lies our security. God loves His glory above all. "For my name's sake I defer my anger, for the sake of my praise I restrain it for you, that I may not cut you off. . . . For my own sake, for my own sake, I do it, for how should my name be profaned? My glory I will not give to another" (Isa. 48: 9, 11).

God performs salvation for *His own sake*. He justifies the people called by His name in order that He may be glorified.

"Therefore say to the house of Israel [and to all the churches], Thus says the Lord GOD: It is not for your sake, O house of Israel, that I am about to act, but for the sake of my holy name, which you have profaned among the nations to which you came. And I will vindicate the holiness of my great name, which has been profaned among the nations, and which you have profaned among them. And the nations will know that I am the LORD. . . . It is not for your sake that I will act, declares the Lord GOD; let that be known to you. Be ashamed and confounded for your ways, O house of Israel'" (Ezek. 36:22–23, 32).

This is no isolated note in the symphony of redemptive history. It is the ever-recurring motif of the all-sufficient Composer. Why did

God predestine us in love to be His sons? That the glory of His grace might be praised (Eph. 1:6, 12, 14). Why did God create a people for Himself? "I created [them] for my glory" (Isa. 43:7). Why did He make from one lump vessels of honor and vessels of dishonor? That He might show His wrath and make known His power and reveal the riches of His glory for the vessels of mercy (Rom. 9:22–23). Why did God raise up Pharaoh and harden his heart and deliver Israel with a mighty arm? That His wonders might be multiplied over Pharaoh (Exod. 14:4) and that His name might be declared in all the earth (Exod. 9:16).

Why did God spare rebellious Israel in the wilderness and finally bring them to the promised land? "I acted for the sake of my name, that it should not be profaned in the sight of the nations" (Ezek. 20:14). Why did He not destroy Israel when they rejected Him from being king over them and demanded to be like all the nations (1 Sam. 8:4–6)? "The LORD will not forsake his people, for his great name's sake" (1 Sam. 12:22). God's love for the glory of His own name is the spring of free grace and the rock of our security.

Why did God bring back the Israelites from Babylonian captivity? Because Daniel prayed: "For your own sake, O Lord, make your face to shine upon your sanctuary, which is desolate" (Dan. 9:17). Why did the Father send the incarnate Son to Israel? "To confirm the promises given to the patriarchs, and in order that the Gentiles might glorify God for his mercy" (Rom. 15:8–9). Why did the Son come to His final hour? "For this purpose I have come to this hour. Father, glorify your name" (John 12:27–28). Christ died to glorify the Father and to repair all the defamation we had brought upon His honor. Our only hope is that the death of Christ satisfied God's righteous claims to receive proper glory from His creatures (Rom. 3:24–26).

Brothers, God loves His glory! He is committed with all His infinite and eternal might to display that glory and to preserve the honor of His name.

When Paul says in 2 Timothy 2:13, "If we are faithless, he remains faithful," it does not mean that we are saved in spite of faithlessness. For the verse before says, "If we deny him, he also will deny us." Rather, as the verse explains, "He remains faithful" means "He cannot deny *Himself*." God's most fundamental allegiance is to His own glory. He is committed to being God before He is committed to being anything else.

Do your people know these things? Do they stake the answer to their prayers on God's love for His own glory? Do they make their case before His throne on the grounds that God does everything for His own name's sake? "Act, O LORD, for your name's sake!" (Jer. 14:7). "Help us, O God of our salvation, for the glory of your name; deliver us, and atone for our sins, for your name's sake!" (Ps. 79:9). "For Your name's sake, O LORD, Pardon my iniquity, for it is great" (Ps. 25:11 NASB). Do our people really know that "Hallowed be thy name!" is a petition for God to glorify Himself as God? "Not to us, O LORD, not to us, but to your name give glory" (Ps. 115:1).

We have told our people a hundred times, "Do all to the glory of God" (1 Cor. 10:31). But have we given them the foundation of this command? God loves His glory. He loves it with infinite energy and passion and commitment. And the Spirit of God is ablaze with this love. That is why children of God love the glory of God; they are led by this blazing Spirit (Rom. 8:14).

Let us declare boldly and powerfully what God loves most—the glory of God. Let us guard ourselves from the ocean of man-centeredness around us. "Stop regarding man in whose nostrils is breath, for of what account is he?" (Isa. 2:22). The foundation, the means, and the goal of God's *agape* for sinners is His prior, deeper, and ultimate love for His own glory. Therefore, brothers, tell your people the great ground of the gospel: God loves His glory!

God is love.

1 JOHN 4:8

Then the LORD passed by in front of him and proclaimed,
"The LORD, the LORD God,
compassionate and gracious,
slow to anger,
and abounding in lovingkindness and truth."

EXODUS 34:6 NASB

His holiness is the absolute uniqueness and infinite value of His glory.
His righteousness is His unswerving commitment
always to honor and display that glory.
And His all-sufficient glory is honored and displayed most
by His working for us
rather than our working for Him. And this is love.

JOHN PIPER

3

BROTHERS, GOD IS LOVE

SOME READERS of the previous chapter will echo the concerns of some of the men at our church. At a men's retreat I defined *spiritual leadership* as "knowing where God wants people to be and taking the initiative to get them there by *God's* means in reliance on *God's* power." I suggested that the way we find out where God wants people to be is to ask where God Himself is going. The answer, I think, is that God loves His glory (see chapter 2) and that He aims to magnify His glory in all He does.

So the goal of spiritual leadership is to muster people to join God in living for God's glory.

The objection arose at the retreat that this teaching makes God out to be a self-centered egomaniac who seems never to act out of love. But God does act out of love. He *is* love. We need to see how God can be for His own glory and be for us too. The best way I know to show this is to explain how God is holy, God is righteous, and God is love, and how these three interrelate.

When we describe God as holy we mean that He is one of a kind. There is none like Him. He is in a class by Himself.

Moses taught Israel to sing, "Who is like you, O LORD, among the gods? Who is like you, majestic in holiness, awesome in glorious deeds, doing wonders?" (Exod. 15:11). Centuries later Hannah, Samuel's mother, taught Israel to sing, "There is none holy like the LORD; there is none besides you" (1 Sam. 2:2). And Isaiah (40:25) quotes God: "'To whom then will you compare me, that I should be like him?' says the Holy One."

God is holy in His absolute uniqueness. Everything else belongs to a class. We are human; Rover is a dog; the oak is a tree; Earth is a planet; the Milky Way is one of a billion galaxies; Gabriel is an angel; Satan is a demon. But only God is God. And therefore He is holy, utterly different, distinct, unique.

All else is creation. He alone creates. All else begins. He alone always was. All else depends. He alone is self-sufficient.

And therefore the holiness of God is synonymous with His infinite value. Diamonds are valuable because they are rare and hard to make. God is infinitely valuable because He is the rarest of all beings and cannot be made at all, nor was He ever made. If I were a collector of rare treasures and could somehow have God, the Holy One, in my treasury, I would be wealthier than all the collectors of all the rarest treasures that exist outside God.

Revelation 4:8–11 recounts the songs that are being sung to God in heaven. The first one says, "Holy, holy, holy, is the Lord God Almighty, who was and is and is to come!" The second says,

"Worthy are you, our Lord and God, to receive glory and honor and power." These two songs mean the same thing. "God is holy" means that He is worthy. His holiness is His immeasurable worth and value. Nothing can be compared with Him, for He made everything. Whatever worth makes a created thing valuable is found a million-fold in the Creator.

One way to highlight the meaning of God's holiness is to compare it with His glory. Are they the same? Not exactly. I would say that His glory is the shining forth of His holiness. His holiness is His intrinsic worth—an utterly unique excellence. His glory is the manifest display of this worth in beauty. His glory is His holiness on display. "Holy, holy, holy is the LORD of hosts; the whole earth is *full* of his glory," say the seraphim above His throne (Isa. 6:3). Habakkuk cries, "God came from Teman, and the Holy One from Mount Paran. His splendor covered the heavens, and the earth was full of his praise" (Hab. 3:3). And the Lord Himself says in Leviticus 10:3: "Among those who are near me I will be sanctified, and before all the people I will be glorified." To *show* Himself holy is the way He is glorified.

The holiness of God is the absolutely unique and infinite value of His being and His majesty. To say that our God is holy means that His value is infinitely greater than the sum of the value of all created beings.

Turn now to consider His righteousness. At root, the righteousness of God means that He has a right assessment of His own ultimate value. He has a just regard for His own infinite worth, and He brings all His actions into conformity to this right judgment of Himself.

God would be unrighteous and unreliable if He denied His ultimate value, disregarded His infinite worth, and acted as though the preservation and display of His glory were worth anything less than His wholehearted commitment. God acts in righteousness when He acts for His own name's sake. For it would not be right for God to esteem anything above the infinite glory of His own name.

Psalm 143:11 says, "For your name's sake, O LORD, preserve my life! In your righteousness bring me out of trouble!" Notice the parallel between "in your righteousness" and "for your name's sake." Similarly, Psalm 31:1 says, "In your righteousness deliver me." And verse 3 adds, "For your name's sake you lead me and guide me." Similarly in Daniel 9:16–17, the prophet prays: "According to all your righteous acts, let your anger and your wrath turn away from your city Jerusalem. . . . For your own sake, O Lord, make your face to shine upon your sanctuary, which is desolate." An appeal to God's righteousness is at root an appeal to His unswerving allegiance to the value of His own holy name.

For God to be righteous, He must devote Himself 100 percent, with all His heart, soul, and strength, to loving and honoring His own holiness in the display of His glory.

And that He does, as we saw in chapter 2. The main point of Ephesians 1 is repeated three times: God "predestined us for adoption through Jesus Christ . . . to the praise of his glorious grace" (vv. 5–6). God's purpose is that "we who were the first to hope in Christ might be to the praise of his glory" (v. 12). "The promised Holy Spirit . . . is the guarantee of our inheritance until we acquire possession of it, to the praise of his glory" (vv. 13–14). Everything in our salvation is designed by God to magnify the glory of God.

God is supremely and unimpeachably righteous because He never shrinks back from a right assessment of His ultimate value, a just regard for His infinite worth, or an unswerving commitment to honor and display His glory in everything He does.

Now we are ready to consider God's love. God's love does not conflict with His holiness and righteousness. On the contrary, the nature of God's holiness and righteousness demands that He be a God of love. His holiness is the absolute uniqueness and infinite value of His glory. His righteousness is His unswerving commitment always to honor and display that glory. And His all-sufficient glory is honored and displayed most by His working for us rather than our working for Him. And this is love.

Love is at the heart of God's being because God's free and sovereign dispensing of mercy is more glorious than would be the demand for humans to fill up some lack in Himself. It is more glorious to give than to receive. Therefore, the righteousness of God demands that He be a giver. Therefore, the Holy and Righteous One is Love.

Jesus Christ is the incarnation of God's love. And when He came, He said, "The Son of Man came not to be served but to serve, and to give his life as a ransom for many" (Mark 10:45).

The Son of Man has not come seeking employees. He has come to employ Himself for our good. We dare not try to work for Him lest we rob Him of His glory and impugn His righteousness. The apostle Paul says, "Now to one who works, his wages are not counted as a gift but as his due. And to one who does not work but trusts him who justifies the ungodly; his faith is counted as righteousness" (Rom. 4:4–5). This is a warning not to pursue justification by working for God. It is a gift. We have it by faith alone (see chapter 4). And even when we "work out" our salvation in fear and trembling, we must see it as a peculiar kind of working: the only reason we can will to lift a finger is that God is the one "who works in you, both to will and to work for his good pleasure" (Phil. 2:13).

Though Paul "worked harder" than any of the other apostles, he declares, "It was not I, but the grace of God that is with me" (1 Cor. 15:10). Therefore, in Romans 15:18, he avows, "I will not venture to speak of anything except what Christ has accomplished through me." Paul is utterly convinced that no blessing in life is finally owing to man's willing or running, but to God, who has mercy (Rom. 9:16).

God aims to get all the glory in our redemption. Therefore He is adamant that He will work for us and not we for Him. He is the workman; we stand in need of His services. He is the doctor; we are the sick patient. We are the weak; He is the strong. We have the broken-down jalopy; He is the gifted mechanic.

We must beware lest we try to serve Him in a way that dishonors Him, for He aims to get the glory. As Peter says (1 Pet. 4:11), "Whoever serves [let him render it] by the strength that God supplies—in order that in everything God may be glorified through Jesus Christ. To him belong glory and dominion forever and ever."

So God is love, not in spite of His passion to promote His glory, but precisely because of it. What could be more loving than the infinite, holy God stooping to work for us? Yet in working for us rather than needing our work, He magnifies His own glorious self-sufficiency. It is the stream that glorifies the fullness of the spring. And the stream that flows from God is love. If He ceased to seek His glory, He would be of no value to us. But, praise God, He is holy. He is righteous, and therefore, He is love.

Now here is a closing test to see if you have penetrated to the essence of God's merciful God-centeredness. Ask yourself and your people: "Do you feel most loved by God because He makes much of you, or because He frees you to enjoy making much of Him forever?" This is the test of whether our craving for the love of God is a craving for the blood-bought, Spirit-wrought capacity to see and glorify God by enjoying Him forever, or whether it is a craving for Him to make us the center and give us the pleasures of esteeming ourselves. Who, in the end, is the all-satisfying Treasure that we are given by the love of God: self or God?

God is love because He is infinitely valuable (His holiness) and is committed to displaying that value for our everlasting enjoyment (His righteousness). God is the one being in all the world for whom the most loving act is self-exaltation. For it is He and He alone who will satisfy our hearts.

And to the one who does not work
but trusts him who justifies the ungodly,
his faith is counted unto righteousness.

ROMANS 4:5 JP

This doctrine is the head and the cornerstone.
It alone begets, nourishes, builds, preserves, and defends
the church of God;
and without it the church of God cannot exist for one hour.

MARTIN LUTHER

Wherever the knowledge of it is taken away,
the glory of Christ is extinguished,
religion abolished,
the Church destroyed,
and the hope of salvation utterly overthrown.

JOHN CALVIN

4

BROTHERS, LIVE AND PREACH JUSTIFICATION BY FAITH

PREACHING AND LIVING justification by faith alone glorifies Christ, rescues hopeless sinners, emboldens imperfect saints, and strengthens fragile churches. It is a stunning truth—that God *justifies the ungodly by faith.* "To the one who does not work but trusts him who justifies the ungodly, his faith is counted as righteousness"

(Rom. 4:5). History bears witness: the preaching of this truth creates, reforms, and revives the church.

This was true in the ministry of the apostle Paul. For example, in Antioch of Pisidia he preached in the synagogue, "Let it be known to you therefore, brethren, that through this man [Jesus] forgiveness of sins is proclaimed to you, and by him every one that believes is justified (*dikaioutai*) from everything from which you could not be justified (*dikaiōthēnai*) by the law of Moses" (Acts 13:38–39, JP). What was the result of this preaching of justification by faith?

> As Paul and Barnabas were going out, the people kept begging that these things might be spoken to them the next Sabbath. Now when the meeting of the synagogue had broken up, many of the Jews and of the God-fearing proselytes followed Paul and Barnabas, who, speaking to them, were urging them to continue in the grace of God. And the next Sabbath nearly the whole city assembled to hear the word of God (Acts 13:42–44 NASB).

As we trace this preaching through the history of the church, sometimes we read that Augustine did not see or preach this doctrine. This is probably not true,[1] though it may not be as clear as later in Luther and Calvin. The move away from justification by faith alone and the resulting confusion of an alien righteousness with sanctification as the basis for our right standing before God probably came after Augustine,[2] although it is doubtful that it ever disappeared completely.

---

1. See the evidences brought forth in *The Basic Writings of St. Augustine*, ed. by Whitney Oates, vol. 2 (New York: Random House, 1968), 142ff; and John H. Gerstner, *The Rational Biblical Theology of Jonathan Edwards*, section on the history of justification, found in *Jonathan Edwards Collection: A Light for Every Age* (CD-ROM), by Michael Bowman and NavPress Software, 1999.

2. See Ian Sellers, "Justification," in *The New International Dictionary of the Christian Church*, ed. by J. D. Douglas (Grand Rapids, Mich.: Wm. B. Eerdmans, 1978), 557.

The great Scholastic theologian, Anselm (1033–1109), was probably also an exponent of justification by faith alone. He described his view in a tract for the consolation of the dying, quoted by A. H. Strong:

"*Question.* Dost thou believe that the Lord Jesus died for thee? *Answer.* I believe it. *Qu.* Dost thou thank him for his passion and death? *Ans.* I do thank him. *Qu.* Dost thou believe that thou canst not be saved except by his death? *Ans.* I believe it." And then Anselm addresses the dying man: "Come then, while life remaineth in thee; in his death alone place thy whole trust; in naught else place any trust; to his death commit thyself wholly; with this alone cover thyself wholly; and if the Lord thy God will to judge thee, say, 'Lord, between thy judgment and me I present the death of our Lord Jesus Christ; no otherwise can I contend with thee.' And if he shall say that thou art a sinner, say thou: 'Lord, I interpose the death of our Lord Jesus Christ between my sins and thee.' If he say that thou hast deserved condemnation, say: 'Lord, I set the death of our Lord Jesus Christ between my evil deserts and thee, and his merits I offer for those which I ought to have and have not.' If he say that he is wroth with thee, say: 'Lord, I oppose the death of our Lord Jesus Christ between thy wrath and me.' And when thou hast completed this, say again: 'Lord, I set the death of our Lord Jesus Christ between thee and me.'" See Anselm, *Opera* (Migne), 1:686, 687. The above quotation gives us reason to believe that the New Testament doctrine of justification by faith was implicitly, if not explicitly, held by many pious souls through all the ages of papal darkness.[3]

And there was darkness. The Reformation was needed. And the discovery and preaching of justification by faith alone was the center of the lightning bolt of truth that lit the world. Luther dates his great discovery of the gospel of justification by faith alone to 1518 during his series of lectures on Psalms.[4] He tells the story in his *Preface to the Complete Edition of Luther's Latin Writings*. This account of the discovery is taken from that *Preface*, written March 5, 1545, the year before his death.

> I had indeed been captivated with an extraordinary ardor for understanding Paul in the Epistle to the Romans. But up till then it was . . . a single word in Chapter 1 [:17], "In it the righteousness of God is revealed," that had stood in my way. For I hated that word "righteousness of God," which according to the use and custom of all the teachers, I had been taught to understand philosophically regarding the formal or active righteousness, as they called it, with which God is righteous and punishes the unrighteous sinner.
>
> Though I lived as a monk without reproach, I felt that I was a sinner before God with an extremely disturbed conscience. I could not believe that he was placated by my satisfaction. I did not love, yes, I hated the righteous God who punishes sinners, and secretly, if not blasphemously, certainly murmuring greatly, I was angry with God, and said, "As if, indeed, it is not enough, that

3. A. H. Strong, *Systematic Theology: A Compendium and Common-place Book Designed for the Use of Theological Students* (Rochester, Minn.: Press of E. R. Andrews, 1886); reprint, three volumes in one (Valley Forge, Pa.: Judson Press, 1972), 849.

4. John Dillenberger, ed., *Martin Luther: Selections from His Writings* (Garden City, N.Y.: Doubleday and Co., 1961), xvii.

miserable sinners, eternally lost through original sin, are crushed by every kind of calamity by the law of the decalogue, without having God add pain to pain by the gospel and also by the gospel threatening us with his righteous wrath!" Thus I raged with a fierce and troubled conscience. Nevertheless, I beat importunately upon Paul at that place, most ardently desiring to know what St. Paul wanted.

At last, by the mercy of God, meditating day and night, I gave heed to the context of the words, namely, "In it the righteousness of God is revealed, as it is written, 'He who through faith is righteous shall live.'" There I began to understand [that] the righteousness of God is that by which the righteous lives by a gift of God, namely by faith. And this is the meaning: the righteousness of God is revealed by the gospel, namely, the passive righteousness with which [the] merciful God justifies us by faith, as it is written, "He who through faith is righteous shall live." Here I felt that I was altogether born again and had entered paradise itself through open gates. Here a totally other face of the entire Scripture showed itself to me. . . . And I extolled my sweetest word with a love as great as the hatred with which I had before hated the word "righteousness of God." Thus that place in Paul was for me truly the gate to paradise.[5]

Oh, that pastors in our pragmatic age would "meditate day and night" and "beat importunately upon Paul" until they see the gospel of justification so clearly that they would "enter paradise itself through open gates." Then we would discover why Luther put such a weight on it: "In it all other articles of our faith are comprehended,

5. Ibid., 11–12.

and when that is safe the others are safe too."[6] "On this article all that we teach and practice is based."[7] "It alone can support us in the face of these countless offenses and can console us in all temptations and persecutions."[8] "This doctrine is the head and the cornerstone. It alone begets, nourishes, builds, preserves, and defends the church of God; and without it the church of God cannot exist for one hour."[9]

John Calvin cherished and preached this truth because "wherever the knowledge of it is taken away, the glory of Christ is extinguished, religion abolished, the Church destroyed, and the hope of salvation utterly overthrown."[10] Concerning his debate with Roman Catholicism, he said that justification by faith alone was "the first and keenest subject of controversy between us."[11] What was this great and central truth? Calvin defined it this way:

> As all mankind are, in the sight of God, lost sinners, we hold that Christ is their only righteousness, since, by his obedience, he has wiped off our transgressions; by his sacrifice, appeased the divine anger; by his blood, washed away our stains; by his cross, borne our curse; and by his death, made satisfaction for us. We maintain that in this way man is reconciled in Christ to God the Father, by no merit of his own, by no value of works, but by gratuitous mercy. When we embrace Christ by faith, and come, as it were, into communion with him, this we term, after the manner of Scripture, the righteousness of faith.[12]

---

6. Martin Luther, quoted in Ewald M. Plass, *What Luther Says: An Anthology*, vol. 2 (St. Louis, Mo.: Concordia Publishing House, 1959), 703.

7. Quoted in Ibid., 718.

8. Ibid.

9. Ibid., 704.

10. John Dillenberger, *John Calvin: Selections from His Writings* (n.p.: Scholars Press, 1975), 95.

11. Ibid.

12. Ibid., 96.

When he and the other reformers and the Puritans after them were challenged that the justification of the ungodly by faith alone would lead to loose living (just as Paul was challenged in Romans 6:1 and 15) he answered:

> I wish the reader to understand that as often as we mention faith alone in this question, we are not thinking of a dead faith, which worketh not by love, but holding faith to be the only cause of justification. It is therefore faith alone which justifies, and yet the faith which justifies is not alone: just as it is the heat alone of the sun which warms the earth, and yet in the sun it is not alone, because it is constantly conjoined with light. Wherefore we do not separate the whole grace of regeneration from faith, but claim the power and faculty of justifying entirely for faith, as we ought.[13]

The Baptist pastor John Bunyan, who wrote *The Pilgrim's Progress,* loved and lived the truth of justification by faith alone. Just before his release from twelve years in prison, he wrote a book entitled *A Defense of the Doctrine of Justification by Faith.* Most of all the message was precious to him because it saved him at a time when he was in hopelessness and despairing in his early twenties.

It's hard to put a date on his conversion, because in retelling the process in *Grace Abounding to the Chief of Sinners* he includes almost no dates or times. But it was a lengthy and agonizing process. "I was all this while ignorant of Jesus Christ, and going about to establish my own righteousness, and [would have] perished therein, had not God in mercy showed me more of my state by nature. . . . The Bible was precious to me in those days."[14]

---

13. Ibid., 198.
14. John Bunyan, *Grace Abounding to the Chief of Sinners* (Hertfordshire, England: Evangelical Press, 1978; original, 1666), 20.

One day as I was passing into the field . . . this sentence
fell upon my soul. Thy righteousness is in heaven. And
methought, withal, I saw with the eyes of my soul Jesus
Christ at God's right hand; there, I say, was my righteousness; so that wherever I was, or whatever I was doing, God
could not say of me, he wants [lacks] my righteousness, for
that was just before him. I also saw, moreover, that it was
not my good frame of heart that made my righteousness
better, nor yet my bad frame that made my righteousness
worse, for my righteousness was Jesus Christ himself, "The
same yesterday, today, and forever." Heb. 13:8. Now did
my chains fall off my legs indeed. I was loosed from my afflictions and irons; . . . now went I also home rejoicing for
the grace and love of God.[15]

During the Great Awakening in the 1730s and '40s, it was the
preaching of justification on both sides of the Atlantic that
grounded the strength of the movement of God. When Jonathan
Edwards finally published the sermons he had preached on justification by faith in 1734, he wrote in the preface:

The beginning of the late work of God in this place
was so circumstanced, that I could not but look upon it as
a remarkable testimony of God's approbation of the doctrine *of justification by faith alone,* here asserted and vin-
dicated. . . . The following discourse of justification . . .
seemed to be remarkably blessed, not only to establish the
judgments of many in this truth, but to engage their hearts
in a more earnest pursuit of justification, in that way that
had been explained and defended; and *at that time,* while
I was greatly reproached for defending this doctrine in the

15. Ibid., 90–91.

pulpit, and just upon my suffering a very open abuse for it, God's work wonderfully brake forth amongst us, and souls began to flock to Christ, as the Savior in whose righteousness alone they hoped to be justified. So that this was the doctrine on which this work in its beginning was founded, as it evidently was in the whole progress of it.[16]

Oh, brothers, do we not want to see souls begin "to flock to Christ as the Savior"? Then let us live and preach this great central truth of justification by faith alone.

Remember what Luther said, and give yourselves to it: "I beat importunately upon Paul." Take hold of Romans and Galatians and wrestle with them the way Jacob wrestled with the angel of God—until these inspired writings bless you with this glorious truth.

In Romans 4, Paul builds his case on Genesis 15:6, which he quotes in verse 3: "For what does the scripture say? 'Abraham believed God, and it was counted to him as righteousness.'" Paul is eager to pick up on the words *faith* and *reckoned* in Genesis 15:6 to show why they rule out boasting and support justification by faith alone. Verse 4: "Now to the one who works, his wage is not reckoned according to grace, but as according to debt" (JP). This is why justification by works would not put an end to boasting. If you work for your justification, what you are doing is trying to put God in your debt. And if you succeed in getting God to owe you something, then you can boast before men and God. If you worked for justification and you succeeded, you would not get grace, but a wage. God would owe it to you. And when you got it, you would be able to say, "I deserve this." And that, Paul says, is not what Abraham did.

Well, what did he do? Romans 4:5 is perhaps the most important verse on justification by faith alone in all the New Testament. Three

---

16. Jonathan Edwards, "Five Discourses," in *The Works of Jonathan Edwards*, vol. 1 (Edinburgh: The Banner of Truth Press, 1974), 620.

bright signals in this verse teach that justification is by faith alone and nothing but faith. "And to one who does not work but trusts him who justifies the ungodly, his faith is reckoned as righteousness." Notice these three signals that justification is by "faith alone."

First, he says, "To the one who does not work." Here is a portrait of the moment of justification. This does not mean there will be no "good works" that follow in sanctification. Paul takes that up in chapter 6. We are dealing here with the moment of justification. This moment could happen for any of your people any Sunday morning in an instant because it is not a long process (like sanctification). Justification is a verdict delivered by God in a moment: not guilty, acquitted, accepted, forgiven, righteous! And Paul says it happens to the person who "does not work"! That means it comes by faith alone.

The second signal that justification is by faith alone is the word *ungodly*. After Paul says, "To the one who does not work," he says, "but trusts him who justifies the ungodly." This is utterly shocking. It jars all of our judicial sentiments (see Exod. 23:7; Prov. 17:15). It makes us cry out, "How can this be?" And the stupendous answer is that "Christ died for the ungodly" (Rom. 5:6). God can justify the ungodly because His Son died for the ungodly.

The point of the word *ungodly* here is to stress that faith is not our righteousness. Faith believes in Him who justifies the ungodly. When faith is born in the soul, we are still ungodly. Faith will begin to overcome our ungodliness. But in the beginning of the Christian life—where justification happens—we are all ungodly. Godly works do not begin to have a role in our lives until we are justified. We are declared righteous[17] by faith alone while we are still ungodly. And that is the only way any of us can have hope that God is on our side

---

17. The word *justify (dikaioō)* means "declare righteous," not "make morally righteous." We see this especially in Romans 3:4 where God is "justified" *(dikaiōthēs)* in his words, that is, declared righteous, not made righteous.

so that we can now make headway in the fight against ungodliness. He is for us. "Who shall bring any charge against God's elect? It is God who justifies. Who is to condemn? Christ Jesus is the one who died" (Rom. 8:33–34).

Finally, the third signal that justification is by faith alone is the last phrase in Romans 4:5, "his faith is counted as righteousness." Not his works or his love or even his fruit of faith, but his faith—his faith alone—is counted as righteousness.

What does this mean, "Faith is reckoned as righteousness"? The idea is clearly crucial for Paul because we meet it in verse 3: "Abraham believed God, and it [his believing] was counted to him as righteousness." Verse 5: "His [the one who believes in him who justifies the ungodly] faith is counted as righteousness." Verse 9: "Faith was counted to Abraham as righteousness." Verse 22: Abraham's "faith was 'counted to him as righteousness.'"

Does reckoning faith as righteousness mean that faith itself is the kind of righteousness we perform and God counts that as good enough to be our justifying righteousness? Does it mean that justification, let's say, costs five million dollars and I can come up with one million dollars (namely, faith), so God mercifully says He will count my one million as five million and cancel the rest? That would make my faith the righteousness imputed to me. So justification would be God's recognizing in me a righteousness that He put there and that He acknowledges and counts for what it really is—righteous. Is that what Paul means when he says, "Faith is counted as righteousness"?

Or is justification something different—not God's seeing any righteousness in me but His reckoning to me His own righteousness in Christ through faith?

My answer is that Paul means faith is what unites us with Christ and all that God is for us in Him. And when God sees us united to Christ—sees us in Christ—He sees the righteousness of Christ as our righteousness. So faith connects us with Christ who is our right-eousness and, in that sense, faith is counted as righteousness. The function of justifying faith is to see and savor all that God is for us in Christ, especially His righteousness.

Now what is the Biblical basis of this interpretation? John Owen gives five arguments,[18] and John Murray gives nine arguments[19] why "faith counted as righteousness" does not mean that faith is our righteousness. Here are some of the reasons that seem compelling to me.

First, notice at the end of Romans 4:6 and at the end of Romans 4:11 a different way of expressing the "imputation" of righteousness (or the "counting" of righteousness). At the end of verse 6, "God counts righteousness apart from works." And at the end of verse 11, "that righteousness might be counted to them." Notice: in both of these, faith is not the thing counted as righteousness, but righteousness is the thing counted to us. "God credits righteousness," not "God credits faith as righteousness." What this does is alert us to the good possibility that when Paul says, "Faith is counted as righteousness," he may well mean, "who thus have right-eousness counted to them." What is counted to our account here is not faith but righteousness. This suggests that speaking of faith being reckoned may be a shorthand way of saying that righteousness is counted through faith.

Second, consider Romans 3:21–22, "But now the righteousness of God has been manifested apart from law, although the Law and the Prophets bear witness to it—the righteousness of God through faith in Jesus Christ for all who believe." Notice that it is God's righteousness that comes to us through faith. Faith is what unites us

---

18. John Owen, *The Doctrine of Justification by Faith,* in *The Works of John Owen,* vol. 5 (Edinburgh: The Banner of Truth Trust, 1965), 318–19.
19. John Murray, *The Epistle to the Romans,* vol. 1 (Grand Rapids, Mich.: Wm. B. Eerdmans Publishing Co., 1959), 353–59.

to God's righteousness. Faith is not God's righteousness which is imputed (reckoned) to us in our union with Christ.

Third, consider 2 Corinthians 5:21, "For our sake he made him to be sin who knew no sin, so that in him we might become the righteousness of God." Here we have a double "imputation." God imputed our sins to Christ who knew no sin. And God imputed His righteousness to us who had no righteousness of our own. The key phrases for us are "the righteousness of God" and "in him." It's not *our* righteousness that we get in Christ. It is *God's* righteousness. And we get it *not* because our faith is righteous but because we are "in Christ." Faith unites us to Christ. And in Christ we have an alien righteousness. It is God's righteousness in Christ. Or you can say it is Christ's righteousness, which is the way Romans 5:18 speaks ("so one act of righteousness leads to justification and life for all men"). He takes our sin. We take His righteousness, imputed to us.[20]

Fourth, consider 1 Corinthians 1:30. John Bunyan said that after the experience in the field where the imputed righteousness of Christ hit him so powerfully, he went home and looked for Biblical support. He came upon 1 Corinthians 1:30. "[God] is the source of

20. The doctrine of the imputation of Christ's righteousness is under heavy attack in our day (again). See for example, Robert H. Gundry, "Why I Didn't Endorse 'The Gospel of Jesus Christ: An Evangelical Celebration,'" in *Books and Culture*, January/February 2001, vol. 7, no. 1, 6–9; Robert H. Gundry, "On Oden's Answer," in *Books and Culture*, March/April 2001, vol. 7, no. 2, 15–16, 39. But this trend in New Testament scholarship may not be able to overthrow four centuries of textual reflection and broad Protestant consensus on God's righteousness in relation to justification. Careful contemporary New Testament exegetes like George Ladd have admitted what Gundry belabors, namely, that an explicit doctrinal statement about the imputation of Christ's righteousness to believers is absent: "Paul never expressly states that the righteousness of Christ is imputed to believers." But from 2 Corinthians Ladd says, "Paul answers the question when he says, 'In him we might become the righteousness of God' (2 Cor. 5:21). Christ was made sin for our sake. We might say that our sins were reckoned to Christ. He, although sinless, identified himself with our sins, suffered their penalty and doom—death. So we have reckoned to us Christ's righteousness even though in character and deed we remain sinners. It is an unavoidable logical conclusion that men of faith are justified because Christ's righteousness is imputed to them." George Eldon Ladd, *A Theology of the New Testament*, revised edition, ed. by Donald A. Hagner (Grand Rapids, Mich.: Wm. B.

your life in Christ Jesus, whom God made our wisdom and our righteousness and sanctification and redemption." "By this scripture," Bunyan said, "I saw that the man Christ Jesus . . . is our righteousness and sanctification before God. Here therefore I lived for some time very sweetly at peace with God, through Christ."[21]

Bunyan's text (1 Cor. 1:30) says that Christ became for us (simple dative, *hēmin*) "righteousness." And the reason Christ is our "righteousness" in this way is that we are "in Christ Jesus." "You are in Christ Jesus who became to [or for] us . . . righteousness." Christ, not faith, is our righteousness. Faith unites us to Christ and all that God is for us in Him. But what He is for us in Him is righteousness.[22]

Eerdmans, 1993), 491. In other words, the absence of doctrinal explicitness and systematization may be no more problematic for the doctrine of the imputation of Christ than it is for the doctrine of the Trinity. For a detailed response to Gundry, see John Piper, *Counted Righteous in Christ: Should We Abandon the Imputation of Christ's Righteousness?* (Wheaton, Ill.: Crossway Books, 2002).

21. Bunyan, *Grace Abounding to the Chief of Sinners*, 91.

22. There is a credible objection to using 1 Corinthians 1:30 to show the imputation of Christ's righteousness. Some say that using the verse to prove the imputation of Christ's righteousness would seem to prove that wisdom and sanctification and redemption are also "imputed" rather than imparted. But each of these is something we actually experience, not just a declaration about us. So if the text says, "God made [Christ to be] our wisdom, our righteousness and sanctification and redemption," can we pick out only "righteousness" and say it was imputed to us while the others are not merely imputed but applied to us so that we experience them?

One answer is that Paul may well have intended each of the four explicit gifts of our union with Christ to be taken in the way that each functions uniquely in meeting our need, rather than all being taken in the exact same way. John Flavel (1630–1691) saw a progression that points in this direction. Thus in this union Christ becomes *wisdom* for us which overcomes our blinding ignorance of Christ (by illumination). Second, in this union Christ becomes righteousness for us which overcomes our guilt and condemnation (by imputation). Third, in this union Christ becomes *sanctification* for us which overcomes our corruption and pollution (by progressive impartation). Fourth, in this union Christ becomes redemption for us which overcomes, in the end, all the miseries and pain and futility that come from sin and guilt (through resurrection, "We wait for adoption as sons, the redemption of our bodies," Rom. 8:23). See John Flavel, *The Method of Grace* (Grand Rapids, Mich.: Baker Book House, 1977), 14. One could also bring to bear Romans 10:4 at this point, which translated literally says, "The goal [or end] of the law is Christ for righteousness to everyone who believes." In other words, the law was pointing toward Christ as our righteousness ("Christ for righteousness for everyone who believes," τελοß γα;ρ νομου Cristo;ß eijß dikaiosunhn panti; tw/' pisteuvonti [telos gar nomou Christos eis dikaiosunēn panti tō pisteuonti]).

My conclusion from these observations is that, when Paul says in Romans 4:3, 5, 9, and 22 that "faith is counted as righteousness," he does not mean that our faith *is* our righteousness. He means that our faith unites us to Christ so that God's righteousness in Christ is reckoned to us.

Here's an imperfect, but I think helpful, analogy. Suppose I say to Barnabas, my teenage son, "Clean up your room before you go to school. You must have a clean room, or you won't be able to go watch the game tonight." Well, suppose he plans poorly and leaves for school without cleaning the room. And suppose I discover the messy room and clean it. His afternoon fills up, and he gets home just before it's time to leave for the game and realizes what he has done and feels terrible. He apologizes and humbly accepts the consequences. No game.

To which I say, "Barnabas, I am going to credit your apology and submission as a clean room. I said, 'You must have a clean room, or you won't be able to go watch the game tonight.' Your room is clean. So you can go to the game." What I mean when I say, "I credit your apology as a clean room," is not that the apology is the clean room nor that he really cleaned his room. I cleaned it. It was pure grace. All I mean is that, in my way of counting—in my grace—his apology connects him with the promise given for a clean room. The clean room is *his* clean room. I credit it to him. Or, I credit his apology as a clean room. You can say it either way. And Paul said it both ways: "Faith is reckoned as righteousness," and "God credits righteousness to us."

So when God says to those who believe in Christ, "I credit your faith as righteousness," He does *not* mean that your faith is your justifying righteousness. He means that your faith connects you to Christ who becomes your righteousness in God's sight—God's righteousness.

For Martin Luther and John Bunyan the discovery of the imputed righteousness of Christ was the greatest life-changing experience they ever had. Luther said it was like entering a paradise of peace with God. For Bunyan it was the end of years of spiritual torture and uncertainty. Brothers, what would your people give to know for sure that their acceptance and approval before God was as sure as the standing of Jesus Christ, His Son?

Say to your beloved flock: "Christ offers you this today as a gift. If you see Him as true and precious, if you receive the gift as your greatest treasure in life and trust in it, you will have a peace with God that passes all understanding. You will be a secure person. You will not need the approval of others. You will not need the ego-supports of wealth or power or revenge. You will be free. You will overflow with love. You will lay down your life in the cause of Christ for the joy that is set before you. Look to Christ and trust Him for your righteousness."

Tell them with joy and passion and power that they can't *give* anything for it. It's free. This is what Christ came to do: fulfill a righteousness and die a death that would remove all our sins and become for us a perfect righteousness. Live in the mighty joy and freedom of this gospel. And preach it! Oh preach this to your people again and again.

> Every good deed we do in dependence on God
> does just the opposite of paying Him back;
> it puts us ever deeper in debt to His grace.
> And that is exactly where God wants us to be
> through all eternity.
>
> JOHN PIPER

> Good deeds do not pay back grace;
> they borrow more grace.
>
> JOHN PIPER

5

BROTHERS, BEWARE OF THE DEBTOR'S ETHIC

WHY CHRISTIANS do what they do is just as important as what they do. Bad motives ruin good acts. "If I give away all I have, and if I deliver my body to be burned, but have not love, I gain nothing" (1 Cor. 13:3). At the last judgment the Lord "will bring to light the things now hidden in darkness and will disclose the purposes of the heart" (1 Cor. 4:5).

Therefore, we must not be content that our people are doing

good things. We must labor to see that they do good things from God-exalting motives—lest they find in the end that their sacrifices were for nothing.

The debtor's ethic has a deadly appeal to immature Christians. It comes packaged as a gratitude ethic and says things like: "God has done so much for you; now what will you do for Him?" "He gave you His life; now how much will you give to Him?"

The Christian life is pictured as an effort to pay back the debt we owe to God. The admission is made that we will never fully pay it off, but the debtor's ethic demands that we work at it. Good deeds and religious acts are the installment payments we make on the unending debt we owe God.

Have you ever tried to find a Biblical text where gratitude or thankfulness is the explicit motive for obedience to God? Stories like the sinful woman (in Luke 7:36–50) and the unforgiving servant (in Matt. 18:23–35) come to mind,[1] but neither speaks *explicitly* of gratitude as a motive.

Why is this explicit motive for obedience—which in contemporary Christianity is probably the most commonly used motive for obedience to God—(almost?) totally lacking in the Bible? Could it be that a gratitude ethic so easily slips over into a debtor's ethic that God chose to protect His people from this deadly motivation by *not* including gratitude as an explicit motive for obedience?

Instead He lures us into obedience with irresistibly desirable promises of enablement (Jer. 31:33; Ezek. 36:27; Matt. 19:26; Rom. 6:14; 1 Cor. 1:8–9; Gal. 5:22; Phil. 2:13; 4:13; 1 Thess. 3:12; Heb.

---

1. Another possible exception is Hebrews 12:28–29, "Since we receive a kingdom which cannot be shaken, let us show gratitude, by which we may offer to God an acceptable service with reverence and awe; for our God is a consuming fire." But the phrase "show gratitude" is a questionable translation. The KJV has, "Wherefore we receiving a kingdom which cannot be moved, let us have grace whereby we may serve God." Even if the KJV is wrong, I take the function of gratitude to be that it empowers service by feeding faith in future grace. I say this because Hebrews, more than any other book in the New Testament, is explicitly insistent that obedience comes "by faith" (Heb. 11).

13:21) and divine reward (Luke 9:24; 10:28; 12:33; 16:9, 25; 10:35–36; Heb. 11:24–26; 12:2; 13:5–6).[2]

God takes pains to motivate us by reminding us that He is now and always will be working for those who follow Him in the obedience of faith. He never stops and waits for us to work for Him "out of gratitude." He guards us from the mindset of a debtor by reminding us that all our Christian labor *for* Him is a gift *from* Him (Rom. 11:35–36; 15:18) and therefore cannot be conceived as payment of a debt. In fact the astonishing thing is that every good deed we do in dependence on Him to "pay Him back" does just the opposite; it puts us ever deeper in debt to His grace. "I labored even more than all of them, yet not I, but the grace of God with me" (1 Cor. 15:10 NASB). Let us teach people that is exactly where God wants us to be through all eternity, going ever deeper in debt to grace.

Should we then stop preaching gratitude as a motivation? I leave that for you to answer. But if we go on urging people to obey "out of gratitude," we should at least show them the lurking dangers, and describe *how* gratitude can motivate obedience without succumbing to a debtor's mentality.

Ponder with me the meaning of gratitude and how it might work to motivate in a good way, not like a debtor's ethic.

First we need a definition. Suppose I wake up to the sound of a robber trying to break into my house. When I turn on the light, he flees. As I get dressed, I smell smoke. A fire had just started in the basement where my sons sleep. I quickly put it out.

The thief had awakened me and, unbeknownst to him, saved my sons. But I do not feel grateful to him. I feel grateful to God. Why? Because the thief had no good intentions toward me, but God did. We do not respond with gratitude to a person who does us a favor *unintentionally.*

2. See chapter 7, "Brothers, Consider Christian Hedonism."

Or suppose I am visiting some Christian friends in a remote jungle village and fall deathly sick. One of the villagers perceives a need for penicillin and sets out on foot to get it from a doctor ten miles away. On his way back he is bitten by a deadly snake but manages to make it to the village before he dies. In his pocket is found the bottle of penicillin—broken by his last fall. He gave his life for me, but I did not get the benefit he died to bring.

Do I feel thankful? Yes! Because gratitude is not merely a response to a benefit received; it is a response to someone's *goodwill* toward us.

This is confirmed by another experience. Suppose you give someone a gift at a party and he opens it and loves it. He fondles it and shows it off and speaks of it the whole evening, but never once does he even look at you or speak to you, the giver. He is totally enthralled with the gift. What do we say of such a person? We say he is an ingrate. Why? Because his emotion of joy over the gift has no reference to the goodwill of the giver.

So I arrive at this definition of *gratitude*. *Gratitude is a species of joy which arises in your heart in response to the goodwill of someone who does or tries to do you a favor.*

The reason this spontaneous response of a heart has a good potential to produce other acts of obedience is that it is a species of *joy.* Whenever we experience joy, it is because our hearts have esteemed something we regard as valuable. The cause of joy is always a perceived value. The greater the value to us, the greater our joy in receiving it.

But not only that. All joy is gregarious. It has in it a demonstrative impulse. It likes to gather others around and savor the value together. Is it not a psychological impossibility to feel intense delight in something good yet feel no impulse to demonstrate to others the value which caused that delight?

In his *Reflections on the Psalms,* C. S. Lewis put it like this:

Just as men spontaneously praise whatever they value, so they spontaneously urge us to join them in praising it: "Isn't she lovely? Wasn't it glorious? Don't you think that magnificent?" It isn't out of compliment that lovers keep on telling one another how beautiful they are; the delight is incomplete until it is expressed.

It is frustrating to have discovered a new author and not be able to tell anyone how good he is; to come suddenly, at the turn of the road, upon some mountain valley of unexpected grandeur and then to have to keep silent because the people you are with care for it no more than for a tin can in the ditch.[3]

So the secret of how gratitude motivates obedience is in the nature of joy. All joy has in it an impulse to demonstrate the beauty and value of its object.

So the question becomes: How should (indeed, how must) our joy in the value of God's gift of Jesus Christ demonstrate itself? Answer: In a way that honors the nature and aim of God's goodwill and does not contradict it. (You should not try to show your gratitude to someone who just paid your way through an alcohol treatment center by throwing him a beer party. That would contradict the aim of his goodwill.)

The nature of God's goodwill in giving His Son was that it was unconditional and undeserved—a gift of free grace. The aim of that act was to unleash a power of forgiveness and renewal that would transform people into reflectors of God's glory. So the way our gratitude to God for His goodwill must express itself is by saying and doing what honors its nature as free and its aim as God's glory.

---

3. C. S. Lewis, *Reflections on the Psalms* (New York: Harcourt, Brace and World, 1958), 93–95.

This immediately excludes the debtor's ethic. Any attempt to express a gratitude by paying God back would contradict the nature of His gift as free and gracious. Any attempt to turn from being a beneficiary of God in order to become God's benefactors would remove the stumbling block of the cross where my debt was so fully paid that I am forever humbled to the status of a receiver, not a giver. "Whoever serves is to do so as one who is serving by the strength which God supplies" (1 Pet. 4:11 NASB).

Instead, the way our joy expresses the value of free grace is by admitting we don't deserve it, and by banking our hope on it and doing everything we do as a recipient of more and more grace. "God is able to make all grace abound to you, [so that] . . . you may have an abundance for every good deed" (2 Cor. 9:8 NASB). Good deeds do not pay back grace; they borrow more grace.

Gratitude will always degenerate into the debtor's ethic if it only looks back on past grace and not forward as well to future grace. We honor the nature and aim of God's goodwill by trusting Him to work for us from now on, which means that gratitude functions well as a motive only as it gives rise to faith. Gratitude says to faith, "Keep trusting your Father for more grace; I know He will supply. I have experienced it, and it was sweet." Gratitude does help motivate the radical obedience of love, but it does so indirectly through the service of faith in future grace.

Perhaps this is why the central ethical affirmation of the New Testament is that "faith works through love" (Gal. 5:6), not "gratitude works through love." Not that this would be untrue, but that it is fraught with legalistic dangers. So Paul would have us beware of the debtor's ethic and lead our people into the life-changing power of ever-dependent joy.[4]

---

4. A full treatment of what I call "living by faith in future grace" and which is the opposite of the debtor's ethic is found in John Piper, *The Purifying Power of Living by Faith in Future Grace* (Sisters, Oreg.: Multnomah Publishers, 1995).

> [God is not] served by human hands,
> as though he needed anything,
> since he himself gives to all mankind life and breath and everything.
>
> ACTS 17:25

> The difference between Uncle Sam and Jesus Christ is that
> Uncle Sam won't enlist you in his service unless you are healthy
> and Jesus won't enlist you unless you are sick.

> What is God looking for in the world?
> Assistants? No.
> The gospel is not a help-wanted ad.
> It is a help-available ad.
> God is not looking for people to work for Him
> but people who let Him work mightily in and through them.
>
> JOHN PIPER

6

BROTHERS, TELL THEM NOT TO SERVE GOD

WE HAVE ALL told our people to serve God. The Bible says, "Serve the LORD with gladness" (Ps. 100:2). But now it may be time to tell them *not* to serve God. For Scripture also says: "The Son of Man . . . came not to be served" (Mark 10:45).

The Bible is concerned to call us back from idolatry to serve the true and living God (1 Thess. 1:9). But it is also concerned to keep us from serving the true God in the wrong way. There is a way to serve God that belittles and dishonors Him. Therefore, we must take heed lest we recruit servants whose labor diminishes the glory of the All-powerful Provider. If Jesus said that He came *not* to be served, service may be rebellion.

God wills not to be served: "The God who made the world and everything in it . . . [is not] served by human hands, as though he needed anything, since he himself gives to all mankind life and breath and everything" (Acts 17:24–25). Paul warns against any view of God which makes Him the beneficiary of our beneficence. He informs us that God cannot be served in any way that implies we are meeting His needs. It would be as though a stream should try to fill a spring that feeds it. "He himself gives to all mankind life and breath and everything."

What is the greatness of our God? What is His uniqueness in the world? Isaiah says, "From of old no one has heard or perceived by ear, no eye has seen a God besides you, who acts for those who wait for him" (Isa. 64:4). All the other so-called gods make man work for them. Our God will not be put in the position of an employer who must depend on others to make his business go. Instead He magnifies His all-sufficiency by doing the work Himself. *Man* is the dependent partner in this affair. His job is to wait for the Lord.

What is God looking for in the world? Assistants? No. The gospel is not a help-wanted ad. It is a help-available ad. Nor is the call to Christian service a help-wanted ad. God is not looking for people to work for Him but people who let Him work mightily in and through them: "The eyes of the LORD run to and fro throughout the whole earth, to give strong support to those whose heart is blameless toward him" (2 Chron. 16:9). God is not a scout looking for the first draft choices to help His team win. He is an unstoppable fullback ready to take the ball and run touchdowns for anyone who trusts Him to win the game.

Well, then, our people will ask as we teach them these things,

"What does God want from us?" Not what they might expect. God rebukes Israel for bringing Him so many sacrifices: "I will not accept a bull from your house. . . . For every beast of the forest is mine. . . . If I were hungry, I would not tell you, for the world and its fullness are mine" (Ps. 50:9–10, 12).

But isn't there something we can give to God that won't belittle Him to the status of beneficiary? Yes. Our anxieties. It's a command: "Cast all your anxieties on him" (1 Pet. 5:7 RSV). God will gladly receive anything from us that shows our dependence and His all-sufficiency.

The difference between Uncle Sam and Jesus Christ is that Uncle Sam won't enlist you in his service unless you are healthy and Jesus won't enlist you unless you are sick. "Those who are well have no need of a physician, but those who are sick. I came not to call the righteous, but sinners" (Mark 2:17). Christianity is fundamentally convalescence. Patients do not serve their physicians. They trust them for good prescriptions. The Sermon on the Mount is our doctor's medical advice, not our employer's job description.

But even that analogy doesn't get it quite right. Even trusting our doctor to tell us wise and healing things to do may leave us trying to do them in our own strength. God is not only the doctor who prescribes. He is the nurse who lifts up our powerless head and puts the spoon in our mouth (or who hangs the bag of intravenous medicine). And He is the medicine.

Our very lives hang on not working for God. "To the one who works, his wages are not counted as a gift but as his due. And to the one who does not work but trusts him who justifies the ungodly, his faith is counted as righteousness" (Rom. 4:4–5). Workmen get no gifts. They get their due. If we would have the gift of justification, we dare not work. God is the workman in this affair. And what He gets is the glory of being the benefactor of grace, not the beneficiary of service.

Nor should we think that after justification our labor for God begins. Those who make a work out of sanctification demean the glory of God. Jesus Christ is "our righteousness *and* sanctification" (1 Cor. 1:30). "Did you receive the Spirit by works of the law or by hearing with faith? Are you so foolish? Having begun with the Spirit, are you now being perfected by the flesh?" (Gal. 3:2–3). God was the workman in our justification, and He will be the workman in our sanctification.

Religious "flesh" always wants to work for God. But "if you live according to the flesh you will die" (Rom. 8:13). That is why our very lives hang on *not* working for God, both in justification and sanctification.

But shall we not then serve Christ? It is commanded: "Serve the Lord" (Rom. 12:11). Those who do not serve Christ are rebuked (Rom. 16:18, "Such persons do not serve our Lord Christ, but their own appetites"). Yes, we will serve Him. But before we do, we will ponder what to avoid in this service. Surely all the warnings against serving God mean that in the idea of service lies something to be avoided. When we compare our relationship with God to the relationship between servant and master, the comparison is not perfect. Some things about servanthood should be avoided in relation to God. Some should be affirmed.

How then shall we serve and not serve? Psalm 123:2 gives part of the answer: "Behold, as the eyes of servants look to the hand of their master, as the eyes of a maidservant to the hand of her mistress, so our eyes look to the LORD our God, till he has mercy upon us." The good way to serve God is be like the maid who looks to the hand of her mistress for mercy.

Any servant who tries to get off the divine dole and strike up a manly partnership with his Heavenly Master is in revolt against the Creator. God does not barter. He gives *mercy* to servants who will have it, and the wages of death to those who won't. Good service is always and fundamentally receiving mercy, not rendering assistance.

But it is not entirely passive. Matthew 6:24 gives another clue to good service. Compare serving money and serving God. "No one can serve two masters, for either he will hate the one and love the other, or he will be devoted to the one and despise the other. You cannot serve God and money."

How does a person serve money? He does not assist money. He is not the benefactor of money. How then do we serve money? Money exerts a certain control over us because it seems to hold out so much promise of happiness. It whispers with great force, "Think and act so as to get into a position to enjoy my benefits." This may include stealing, borrowing, or working.

Money promises happiness, and we serve it by believing the promise and living by that faith. So we don't serve money by putting our power at its disposal for its good. We serve money by doing what is necessary so that money's power will be at our disposal for our good.

I think the same sort of service to God must be in view in Matthew 6:24, since Jesus puts the two side by side: "You cannot serve God and money." So if we are going to serve God and not money, then we are going to have to open our eyes to the vastly superior happiness which God offers. Then God will exert a greater control over us than money does. We will serve by believing His promise of fullest joy and walking by that faith. We will not serve by trying to put our power at His disposal for His good, but by doing what is necessary so that His power will be ever at our disposal for our good.

Of course, this means obedience. A patient obeys his doctor in hopes of getting well. A convalescent sinner trusts the painful directions of his therapist, and follows them. Or, most accurately, a paralyzed patient lets the nurse serve him the medicine that will give him healing and strength. Only in this way do we keep ourselves in a position to benefit from what the divine Physician has to offer. In all this obedience we are the beneficiaries. God is ever the giver. For it is the giver who gets the glory.

And that, perhaps, is the most important thing of all. The only right way to serve God is in a way that reserves for Him all the glory. "Whoever serves [must do it] as one who serves by the strength that God supplies—*in order that in everything God may be glorified*" (1 Pet. 4:11). How do we serve so God is glorified? We serve by the strength He supplies. When we are at our most active for God, we are still the recipients. God will not surrender the glory of the benefactor, ever!

So let us work hard but never forget that it is not us but the grace of God which is with us (1 Cor. 15:10). Let us obey now, as always, but never forget that it is God who works in us both the will and the deed (Phil. 2:13). Let us spread the gospel far and wide and spend ourselves for the sake of the elect but never venture to speak of anything except what Christ has wrought in us (Rom. 15:18). In all our serving may God be the giver, and may God get the glory.

Until the people understand this, brothers, tell them not to serve God!

> Delight yourself in the LORD.
>
> PSALM 37:4

> Rejoice in the Lord always; again, I say, Rejoice!
>
> PHILIPPIANS 4:4

> God is most glorified in us
> when we are most satisfied in Him.
>
> JOHN PIPER

> The desire to be happy is a proper motive for every good deed,
> and if you abandon the pursuit of your own joy,
> you cannot love man or please God.
>
> JOHN PIPER

7

BROTHERS, CONSIDER CHRISTIAN HEDONISM

IF YOU MUST, forgive me for the label. But don't miss the truth because you don't like my tag. My shortest summary of it is: God is most glorified in us when we are most satisfied in Him. Or: The chief end of man is to glorify God *by* enjoying Him forever. Does Christian hedonism[1] make a god out of pleasure? No. It says that

---

1. For the full story of what I call "Christian hedonism," see John Piper, *Desiring God: Meditations of a Christian Hedonist* (Sisters, Oreg.: Multnomah Publishers, 1996);

we all make a god out of what we take most pleasure in. My life is devoted to helping people make God their God, by wakening in them the greatest pleasures in Him.

When Jesus warned His disciples that they might get their heads chopped off (Luke 21:16), He comforted them with the promise that, nevertheless, not a hair on their heads would perish (v. 18). When He warned them that discipleship means self-denial and crucifixion (Mark 8:34), He consoled them with the promise that "whoever loses his life for my sake and the gospel's will save it" (v. 35). When He commanded them to leave all and follow Him, He assured them that they would "receive a hundredfold now . . . with persecutions, and in the age to come eternal life" (Mark 10:30–31).

If we must sell all, we should do it, Jesus said, "with joy" because the field we aim to buy contains a hidden treasure (Matt. 13:44).

By Christian hedonism I do not mean that our happiness is the highest good. I mean that pursuing the highest good will always result in our greatest happiness in the end. But almost all Christians believe this. Christian hedonism says more, namely, that we should *pursue* happiness, and pursue it with all our might. The desire to be happy is a proper motive for every good deed, and if you abandon the pursuit of your own joy, you cannot love man or please God. That's what makes Christian hedonism controversial.

Christian hedonism aims to replace a Kantian morality with a Biblical one. Immanuel Kant, the German philosopher who died in 1804, was the most powerful exponent of the notion that the moral value of an act decreases as we aim to derive any benefit from it. Acts are good if the doer is "disinterested." We should do the good because it is good. Any motivation to seek joy or reward corrupts

---

or the small version: John Piper, *The Dangerous Duty of Delight: The Glorified God and the Satisfied Soul* (Sisters, Oreg.: Multnomah Publishers, 2001).

the act. Cynically, perhaps, but not without warrant, the novelist Ayn Rand captured the spirit of Kant's ethic:

> An action is moral, said Kant, only if one has no desire to perform it, but performs it out of a sense of duty and derives no benefit from it of any sort, neither material nor spiritual. A benefit destroys the moral value of an action. (Thus if one has no desire to be evil, one cannot be good; if one has, one can.)[2]

Against this Kantian morality—which has passed as Christian for too long!—we must herald the unabashedly hedonistic Biblical morality. Jonathan Edwards, who died when Kant was thirty-four, expressed it like this in one of his early resolutions: "Resolved, To endeavor to obtain for myself as much happiness in the other world as I possibly can, with all the power, might, vigor, and vehemence, yea violence, I am capable of, or can bring myself to exert, in any way that can be thought of."[3]

C. S. Lewis put it like this in a letter to Sheldon Vanauken: "It is a Christian duty, as you know, for everyone to be as happy as he can."[4]

And southern novelist Flannery O'Connor gives her view of self-denial like this: "Always you renounce a lesser good for a greater; the opposite is sin. Picture me with my ground teeth stalking joy—fully armed too, as it's a highly dangerous quest."[5]

The Kantian notion says that it's OK to get joy as an *unintended result* of your action. But all these people (myself included) are *aiming* at joy. We repudiate both the possibility and desirability of

---

2. Ayn Rand, *For the Intellectual* (New York: Signet, 1961), 32.
3. Resolution 22 in Edwards' *Memoirs in The Works of Jonathan Edwards*, vol. 1 (Edinburgh: The Banner of Truth Trust, 1974), xxi.
4. From a letter to Sheldon Vanauken in Vanauken's book, *A Severe Mercy* (New York: Harper and Row, 1977), 189.
5. *The Habit of Being*, ed. Sally Fitzgerald (New York: Farrar, Straus, Giroux, 1979), 126.

disinterested moral behavior. It is impossible, because the will is not autonomous; it always inclines to what it perceives will bring the most happiness (John 8:34; Rom. 6:16; 2 Pet. 2:19).

Pascal was right when he said: "All men seek happiness without exception. They all aim at this goal however different the means they use to attain it. . . . They will never make the smallest move but with this as its goal. This is the motive of all the actions of all men, even those who contemplate suicide."[6]

But not only is disinterested morality (doing good "for its own sake") impossible; it is undesirable. That is, it is unbiblical because it would mean that the better a man became the harder it would be for him to act morally. The closer he came to true goodness the more naturally and happily he would do what is good. A good man in Scripture is not the man who dislikes doing good but toughs it out for the sake of duty. A good man *loves* kindness (Mic. 6:8) and *delights* in the law of the Lord (Ps. 1:2) and the will of the Lord (Ps. 40:8). But how shall such a man do an act of kindness disinterestedly? The better the man, the more joy in obedience.

Kant loves a disinterested giver. God loves a cheerful giver (2 Cor. 9:7). Disinterested performance of duty displeases God. He wills that we *delight* in doing good and that we do it with the confidence that our obedience secures and increases our joy in God.

Oh, that I could drive the notion out of our churches that virtue requires a stoical performance of duty—the notion that good things are promised merely as the *result* of obedience but not as an *incentive* for it. The Bible is replete with promises which are not appended carefully as nonmotivational *results,* but which clearly and boldly and hedonistically aim to motivate our behavior.

What sets off Biblical morality from worldly hedonism is not

---

6. Blaise Pascal, *Pascal's Pensées,* trans. W. F. Trotter (New York: E. P. Dutton, 1958), 113 (thought 425).

that Biblical morality is disinterested but that it is interested in vastly greater and purer things. Some examples:

Luke 6:35 says, "Love your enemies, and do good, and lend, expecting nothing in return, and your reward will be great." Note: We should never be motivated by worldly aggrandizement ("expect nothing in return"); but we are given strength to suffer loss in service of love by the promise of a future reward.

Again, in Luke 14:12–14: "When you give a dinner or a banquet, do not invite your friends or your brothers or your relatives or rich neighbors, lest they also invite you in return and you be repaid. But when you give a feast, invite the poor, . . . and you will be blessed, because they cannot repay you. You will be repaid at the resurrection of the just." Note: Don't do good deeds for worldly advantage; but do them for spiritual, heavenly benefits.

The Kantian philosopher will say, "No, no. These texts only describe what reward will *result* if you act disinterestedly. They do not teach us to seek the reward."

Two answers: (1) It is bad pedagogy to say, "Take this pill, and I will give you a nickel," if you think the desire for the nickel will ruin the taking of the pill. But Jesus was a wise teacher, not a foolish one. (2) Even more importantly, there are texts which not only commend but command that we do good in the hope of future blessing.

Luke 12:33 says, "Sell your possessions, and give to the needy. Provide yourselves with moneybags that do not grow old, with a treasure in the heavens that does not fail." The connection here between alms and having eternal treasure in heaven is not mere *result* but *aim*: "Make it your aim to have treasure in heaven, and the way to do this is to sell your possessions and give alms."

And again, Luke 16:9 says, "Make friends for yourselves by means of unrighteous wealth, so that when it fails they may receive you into the eternal dwellings." Luke does not say that the *result* of a proper use of possessions is to receive eternal habitations. He says, "Make it your *aim* to secure an eternal habitation by the way you use your possessions."

Therefore, a resounding *no* to Kantian morality. No in the pew and no in the pulpit. In the pew, the heart is ripped out of worship by the notion that it can be performed as a mere duty. There are two possible attitudes in genuine worship: delight in God or repentance for the lack of it.

Sunday at 11 A.M., Hebrew 11:6 enters combat with Immanuel Kant. "Without faith it is impossible to please him, for whoever would draw near to God must believe that he exists and that *he rewards those who seek him*." You cannot please God if you do not come to Him as *rewarder*. Therefore, worship which pleases God is the hedonistic pursuit of God in whose presence is fullness of *joy* and in whose hand are *pleasures* forevermore (Ps. 16:11).

And in the pulpit, brothers, what a difference it will make if we are Christian hedonists and not Kantian commanders of duty! Jonathan Edwards, the greatest preacher-theologian that America has ever produced, daringly said, "I should think myself in the way of my duty to raise the affections of my hearers as high as possibly I can, provided that they are affected with nothing but truth, and with affections that are not disagreeable to the nature of what they are affected with."[7] The ultimate reason Edwards believed this was his duty is his profound and Biblical conviction that

> God glorifies Himself toward the creatures . . . in two ways: 1. By appearing to . . . their understanding. 2. In communicating Himself to their hearts, and in their rejoicing and delighting in, and enjoying, the manifestations which He makes of Himself. . . . *God is glorified*

7. Jonathan Edwards, *Some Thoughts Concerning the Revival,* in *The Works of Jonathan Edwards,* vol. 4, ed. by C. Goen (New Haven, Conn.: Yale University Press, 1972), 87.

*not only by His glory's being seen, but by its being re-
joiced in.* When those that see it delight in it, God is
more glorified than if they only see it. . . . He that testifies his idea of God's glory [doesn't] glorify God so much
as he that testifies also his approbation of it and his delight in it.[8]

This is the ultimate foundation for Christian hedonism and profoundly shapes a pastor's pulpit ministry.

As Christian hedonists we know that every listener longs for
happiness. And we will never tell them to deny or repress that desire. Their problem is not that they want to be satisfied but that
they are far too easily satisfied. We will instruct them how to glut
their soul-hunger on the grace of God. We will paint God's glory in
lavish reds and yellows and blues, and hell we will paint with
smoky shadows of gray and charcoal. We will labor to wean them
off the milk of the world onto the rich fare of God's grace and
glory.

We will bend all our effort, by the Holy Spirit, to persuade our
people

- that "the reproach of Christ [is] greater wealth than the
  treasures of Egypt" (Heb. 11:26)
- that they can be happier in giving than receiving (Acts
  20:35)
- that they should count everything as loss for the surpassing worth of knowing Christ Jesus their Lord (Phil. 3:8)
- that the aim of all of Jesus' commandments is that their
  joy might be full (John 15:11)

8. Jonathan Edwards, The "Miscellanies," a-500, ed. by Thomas Schafer, *The Works of Jonathan Edwards*, vol. 13 (New Haven, Conn.: Yale University Press, 1994), 495. Miscellany 448; see also 87, 251–252; 332, 410; #679 (not in the New Haven vol.). Emphasis added. These Miscellanies were the private notebooks of Edwards from which he built his books, like *The End for Which God Created the World*.

- that if they delight themselves in the Lord He will give them the desires of their heart (Ps. 37:4)
- that there is great gain in godliness with contentment (1 Tim. 6:6)
- that the joy of the Lord is their strength (Neh. 8:11)

We will not try to motivate their ministry by Kantian appeals to mere duty. We will tell them that delight in God *is* their highest duty. But we will remind them that Jesus endured the cross for the *joy* that was set before Him (Heb. 12:2), and that Hudson Taylor, at the end of a life full of suffering and trial, said, "I never made a sacrifice."[9]

---

9. Howard and Geraldine Taylor, *Hudson Taylor's Spiritual Secret* (Chicago, Ill.: Moody Press, n.d.), 30.

> Prayer is the coupling of primary and secondary causes.
> It is the splicing of our limp wire to the lightning bolt of heaven.
>
> JOHN PIPER
>
> A pastor who feels competent in himself to produce eternal fruit
> knows neither God nor himself.
> A pastor who does not know the rhythm of desperation and deliverance
> must have his sights only on what man can achieve.
>
> JOHN PIPER
>
> When we depend upon organizations,
> we get what organizations can do;
> when we depend upon education,
> we get what education can do;
> when we depend upon man,
> we get what man can do;
> but when we depend upon prayer,
> we get what God can do.
>
> A. C. DIXON

8

BROTHERS, LET US PRAY

PRAYER IS THE coupling of primary and secondary causes. It is the splicing of our limp wire to the lightning bolt of heaven. How astonishing it is that God wills to do His work through people. It is doubly astonishing that He ordains to fulfill His plans by being asked to do so by us. God loves to bless His people. But even more He loves to do it in answer to prayer.

For example, God knew that His purpose was to increase the men of Israel. But He said, "This also *I will let the house of Israel ask me* to do for them: to increase their people like a flock" (Ezek.

36:37). He wills to convey to us our blessings through the coupling of prayer.

God knew He would preserve Abimelech's life if the king would return Sarah to Abraham. But He said to him: "Return the man's wife, for he is a prophet, *so that he will pray for you,* and you shall live" (Gen. 20:7). God desired to save Abimelech, but He wanted to do it through Abraham's prayer.

And who would say that God does not love the world or that He is hesitant to gather His harvest? Yet Jesus said, "*Pray . . . the Lord of the harvest* to send out laborers into his harvest" (Matt. 9:38). Why must the owner of the farm be implored by his farmhands to send out more laborers? Because there is one thing God loves to do more than bless the world. He loves to bless the world in answer to prayer.

I was amazed once to hear a seminary graduate say how adequate he felt for the ministry after his years of schooling. This was supposed to be a compliment to the school. The reason this amazed me is that the greatest theologian and missionary and pastor who ever lived cried out, "Who is sufficient for these things?" (2 Cor. 2:16). Not because he was a bungler, but because the awful calling of emitting the fragrance of eternal life for some and eternal death for others was a weight he could scarcely bear.

A pastor who feels competent in himself to produce eternal fruit—which is the only kind that matters—knows neither God nor himself. A pastor who does not know the rhythm of desperation and deliverance must have his sights only on what man can achieve.

But brothers, the proper goals of the life of a pastor are unquestionably beyond our reach. The changes we long for in the hearts of our people can happen only by a sovereign work of grace.

Salvation is a gift of God (Eph. 2:8). Love is a gift of God (1 Thess. 3:12). Faith is a gift of God (1 Tim. 1:14). Wisdom is a gift of God (Eph. 1:17). Joy is a gift of God (Rom. 15:13). Yet as pastors *we* must labor to "save some" (1 Cor. 9:22). *We* must stir up the people to love

(Heb. 10:24). *We* must advance their faith (Phil. 1:25). *We* must impart wisdom (1 Cor. 2:7). *We* must work for their joy (2 Cor. 1:24).

We are called to labor for that which is God's alone to give. The essence of the Christian ministry is that its success is not within our reach.

God's purpose is that *we* get the joy of service but that *He* gets the glory. "Whoever serves, [let him do so] as one who serves by the strength that God supplies—in order *that in everything God may be glorified*" (1 Pet. 4:11). "Neither he who plants nor he who waters is anything, but only God who gives the growth" (1 Cor. 3:7). God does all His gracious work in such a way "that no human being might boast in the presence of God" (1 Cor. 1:29), which means He usually does it in answer to prayer.

A cry for help from the heart of a childlike pastor is sweet praise in the ears of God. Nothing exalts Him more than the collapse of self-reliance which issues in passionate prayer for help. "*Call upon me* in the day of trouble; I will deliver you, and you shall *glorify me*" (Ps. 50:15). Prayer is the translation into a thousand different words of a single sentence: "Apart from me [Christ] you can do nothing" (John 15:5).

Oh, how we need to wake up to how much "nothing" we spend our time doing. Apart from prayer, all our scurrying about, all our talking, all our study amounts to "nothing." For most of us the voice of self-reliance is ten times louder than the bell that tolls for the hours of prayer. The voice cries out: "You must open the mail, you must make that call, you must write this sermon, you must prepare for the board meeting, you must go to the hospital." But the bell tolls softly: "Without Me you can do nothing."

Both our flesh and our culture scream against spending an hour on our knees beside a desk piled with papers. It is un-American to be so impractical as to devote oneself to prayer and meditation two hours a day. And sometimes I fear that our seminaries conform to this deadly pragmatism which stresses management and maneuvering as ways to get things done with a token mention of prayer and reliance on the Holy Spirit.

A. C. Dixon said,

> When we depend upon organizations, we get what organizations can do; when we depend upon education, we get what education can do; when we depend upon man, we get what man can do; but when we depend upon prayer, we get what God can do.[1]

I do not become excited when denominations or churches react to their lack of growth by merely adding a new program. I know that the reason so few conversions are happening through my church is *not* because we lack a program or staff. It is because we do not love the lost and yearn for their salvation the way we should. And the reason we do not love them as we ought is because such love is a miracle that overcomes our selfish bent. It cannot be managed or maneuvered into existence. It is an astonishing miracle.

Examine yourself: Does it lie within your power right now to weep over the spiritual destruction of the people on your street? Such tears come only through a profound work of God. If we want this work of God in our lives and in our churches, there will be agonizing prayer: "God, break my heart!" I choose the word "agonize" carefully. It is the word Paul used in Romans 15:30, "Now I appeal to you, brothers, by our Lord Jesus Christ and by the love of the Spirit, to strive together [*sunagōnizasthai*] with me in your prayers to God on my behalf." With such "agonizing together" God may grant tears. And without those tears we may shuffle

---

1. Quoted in G. Michael Cocoris, *Evangelism: A Biblical Approach* (Chicago, Ill.: Moody Press, 1984), 108.

members from church to church, but few people will pass from darkness to light.

Take one of your days off and go away by yourself and pray about how you should pray. Say to yourself right now: "God help me to do something radical in regard to prayer!" Refuse to believe that the daily hours Luther and Wesley and Brainerd and Judson spent in prayer are idealistic dreams of another era.

William Wilberforce, who fought unrelentingly in Parliament for the abolition of the slave trade in England, took his own spiritual temperature by consulting "the experience of all good men" and lamented:

> This perpetual hurry of business and company ruins me in soul if not in body. More solitude and earlier hours! I suspect I have been allotting habitually too little time to religious exercises, as private devotion and religious meditation, Scripture-reading, etc. Hence I am lean and cold and hard. I had better allot two hours or an hour and a half daily. I have been keeping too late hours, and hence have had but a hurried half-hour in the morning to myself. Surely the experience of all good men confirms the proposition that without a due measure of private devotions the soul will grow lean. But all may be done through prayer—almighty prayer, I am ready to say—and why not? For that it is almighty is only through the gracious ordination of the God of loving truth. On then, pray, pray, pray![2]

Are our packed calendars and handheld computers really fulfilling our own hunger for life in Christ, let alone the hunger of our

---

2. Quoted in E. M. Bounds, *Power Through Prayer* (Grand Rapids, Mich.: Baker Book House, 1972), 116.

people and the world? Are not our people really yearning to be around a man who has been around God? Is it not the lingering aroma of prayer that gives a sense of eternity to all our work?

Read about men of prayer, and you will get hungry to pray. Dozens of stories about praying saints have stirred me up to renewed prayer. I close with one from Charles Spurgeon, who writes:

> That was a grand action by Jerome, one of the Roman fathers. He laid aside all pressing engagements and went to fulfill the call God gave him, *viz.,* to translate the Holy Scriptures. His congregations were larger than many preachers of today, but he said to his people, "Now it is necessary that the Scriptures be translated; you must find another minister: I am bound for the wilderness and shall not return until my task is finished." Away he went and labored and prayed until he produced the Latin Vulgate, which will last as long as the world stands. So we must say to our friends, "I must go away and have time for prayer and solitude." And though we did not write Latin Vulgates, yet our work will be immortal: Glory to God.[3]

---

3. Charles Spurgeon, "The Christian Minister's Private Prayer," *The Sword and Trowel,* November 1868, 165.

> Ministry is its own worst enemy.
> It is not destroyed by the big, bad wolf of the world.
> It destroys itself.
>
> JOHN PIPER

> Those incessant knocks at our door,
> and perpetual visits from idle persons,
> are so many buckets of cold water thrown upon our devout zeal.
> We must by some means secure uninterrupted meditation,
> or we shall lose power.
>
> CHARLES SPURGEON

> The great threat to our prayer and our meditation on the Word of God
> is good ministry activity.
>
> JOHN PIPER

9

BROTHERS, BEWARE OF SACRED SUBSTITUTES

MINISTRY IS ITS own worst enemy. It is not destroyed by the big, bad wolf of the world. It destroys itself. One survey of pastors asked, "What are the most common obstacles to spiritual growth?" The top three were busyness (83 percent), lack of discipline (73 percent), and interruptions (47 percent). Most of these interruptions and most of our busyness is ministry-related, not "worldly." The great threat to our prayer and our meditation on the Word of God is good ministry activity. Charles Spurgeon put it like this: "Those incessant knocks at our door, and perpetual visits from idle persons, are so many buckets of cold water thrown upon our devout zeal. We must by some means secure uninterrupted meditation, or we shall lose power."[1]

That is the point of Acts 6:2–4:

> And the twelve summoned the full number of the disciples and said, "It is not right that we should give up preaching the word of God to serve tables. Therefore, brothers, pick out from among you seven men of good repute, full of the Spirit and of wisdom, whom we will appoint to this duty. But *we will devote ourselves to prayer* and to the ministry of the word."

Without extended and consecrated prayer, the ministry of the Word withers up and bears no fruit. The 120 were devoting themselves to *prayer* (Acts 1:14) when the Spirit fell and gave them utterance with three thousand converts (Acts 2:41). These converts were also devoting themselves to *prayer* (Acts 2:42) when signs and wonders were done and people were added to the church daily (Acts 2:43, 47). Peter and his friends were engaged in *prayer* when the place was shaken and they were filled with the Spirit and spoke the Word boldly (Acts 4:31). Paul relied on *prayer* that he might be given utterance to open his mouth and proclaim the mystery of the gospel (Eph. 6:19).

Without extended, concentrated prayer, the ministry of the Word withers. And when the ministry of the Word declines, faith (Rom. 10:17; Gal. 3:2, 5) and holiness (John 17:17) decline. Activity may continue, but life and power and fruitfulness fade away. Therefore, whatever opposes prayer opposes the whole work of ministry.

1. Charles H. Spurgeon, *Lectures to My Students* (Grand Rapids, Mich.: Zondervan Publishing House, 1972), 309.

And what opposes the pastor's life of prayer more than anything? The ministry. It is not shopping or car repairs or sickness or yard work that squeezes our prayers into hurried corners of the day. It is budget development and staff meetings and visitation and counseling and answering mail and writing reports and reading journals and answering the phone and preparing messages.

The effort to meet needs is, ironically, often the enemy of prayer. Literally, Acts 6:3 says, "Brothers, pick out from among you seven men of good repute, full of the Spirit and wisdom, whom we may appoint over *this need*." The care of the widows was a *real need*. And it was precisely this need which threatened apostolic prayer.

But the apostles would not yield to the temptation. This must mean that prayer demanded a large part of their uninterrupted time. If they had thought of prayer as something you do while washing dishes or cooking (or driving a car between hospitals), they would not have seen table-serving as a threat to prayer. Prayer was a time-consuming labor during which other duties had to be set aside.

They had learned from Jacob and from Jesus that whole nights may have to be spent in prayer (Gen. 32:24; Luke 6:12). Under the drain of ministry, we must "withdraw to desolate places and pray" (Luke 5:16). Before significant pastoral encounters we must pray *alone* (Luke 9:18). For Jesus and the apostles the work of prayer demanded significant amounts of solitude: "In the morning, while it was still dark, he departed and went out to a desolate place, and there he prayed" (Mark 1:35).

The apostles said, "We will *devote* ourselves to prayer" (Acts 6:4). The word translated "devote ourselves" *(proskartereō)* emphasizes the unbending commitment of the apostles to preserve time for prayer. It means "to persist at" and "remain with." It is used in Acts 10:7 to refer to the loyalty with which some soldiers served Cornelius. The idea is to be strong and persistent and unwavering in one's assignment.

So the apostles were saying: No matter how urgent the pressures upon us to spend our time doing good deeds, we will not forsake our chief work. We will persist in it. We will not waver or turn aside from the work of prayer.

This word *(proskartereō)* becomes firmly attached to the ministry of prayer in the early church. In Acts 1:14 the disciples were *"devoting themselves* to prayer," and in Acts 2:42 they "devoted themselves" to "prayers." Then in the epistles of Paul, this practice becomes a command: *"Be constant* in prayer" (Rom. 12:12). *"Continue steadfastly* in prayer" (Col. 4:2). "Keep alert *with all perseverance,* making supplication for all the saints" (Eph. 6:18). The more heavily engaged one is in battling the powers of darkness, the greater will be one's sense of need to spend time in prayer. Therefore, the apostles combine "prayer" and "the ministry of the Word" and free themselves from time-consuming good deeds.

The importance of prayer rises in proportion to the importance of the things we should give up in order to pray. If the work we are to give up is a work which requires great spiritual depth and power, then how much more crucial and demanding must be the work of prayer? And this is just the case in Acts 6:3.

The text does not say, "Apostles should do the spiritual work of prayer and get some practical folks to serve tables." It says, "Pick out from among you seven men of good repute, *full of the Spirit and of wisdom."* (Deacons and trustees ought not to be worldly financiers. They ought to be full of the Spirit and of wisdom.) It is not just the daily, routine demands of the pastorate that threaten our life of prayer. Prayer is also menaced by opportunities for ministry which demand fullness of the Spirit and wisdom. Even this we must forsake in order to devote ourselves to prayer.

Martin Luther was once asked by his barber, "Dr. Luther, how do you pray?" Astonishingly, one of the busiest men of the

Reformation wrote a forty-page response for his barber, Peter Beskendorf. His words are a great inspiration for us to beware of sacred substitutes.

> A good clever barber must have his thoughts, mind and eyes concentrated upon the razor and the beard and not forget where he is in his stroke and shave. If he keeps talking or looking around or thinking of something else, he is likely to cut a man's mouth or nose—or even his throat. So anything that is to be done well ought to occupy the whole man with all his faculties and members. As the saying goes: he who thinks of many things thinks of nothing and accomplishes no good. How much more must prayer possess the heart exclusively and completely if it is to be a good prayer![2]

Luther knew well the struggle to get down to praying when a dozen good things press for our time. So he exhorted himself and his barber:

> It is a good thing to let prayer be the first business in the morning and the last in the evening. Guard yourself against such false and deceitful thoughts that keep whispering: Wait a while. In an hour or so I will pray. I must first finish this or that. Thinking such thoughts we get away from prayer into other things that will hold us and involve us till the prayer of the day comes to naught.[3]

Oh, how we need to hear the earnest exhortations of our brothers. I preach to myself here. I long to know God in prayer better than I do. I hear the plea of A. A. Bonar, and I am prompted to get up from

2. Quoted from Walter Trobisch, *Martin Luther's Quiet Time* (Downers Grove, Ill.: InterVarsity Press, 1975), 4.
3. Ibid., 5.

my desk and go to my prayer bench and linger for a while with the Lord in prayer:

> O brother, pray; in spite of Satan, pray; spend hours in prayer; rather neglect friends than not pray; rather fast, and lose breakfast, dinner, tea, and supper—and sleep too—than not pray. And we must not talk about prayer, we must pray in right earnest. The Lord is near. He comes softly while the virgins slumber.[4]

Brothers, beware of sacred substitutes. Devote yourselves to prayer and to the ministry of the Word.

4. Quoted in *Free Grace Broadcaster* (Pensacola, Fla.: Mount Zion Bible Church) Issue 153, Summer 1995, 25.

> Few things frighten me more than the beginnings of barrenness
> that come from frenzied activity
> with little spiritual food and meditation.
>
> JOHN PIPER

> A student will find that his mental constitution
> is more affected by one book thoroughly mastered
> than by twenty books
> which he has merely skimmed, lapping at them.
>
> CHARLES SPURGEON

> It is a good rule, after reading a new book,
> never to allow yourself another new one
> till you have read an old one in between.
>
> C. S. LEWIS

10

BROTHERS, FIGHT FOR YOUR LIFE

I AGREE WITH Martyn Lloyd-Jones that the fight to find time to read is a fight for one's life. "Let your wife or anyone else take messages for you, and inform the people who are telephoning that you are not available. One literally has to fight for one's life in this sense!"[1]

---

1. D. Martyn Lloyd-Jones, *Preaching and Preachers* (Grand Rapids, Mich.: Zondervan Publishing House, 1971), 167.

Most of our people have no idea what two or three new messages a week cost us in terms of intellectual and spiritual drain. Not to mention the depletions of family pain, church decisions, and imponderable theological and moral dilemmas. I, for one, am not a self-replenishing spring. My bucket leaks, even when it is not pouring. My spirit does not revive on the run. Without time of unhurried reading and reflection, beyond the press of sermon preparation, my soul shrinks, and the specter of ministerial death rises. Few things frighten me more than the beginnings of barrenness that come from frenzied activity with little spiritual food and meditation.

The great pressure on us today is to be productive managers. But the need of the church is for prayerful, spiritual poets. I don't mean (necessarily) pastors who write poems. I mean pastors who feel the weight and glory of eternal reality even in the midst of a business meeting; who carry in their soul such a sense of God that they provide, by their very presence, a constant life-giving reorientation on the infinite God. For your own soul and for the life of your church, fight for time to feed your soul with rich reading. Almost all the forces in our culture are trivializing. If you want to stay alive to what is great and glorious and beautiful and eternal, you will have to fight for time to look through the eyes of others who were in touch with God. Here are a few suggestions that have helped me.

We think we don't have time to read. We despair of reading anything spiritually rich and substantial because life seems to be lived in snatches. One of the most helpful discoveries I have made is how much can be read in disciplined blocks of twenty minutes a day.

Suppose that you read slowly, say about 250 words a minute (as I do). This means that in twenty minutes you can read about five thousand words. An average book has about four hundred words to a page. So you could read about twelve-and-a-half pages in twenty minutes. Suppose you discipline yourself to read a certain author or topic twenty minutes a day, six days a week, for a year. That would be 312 times 12.5 pages for a total of 3,900 pages. Assume that an average book is 250 pages long. This means you could read fifteen books like that in one year.

Or take a longer classic like John Calvin's *Institutes* (fifteen hundred pages in the Westminster edition). At twenty minutes a day and 250 words a minute and six days a week, you could finish it in twenty-five weeks. Then Augustine's *The City of God* and B. B. Warfield's *Inspiration and Authority of the Bible* could be finished before year's end.

This astonishing discovery freed me from the paralysis of not starting great, mind-shaping, heart-enriching books because I lacked enough big blocks of time. It turns out that I don't need long periods of time in order to read three masterpieces in one year! I needed twenty minutes a day, six days a week.

Several other thoughts made the discovery even more exciting. Is it too hard to imagine disciplining yourself to set aside twenty minutes early in the morning, twenty minutes after lunch, and twenty minutes before you go to bed to read on various topics for your soul and mind? If not, then think what you could read! Thirty-six medium-sized books! John Stott says that an hour a day is an "absolute minimum for time for study which even the busiest pastors should be able to manage."

> Many will achieve more. But the minimum would amount to this: every day at least one hour; every week one morning, afternoon or evening; every month a full day; every year a week. Set out like this, it sounds very little. Indeed, it is too little. Yet everybody who tries it is surprised to discover how much reading can be done within such a disciplined framework. It tots up to nearly six hundred hours in the course of a year.[2]

2. John Stott, *Between Two Worlds: The Art of Preaching in the Twentieth Century* (Grand Rapids, Mich.: Wm. B. Eerdmans Publishing Company, 1982), 204.

Now don't get me wrong. I don't mean we should limit our reading to quick shots one or two times a day. But if you will use severe discipline to make regular short appointments with a given book, you can live in another great mind more than you thought you could—*beyond the more extended times you set aside for study and sermon preparation.*

Nor do I want to give the impression that I think there is virtue in reading many books. In fact one of my greatest complaints in seminary was that professors trained students in bad habits of superficial reading because they assigned too many books. I agree with Spurgeon: "A student will find that his mental constitution is more affected by one book thoroughly mastered than by twenty books which he has merely skimmed, lapping at them."[3] God save us from the allurement of "keeping up with Pastor Jones" by superficial skimming. Forget about "keeping up." It only feeds pride and breeds spiritual barrenness. Instead devote yourself to boring in and going deep. There is so much soul-refreshing, heart-deepening, mind-enlarging truth to be had from great books! Your people will know if you are walking with the giants (as Warren Wiersbe says) or watching television.

Take that early morning twenty minutes, for example. Perhaps you should not view it in isolation from your season of morning prayer but as an organic part of it and help to it. Lloyd-Jones again confesses for many of us:

> I have often found it difficult to start praying in the
> morning. . . . I have found nothing more important than
> to learn how to get oneself into that frame and condition
> in which one can pray. . . . To read something which can
> be characterized in general as devotional is of great value.

3. Charles H. Spurgeon, *Lectures to My Students* (Grand Rapids, Mich.: Zondervan Publishing House, 1972), 177.

By devotional I do not mean something sentimental, I mean something with a true element of worship in it. . . . Start by reading something that will warm your spirit. . . . You have to learn how to kindle a flame in your spirit. . . . You have to learn how to use a spiritual choke.[4]

For him (and for me) that meant primarily the Puritans, because there is so much "devotional" material today that is too light and too shallow and too a-theological to be helpful. It just doesn't carry a sense of the greatness of God. And so it leaves the soul starving for what we were created for—seeing all that God is for us in Jesus (2 Cor. 3:18).

C. S. Lewis helps us here with our prejudice against old books when he writes,

There is a strange idea abroad that in every subject the ancient books should be read only by the professionals, and that the amateur should content himself with the modern books. . . . This mistaken preference for the modern books and this shyness of the old ones is nowhere more rampant than in theology.

Now this seems to me topsy-turvy. Naturally, since I myself am a writer, I do not wish the ordinary reader to read no modern books. But if he must read only the new or only the old, I would advise him to read the old. . . . It is a good rule, after reading a new book, never to allow yourself another new one till you have read an old one in between. If that is too much for you, you should at least read one old one to every three new ones. . . . We all . . . need the books that will correct the characteristic mistakes of our own period. And that means the old books. . . . We

4. Lloyd-Jones, *Preaching and Preachers*, 170.

may be sure that the characteristic blindness of the twentieth century . . . lies where we have never suspected it. . . .
None of us can fully escape this blindness. . . . The only
palliative is to keep the clean sea breeze of the centuries
blowing through our minds, and this can be done only by
reading old books.[5]

I can think of no better way to begin an early morning season of
prayer than to mingle Scripture with a fifteen- or twenty-minute
taste of Jonathan Edwards' *Religious Affections,* or Bunyan's
Pilgrim's Progress, or Sibbes' *Bruised Reed,* or Baxter's *Saints'
Everlasting Rest,* or Boston's *Fourfold State,* or Burrough's
Christian Contentment, or Ryle's *Holiness,* or Bridges' *Christian
Ministry,* or Brook's *Precious Remedies,* or Flavel's *Method of
Grace.* It is amazing how many pastors, immersed in contemporary
reading on management and leadership and church growth, don't
even know such treasures for the soul exist. But, to our great benefit
they not only exist but are almost all still in print from publishers
like Banner of Truth Trust and Soli Deo Gloria. J. I. Packer is so
right when he says, "Not many believers seem to read the Puritan
reprints that are nowadays happily available. I believe that this neglect impoverishes us grievously, and I would like to see it end."[6]
My heart resonates with Lloyd-Jones:

I shall never cease to be grateful to one of [the
Puritans] called Richard Sibbes, who was a balm to my
soul at a period in my life when I was overworked and
badly overtired, and therefore subject in an unusual man-

5. C. S. Lewis, "On the Reading of Old Books," in *God in the Dock* (Grand Rapids:
Wm. B. Eerdmans Publishing Co., 1970), 200–207. This essay was first published as the
introduction to St. Athanasius, *The Incarnation of the Word of God,* trans. A Religious
of C.S.M.V. (London, 1944), 200–201.

6. J. I. Packer, *A Quest for Godliness: The Puritan Vision of the Christian Life*
(Wheaton, Ill.: Crossway Books, 1990), 50.

ner to the onslaughts of the Devil. In that state and condition, to read theology does not help, indeed it may be well-nigh impossible; what you need is some gentle treatment for your soul. . . . Sibbes' book *The Bruised Reed* and *The Soul's Conflict* quieted, soothed, comforted, encouraged and healed me.[7]

No, the point is not to read many books. The point is to stay alive in your soul, to keep the juices flowing, to fan the flame again on Monday and have it burning bright on Saturday night.

Brothers, fight for your life. Fight for your mornings! Protect those life-giving hours! But also gather up some of the vanishing moments, venture a new kind of daily discipline, and read the great life-giving books of the centuries in twenty-minute blocks.

7. Lloyd-Jones, *Preaching and Preachers*, 175.

> Think over what I say,
> for the Lord will give you understanding in everything.
>
> 2 TIMOTHY 2:7

> Sometimes we hear it said that ten minutes on your knees
> will give you a truer, deeper, more operative knowledge of God
> than ten hours over your books.
> "What!" is the appropriate response,
> "than ten hours over your books, on your knees?"
>
> BENJAMIN WARFIELD

> Resolved:
> To study the Scriptures so steadily, constantly, and frequently,
> as that I may find, and plainly perceive,
> myself to grow in the knowledge of the same.
>
> JONATHAN EDWARDS

11

BROTHERS, LET US QUERY THE TEXT

IF THE BIBLE is coherent, then understanding the Bible means grasping how things fit together. Becoming a Biblical theologian, which every pastor should be, means seeing more and more pieces fit together into a glorious mosaic of the divine design. And doing exegesis means querying the text about how its many propositions cohere in the author's mind, and through that, in God's mind.

If we are going to feed our people, we must ever advance in our grasp of Biblical truth. We must be like Jonathan Edwards who resolved in his college days, and kept the resolution all his life, "Resolved: To study the Scriptures so steadily, constantly, and frequently, as that I may find, and plainly perceive, myself to grow in the knowledge of the same."[1] Growing, advancing, increasing—that is the goal. And to advance we must be troubled by Biblical affirmations.

It must bother us that James and Paul don't seem to fit together. Only when we are troubled and bothered do we think hard. Paul told young pastor Timothy to think hard: "Think over what I say, for the Lord will give you understanding in everything" (2 Tim. 2:7). And if we don't think hard about how Biblical affirmations fit together, we will never penetrate to their common root and discover the beauty of unified divine truth—what David calls "wondrous things out of your law" (Ps. 119:18). The end result is that our Bible reading will become insipid, we will turn to fascinating "secondary literature," our sermons will be the lame work of "second-handers," and the people will go hungry.

"People only truly think when they are confronted with a problem," said John Dewey. "Without some kind of dilemma to stimulate thought, behavior becomes habitual rather than thoughtful." He was right. And that is why we will never think hard about Biblical truth until we are troubled by our faltering efforts to grasp its complexity.

We must form the habit of being systematically disturbed by things that at first glance don't make sense. Or to put it a different way, we must relentlessly query the text. One of the greatest honors I received while teaching Biblical studies at Bethel College in St. Paul, Minnesota, was when the teaching assistants in the Bible department gave me a T-shirt which had the initials of Jonathan

---

1. The seventy resolutions of the young Edwards are found in Sereno Dwight, *Memoirs of Jonathan Edwards*, in *The Works of Jonathan Edwards*, vol. 1 (Edinburgh: The Banner of Truth Trust, 1974), xx–xxi. This is resolution 28 from page xxi.

Edwards on the front and on the back the words: "Asking questions is the key to understanding."

But several strong forces oppose our relentless and systematic interrogating of Biblical texts. One is that it consumes a great deal of time and energy on one small portion of Scripture. We have been schooled (quite erroneously) that there is a direct correlation between reading a lot and gaining insight. But, in fact, there is no positive correlation at all between the quantity of pages read and the quality of insight gained. Just the reverse for most of us. Insight diminishes as we try to read more and more.

Insight or understanding is the product of intensive, headache-producing meditation on two or three propositions and how they fit together.[2] This kind of reflection and rumination is provoked by asking questions of the text. And you cannot do it if you hurry. Therefore, we must resist the deceptive urge to carve notches in our bibliographic gun. Take two hours to ask ten questions of Galatians 2:20, and you will gain one hundred times the insight you would have attained by quickly reading thirty pages of the New Testament or any other book. Slow down. Query. Ponder. Chew.

Another reason it is hard to spend hours probing for the roots of coherence is that it is fundamentally unfashionable today to systematize things and seek for harmony and unity. This noble quest has fallen on hard times because so much artificial harmony has been discovered by impatient and nervous Bible defenders. But if God's mind is truly coherent and not confused, and if the Bible is really His God-breathed book (2 Tim. 3:16), then exegesis must aim to see the coherence of Biblical revelation and the profound unity of divine truth. Unless we are to dabble forever on the surface of things

2. For the method I have found most helpful to interpret the Bible and fit propositions together, see John Piper, "Biblical Exegesis: Discovering the Original Meaning of Scriptural Texts" (Minneapolis, Minn.: Desiring God Ministries, 1999); and Thomas R. Schreiner, "Tracing the Argument," in *Interpreting the Pauline Epistles* (Grand Rapids, Mich.: Baker Book House, 1990), 97–126.

(content to turn up "tensions" and "difficulties"), then we must resist the atomistic (and basically anti-intellectual) fashions in the contemporary theological establishment. There is far too much debunking of past failures and far too little constructive, coherence-discovering thinking going on.

A third force that opposes the effort to ask questions of the Bible is this: Asking questions is the same as posing problems, and we have been discouraged all our lives from finding problems in God's Holy Book.

It is impossible to respect the Bible too highly, but it is possible to respect it wrongly. If we do not ask seriously how differing texts fit together, then we are either superhuman (and see all truth at a glance) or indifferent (and don't care about seeing the coherence of truth). But I don't see how anyone who is indifferent or superhuman can have a proper respect for the Bible. Therefore reverence for God's Word demands that we ask questions and pose problems *and* that we believe that there are answers and solutions which will reward our labor with treasures new and old (Matt. 13:52).

We must train our people that it is not irreverent to see difficulties in the Biblical text and to think hard about how they can be resolved. Preaching should model this for them week after week.

I do not accuse my six-year-old daughter, Talitha, of irreverence when she cannot make sense out of a Bible verse and asks me about it. She is just learning to read. But have *our* abilities to read been perfected? Can any of us pastors, at one reading, grasp the logic of a paragraph and see how every part relates to all the other parts and how they all fit together to make a unified point? How much less the thought of an entire epistle, the New Testament, the Bible! If we care about truth, we must relentlessly query the text and form the habit of being humbly bothered by things we read.

This is just the opposite of irreverence. It is what we do if we crave the mind of Christ. Nothing sends us deeper into the counsels of God than seeing apparent theological discrepancies in the Bible and pondering them day and night until they grow into an emerging vision of unified truth. For example, at one point I struggled for days with how Paul could say on the one hand, "Do not be anxious about anything" (Phil. 4:6), but on the other hand say (with apparent impunity) that his "anxiety for all the churches" was a daily pressure on him (2 Cor. 11:28). How could he say, "Rejoice always" (1 Thess. 5:16), and "Weep with those who weep" (Rom. 12:15)? How would he say to give thanks "always and for everything" (Eph. 5:20) and then admit, "I have great sorrow and *unceasing* anguish in my heart" (Rom. 9:2)?

More recently I have asked: "What does it mean that Jesus said in Matthew 5:39 to turn the other cheek when struck, but said in Matthew 10:23, 'When they persecute you in one town, flee'? When do you flee, and when do you endure hardship and turn the other cheek?" I have also been pondering in what sense it is true that God is "slow to anger" (Exod. 34:6) and in what sense "his wrath is quickly kindled" (Ps. 2:12).

There are hundreds and hundreds of such apparent disparities in the Holy Scripture, and we dishonor the text not to see them and think them through to the root of unity. God is not a God of confusion. His tongue is not forked. There are profound and wonderful resolutions to all problems—whether we see them in this life or not. He has called us to an eternity of discovery so that every morning for ages to come we might break forth in new songs of praise.

I already quoted 2 Timothy 2:7. But I close now by pointing out the relationship between the two halves of this verse. There is a command and a promise. Paul commanded, "*Think* over what I say." And then he promised, "God will give you understanding in everything." Some people see tension between cogitation and illumination. Not Paul. He commands cogitation. And he promises illumination. How do the command and promise fit together? The little connecting word *for* gives the answer. "Think . . . *because* God will reward you with understanding."

A text like this explains why Benjamin Warfield reacted with dismay at those who elevated prayer for divine illumination above rigorous observation of God's written Word and serious intellectual reflection on what it says. Warfield taught at Princeton Seminary for thirty-four years until his death in 1921. In 1911, he gave an address to students with this exhortation. "Sometimes we hear it said that ten minutes on your knees will give you a truer, deeper, more operative knowledge of God than ten hours over your books. 'What!' is the appropriate response, 'than ten hours over your books, on your knees?'"[3]

This is why the Bible has so many appeals to us that we should both meditate on the written Word of God with our minds and pray that God do His revelatory work in our hearts. "This Book of the Law shall not depart from your mouth, but you shall meditate on it day and night" (Josh. 1:8). "His delight is in the law of the LORD, and on his law he meditates day and night" (Ps. 1:2). "Oh how I love your law! It is my meditation all the day" (Ps. 119:97). "I will meditate on your precepts and fix my eyes on your ways" (Ps. 119:15). "I will lift up my hands to your commandments, which I love, and I will meditate on your statutes" (Ps. 119:48). "My eyes anticipate the night watches, that I may meditate on Your word" (Ps. 119:148 NASB). "I remember the days of old; I meditate on all that you have done; I ponder the work of your hands" (Ps. 143:5). "Those who are according to the flesh set their minds on the things of the flesh, but those who are according to the Spirit, the things of the Spirit" (Rom. 8:5 NASB). "Set your mind on things that are above, not on things that are on earth" (Col. 3:2).

To all the commands to meditate and think about God's Word, the Bible adds the promise, "The Lord will give you understanding."

---

3. Benjamin Warfield, "The Religious Life of Theological Students," in Mark Noll, ed., *The Princeton Theology* (Grand Rapids, Mich.: Baker Book House, 1983), 263.

The gift of illumination does not replace meditation. It comes through meditation. The promise of divine light is not made to all. It is made to those who *think*. "Think over what I say, for God will give you understanding in everything." And we do not think until we are confronted with a problem. Therefore, brothers, let us query the text.

> The more a theologian detaches himself
> from the basic Hebrew and Greek text of Holy Scripture,
> the more he detaches himself from the source of real theology!
> And real theology is the foundation of a fruitful and blessed ministry.
>
> HEINRICH BITZER
>
> Languages are the scabbard that contains the sword of the Spirit;
> they are the casket which contains the priceless jewels of antique thought;
> they are the vessel that holds the wine;
> and as the gospel says, they are the baskets
> in which the loaves and fishes are kept to feed the multitude. . . .
> As dear as the gospel is to us all,
> let us as hard contend with its language.
>
> MARTIN LUTHER
>
> The original Scriptures well deserve your pains,
> and will richly repay them.
>
> JOHN NEWTON

12

BROTHERS, BITZER WAS A BANKER

IN 1982, Baker Book House reissued a 1969 book of daily Scripture readings in Hebrew and Greek called *Light on the Path*. The readings were short, and vocabulary helps were given with the Hebrew verses. The aim of the editor, who died in 1980, was to help pastors preserve and improve their ability to interpret the Bible from the original languages.

His name was Heinrich Bitzer. He was a banker.

A banker! Brothers, must we be admonished by the sheep as to what our responsibility is as shepherds? Evidently so. For we are surely not admonishing and encouraging each other to press on in Greek and Hebrew. And most seminaries, evangelical as well as liberal, have communicated by their curriculum emphases that learning Greek and Hebrew may have some value for a few rare folks but is optional for the pastoral ministry.

I have a debt to pay to Heinrich Bitzer, and I would like to discharge it by exhorting all of us to ponder his thesis: "The more a theologian detaches himself from the basic Hebrew and Greek text of Holy Scripture, the more he detaches himself from the source of real theology! And real theology is the foundation of a fruitful and blessed ministry."[1]

What happens to a denomination when a useful knowledge of Greek and Hebrew is not cherished and encouraged for the pastoral office? I don't mean simply offered and admired. I mean cherished, promoted, and sought.

Several things happen as the original languages fall into disuse among pastors. First, the confidence of pastors to determine the precise meaning of Biblical texts diminishes. And with the confidence to interpret rigorously goes the confidence to preach powerfully. It is difficult to preach week in and week out over the whole range of God's revelation with depth and power if you are plagued with uncertainty when you venture beyond basic gospel generalities.

Second, the uncertainty of having to depend on differing translations—which always involve much interpretation—will tend to discourage careful textual analysis in sermon preparation. For as soon as you start attending to crucial details like tenses, conjunctions, and vocabulary repetitions, you realize the translations are too diverse to provide a sure basis for such analysis. For example,

1. Heinrich Bitzer, ed., *Light on the Path: Daily Scripture Readings in Hebrew and Greek* (Grand Rapids. Mich.: Baker Book House, 1982), 10.

most of the modern English translations (RSV, NIV, NASB, NLT) do not enable the expositor to see that "have fruit" in Romans 6:22 links with "bear fruit" five verses later in Romans 7:4.[2] They all translate Romans 6:22 without the word *fruit*.

So the preacher often contents himself with the general focus or flavor of the text, and his exposition lacks the precision and clarity which excite a congregation with the Word of God. Boring generalities are a curse in many pulpits.

Expository preaching, therefore, falls into disuse and disfavor. I say disfavor because we often tend to protect ourselves from difficult tasks by minimizing or ignoring their importance. So what we find in groups where Greek and Hebrew are not cherished and pursued and promoted is that expository preaching—which devotes a good bit of the sermon to explaining the meaning of the text—is not much esteemed by the preachers or taught in the seminaries.

Sometimes this is evident in outright denunciation of exposition as pedantic and schoolish. More often there is simply a benign neglect; and an emphasis on sermonic features like order, diction, illustration, and relevance crowds out the need for careful textual exposition.

Another result when pastors do not study the Bible in Greek and Hebrew is that they, and their churches with them, tend to become second-handers. The harder it is for us to get at the original meaning of the Bible, the more we will revert to the secondary literature. For one thing, it is easier to read. It also gives us a superficial glow that we are "keeping up" on things. And it provides us with ideas and insights which we can't dig out of the original for ourselves.

We may impress one another for a while by dropping the name of the latest book we've read, but secondhand food will not sustain and deepen our people's faith and holiness.

---

2. Of modern translations, the ESV is one of the few that gets it right.

Weakness in Greek and Hebrew also gives rise to exegetical imprecision and carelessness. And exegetical imprecision is the mother of liberal theology.

Where pastors can no longer articulate and defend doctrine by a reasonable and careful appeal to the original meaning of Biblical texts, they will tend to become close-minded traditionalists who clutch their inherited ideas, or open-ended pluralists who don't put much stock in doctrinal formulations. In both cases the succeeding generations will be theologically impoverished and susceptible to error.

Further, when we fail to stress the use of Greek and Hebrew as valuable in the pastoral office, we create an eldership of professional academicians. We surrender to the seminaries and universities essential dimensions of our responsibility as elders and overseers of the churches. I am deeply grateful for seminaries and for Bible-believing, God-centered, Christ-exalting scholars. But did God really intend that the people who interpret the Bible most carefully be one step removed from the weekly ministry of the Word in the church?

Acts 20:27 charges *us* with the proclamation of "the whole counsel of God." But we look more and more to the professional academicians for books which fit the jagged pieces of revelation into a unified whole. Acts 20:28 charges *us* to take heed for the flock and guard it from wolves who rise up in the church and speak perverse things. But we look more and more to the linguistic and historical specialists to fight our battles for us in books and articles. We have, by and large, lost the Biblical vision of a pastor as one who is mighty in the Scriptures, apt to teach, competent to confute opponents, and able to penetrate to the unity of the whole counsel of God. Is it healthy or biblical for the church to cultivate an eldership of pastors (weak in the Word) and an eldership of professors (strong in the Word)?

One of the greatest tragedies in the church today is the depreciation of the pastoral office. From seminaries to denominational headquarters, the prevalent mood and theme is managerial, organizational, and psychological. And we think thereby to heighten our professional self-esteem! Hundreds of teachers and leaders put the mastery of the Word first *with their lips* but by their curriculums, conferences, seminars, and personal example, show that it is not foremost.

One glaring example is the nature of the doctor of ministry programs across the country.

The theory is good: continuing education makes for better ministers. But where can you do a D.Min. in Hebrew language and exegesis? Yet what is more important and more deeply *practical* for the pastoral office than advancing in Greek and Hebrew exegesis by which we mine God's treasures?

Why then do hundreds of young and middle-aged pastors devote years of effort to everything but the languages when pursuing continuing education? And why do seminaries not offer incentives and degrees to help pastors maintain the most important pastoral skill— exegesis of the original meaning of Scripture?

No matter what we say about the inerrancy of the Bible, our actions reveal our true convictions about its centrality and power.

We need to recover our vision of the pastoral office—which embraces, if nothing else, the passion and power to understand the original revelation of God. We need to pray for the day when pastors can carry their Greek Testaments to conferences and seminars without being greeted with one-liners—the day when the esteem of God's Word and its careful exposition is so high among pastors that those who do not have the skill will humbly bless and encourage those who do and will encourage younger men to get what they never got. Oh, for the day when prayer and grammar will meet each other with great spiritual combustion!

In 1829, twenty-four-year-old George Mueller, famous for his faith and prayer and orphanages, wrote:

> I now studied much, about 12 hours a day, chiefly
> Hebrew . . . [and] committed portions of the Hebrew Old
> Testament to memory; and this I did with prayer, often
> falling on my knees. . . . I looked up to the Lord even
> whilst turning over the leaves of my Hebrew dictionary.[3]

In the Methodist Archives of Manchester you can see the two-volume Greek Testament of the evangelist George Whitefield liberally furnished with notes on the interleaved paper. He wrote of his time at Oxford, "Though weak, I often spent two hours in my evening retirements and prayed over my Greek Testament, and Bishop Hall's most excellent *Contemplations,* every hour that my health would permit."[4]

Luther said, "If the languages had not made me positive as to the true meaning of the word, I might have still remained a chained monk, engaged in quietly preaching Romish errors in the obscurity of a cloister; the pope, the sophists, and their anti-Christian empire would have remained unshaken."[5] In other words, he attributes the breakthrough of the Reformation to the penetrating power of the original languages.

Luther spoke against the backdrop of a thousand years of church darkness without the Word when he said boldly, "It is certain that unless the languages remain, the Gospel must finally perish."[6] He asks, "Do you inquire what use there is in learning the languages . . .? Do you say, 'We can read the Bible very well in German?'" And he answers:

3. George Mueller, *Autobiography of George Mueller* (London: J. Nisbet and Co., 1906), 31.

4. Arnold Dallimore, *George Whitefield,* vol. 1 (Edinburgh: The Banner of Truth Trust, 1970), 77.

5. W. Carlos Martyn, *The Life and Times of Martin Luther* (New York: American Tract Society, 1866), 474.

6. Hugh T. Kerr, *A Compend of Luther's Theology* (Philadelphia, Pa.: The Westminster Press, 1943), 17.

Without languages we could not have received the Gospel. Languages are the scabbard that contains the sword of the Spirit; they are the casket which contains the priceless jewels of antique thought; they are the vessel that holds the wine; and as the gospel says, they are the baskets in which the loaves and fishes are kept to feed the multitude.

If we neglect the literature we shall eventually lose the gospel. . . . No sooner did men cease to cultivate the languages than Christendom declined, even until it fell under the undisputed dominion of the pope. But no sooner was this torch relighted, than this papal owl fled with a shriek into congenial gloom. . . . In former times the fathers were frequently mistaken, because they were ignorant of the languages and in our days there are some who, like the Waldenses, do not think the languages of any use; but although their doctrine is good, they have often erred in the real meaning of the sacred text; they are without arms against error, and I fear much that their faith will not remain pure.[7]

Brothers, perhaps the vision can grow with your help. It is never too late to learn the languages. There are men who began after retirement! It is not a question of time but of values. John Newton, the author of "Amazing Grace" and former sea captain, was a pastors' pastor with a winsome, gentle love for people who, nevertheless, thought it important to pursue the languages. He once counseled a younger minister, "The original Scriptures well deserve your pains, and will richly repay them."[8] Concerning the early years of studying the languages he says:

7. Martyn, *The Life and Times of Martin Luther,* 474–75.
8. John Newton, *The Works of the Rev. John Newton,* vol. 1 (Edinburgh: The Banner of Truth Trust, 1985), 143.

You must not think that I have attained, or ever aimed at, a critical skill in any of these: . . . In the Hebrew, I can read the Historical Books and Psalms with tolerable ease; but, in the Prophetical and difficult parts, I am frequently obliged to have recourse to lexicons, etc. However, I know so much as to be able, with such helps as are at hand, to judge for myself the meaning of any passage I have occasion to consult.[9]

Continuing education is being pursued everywhere. Let's give heed to the word of Martin Luther: "As dear as the gospel is to us all, let us as hard contend with its language." Bitzer did. And Bitzer was a banker!

---

9. Richard Cecil, *Memoirs of the Rev. John Newton,* in *The Works of the Rev. John Newton,* vol. 1, 49–50. For the story of Newton's life and ministry see John Piper, *The Roots of Endurance: Invincible Perseverance in the Lives of John Newton, Charles Simeon, and William Wilberforce* (Wheaton, Ill.: Crossway Books, 2002).

> Christian biography is the means by which
> the body life of the church cuts across the centuries.
>
> JOHN PIPER

> Biographies have served
> as much as any other human force in my life
> to resist the inertia of mediocrity.
> Without them I tend to forget
> what joy there is
> in relentless God-besotted labor and aspiration.
>
> JOHN PIPER

13

BROTHERS, READ CHRISTIAN BIOGRAPHY

HEBREWS 11 is a divine mandate to read Christian biography. The unmistakable implication of the chapter is that if we hear about the faith of our forefathers (and mothers), we will "lay aside every weight, and sin" and "run with endurance the race that is set before us" (Heb. 12:1). If we asked the author, "How shall we stir one another up to love and good works?" (10:24), his answer would be: "Through encouragement from the living (10:25) and *the dead*

(11:1–40)." Christian biography is the means by which the body life of the church cuts across the centuries.

This fellowship of the living and the dead is especially crucial for pastors. As leaders in the church, we are supposed to have vision for the future. We are supposed to declare prophetically where our church should be going. We are supposed to inspire people with great possibilities.

Not that *God* can't give vision and direction and inspiration. But He regularly uses human agents to stir up His people. So the question for us pastors is: Through what human agents does God give *us* vision and direction and inspiration? For me, one of the most important answers has been great men and women of faith who, though dead, are yet speaking (Heb. 11:4).

Christian biography, well chosen, combines all sorts of things pastors need but have so little time to pursue. Good biography is history and guards us against chronological snobbery (as C. S. Lewis calls it). It is also theology—the most powerful kind—because it bursts forth from the lives of people. It is also adventure and suspense, for which we have a natural hunger. It is psychology and personal experience, which deepen our understanding of human nature (especially ourselves). Good biographies of great Christians make for remarkably efficient reading.

Since biography is its own best witness, let me tell a little of my own encounter with biographies. Biographies have served as much as any other human force in my life to resist the inertia of mediocrity. Without them I tend to forget what joy there is in relentless God-besotted labor and aspiration. I have devoted more time to the life of Jonathan Edwards (great biography by Iain Murray[1]) than to any other nonbiblical person. Before he was twenty years

---

1. Iain Murray, *Jonathan Edwards: A New Biography* (Edinburgh: The Banner of Truth Trust, 1987).

old, Edwards wrote seventy resolutions, which for years have inspired my work. Number 6 was: "To live with all my might, while I do live." Number 11: "When I think of any theorem in divinity to be solved, immediately to do what I can towards solving it, if circumstances do not hinder." Number 28: "To study the Scriptures so steadily, constantly and frequently, as that I may find, and plainly perceive, myself to grow in the knowledge of the same."[2]

When I came to be pastor of Bethlehem Baptist Church in 1980, I began to hunger for biographies to charge my pastoral batteries and give me guidance and encouragement. Since I believe very much in the pastor-theologian, I recalled not only Edwards but, of course, John Calvin. (T. H. L. Parker has a small *Portrait* and a major biography.[3])

How Calvin could work! After 1549, his special charge in Geneva was to preach twice on Sunday and once *every day* of alternate weeks. On Sunday, August 25, 1549, Calvin began to preach on Acts and continued weekly in that book until March 1554. On weekdays during this time, he preached through eight of the minor prophets as well as Daniel, Lamentations, and Ezekiel. But what amazes me is that between 1550 and 1559 he took 270 weddings. That's one every other week! He also baptized (about once a month), visited the sick, carried on extensive correspondence, and sustained heavy organizational responsibilities.

When I look at Calvin and Edwards and their output, it is hard for me to feel sorry for myself in my few burdens. These brothers inspire me to break out of mediocre plodding.

Parker (who, by the way, spent most of his forty-plus-years' ministry in country parishes) also published a short biography of Karl

---

2. Edwards's resolutions are found in Sereno Dwight, *Memoirs of Jonathan Edwards,* in *The Works of Jonathan Edwards*, vol. 1 (Edinburgh: The Banner of Truth Trust, 1974), xx–xxi.

3. T. H. L Parker, *Portrait of Calvin* (Philadelphia, Pa.: Westminster Press, 1954); *John Calvin: A Biography* (Philadelphia, Pa.: Westminster Press, 1975).

Barth in 1970, which I devoured in my middler year in seminary. Besides being just plain interesting, because of tidbits like Barth's playing Mozart before he took up his pen,[4] it had a tremendous impact on me because of two simple sentences. One was: "That evening Barth began [writing] a pamphlet which he finished the next day, a Sunday (13,000 words in a day!)."[5] I responded, "If neo-orthodoxy merits such phenomenal labor, how much more evangelical orthodoxy!"

The other sentence was, "Barth retired from his chair in Basel in March 1962 and so lost the stimulus provided by the need to give lectures."[6] I wrote in the flap of the book, "Has greatness emerged from anything but pressure? If greatness is to be the servant of all, must we not be under authority, under demand, pushed, pressed?"

There was also a season in my pastoral ministry when I was greatly encouraged in my work by Warren Wiersbe's *Walking with the Giants* and *Listening to the Giants*.[7] The main reason these collections of mini-biographies have been helpful is that they showed diversity of pastoral styles God has chosen to bless. There have been great and fruitful pastors whose preaching patterns, visitation habits, and personalities were so different that all of us may take courage.

One humorous example: Over against the austere Jonathan Edwards, who measured his food intake so as to maximize his alertness for study, you can put Spurgeon, who weighed more than three

---

4. T. H. L. Parker, *Karl Barth* (Grand Rapids, Mich.: Wm. B. Eerdmans Publishing Company, 1970), 110. "He made Mozart's music a part of his preparation for writing the *Church Dogmatics*, so that his custom was to listen to Mozart on the gramophone before he took up his pen."

5. Ibid., 87.

6. Ibid., 124.

7. Warren Wiersbe, *Walking with the Giants: A Minister's Guide to Good Reading and Great Preaching* (Grand Rapids, Mich.: Baker Book House, 1976); *Listening to the Giants: A Guide to Good Reading and Great Preaching* (Grand Rapids, Mich.: Baker Book House, 1980).

hundred pounds and smoked cigars. Yet both of these men won more converts to Christ than most of us will.

Spurgeon said to a Methodist critic, "If I ever find myself smoking to excess, I promise I shall quit entirely." "What would you call smoking to excess?" the man asked. "Why, smoking two cigars at the same time!" was the answer.[8]

George Mueller has been a pacesetter for me in prayer. His *Autobiography* is an orchard of faith-building fruit. In one section he tells us, after forty years of trials, "how to be constantly happy in God." He said, "I saw more clearly than ever that the first great and primary business to which I ought to attend every day was to have my soul happy in the Lord."[9] For ten years, he explained, he went at this backward. "Formerly, when I rose I began to pray as soon as possible and generally spent all my time till breakfast in prayer." The result: "Often after having suffered much from wandering of mind for the first ten minutes, or quarter of an hour, or even half an hour, I only then began really to pray."

So Mueller changed his pattern and made a discovery which sustained him forty years.

> I began to meditate on the New Testament, from the beginning, early in the morning . . . searching into every verse for the sake of obtaining food for my own soul. The result I have found almost invariably this, that after a very few minutes my soul has been led to confession or to thanksgiving, or to intercession, or to supplication; so that though I did not, as it were, give myself to *prayer,* but to meditation; yet, it turned almost immediately more or less into prayer.[10]

8. Wiersbe, *Walking with the Giants,* 74.
9. George Mueller, *Autobiography of George Mueller* (London: J. Nisbet and Co., 1906), 152.
10. Ibid., 153.

I have found Mueller's way absolutely crucial in my own life: be with the Lord before I am with anyone else and let *Him* speak to me first.

Something else surprised me and inspired me from Mueller's life. He prayed with astonishing confidence for supplies for his orphanage. But when his wife became ill with rheumatic fever, he prayed:

> Yes, my Father, the times of my darling wife are in Thy hands. Thou wilt do the very best thing for her and for me, whether life or death. If it may be, raise up yet again my precious wife—Thou art able to do it, though she is so ill; but howsoever Thou dealest with me, only help me to continue to be perfectly satisfied with Thy holy will.[11]

His wife died, and Mueller preached her funeral sermon from Psalm 119:68: "Thou art good and doest good" (KJV).[12]

What a world of difference between this view of God and the one I found when I read William Barclay's *Spiritual Autobiography*. Barclay was for many years on the divinity faculty at the University of Glasgow, Scotland, and a popular commentator. He lost a daughter at sea, but his response was not that of George Mueller, who said, "I know, O LORD, that . . . in faithfulness you have afflicted me" (Ps. 119:75). Instead, Barclay said, "I believe that pain and suffering are never the will of God for His children." To call a fatal accident an "act of God," he said, is blasphemous.[13]

Barclay's *Autobiography* is the more depressing when I think how many evangelical pastors have fed on Barclay's commentaries for almost every sermon. He scorned a view of the atonement in which the death of Christ propitiates the wrath of God.[14] And he wrote, "I

11. Ibid., 442.
12. Ibid., 431.
13. William Barclay, *A Spiritual Autobiography* (Grand Rapids, Mich.: Wm. B. Eerdmans Publishing Co., 1975), 44.
14. Ibid., 52.

am a convinced universalist. I believe that in the end all men will be gathered into the love of God."[15] I can't help wondering whether the theological weakness of many pulpits today is owing to the facile dependence on the anemic, unbiblical theology of commentators like Barclay.

I would rather stake my life on the theology of Sarah Edwards. When she heard that her husband Jonathan had died of a smallpox vaccination at the age of fifty-four, leaving her with ten children, she wrote to her daughter:

> What shall I say? A holy and good God has covered us with a dark cloud. O that we may kiss the rod and lay our hands on our mouths! The Lord has done it. He has made me adore His goodness, that we had him so long. But my God lives; and He has my heart. O what a legacy my husband, and your father, has left us. We are all given to God; and there I am and love to be.[16]

To show you one of the incidental values of reading Christian biography, I close with a word of appreciation for Carl Lundquist, the former president of Bethel College and Seminary. As he was completing his twenty-eight-year presidency, I wanted to write to him and express my love and appreciation to him. He was the president during my six years on the faculty and treated me with great kindness.

It so happened that I was reading the autobiography of A. H. Strong, who himself had been the president of Rochester Theological Seminary. Here I found the words to add spicy truth to my letter of gratitude. Strong wrote, "I have always thought that there must be a future life for canal horses, washerwomen and

15. Ibid., 58.
16. Quoted in Murray, *Jonathan Edwards*, 442.

college presidents; since they do not get their desserts in this life, there must be another life, to justify the ways of God."[17]

Living theology. Flawed and encouraging saints. Stories of grace. Deep inspiration. The best entertainment. Brothers, it is worth your precious hours. Remember Hebrews 11. And read Christian biography.[18]

17. Augustus Hopkins Strong, *Autobiography of Augustus Hopkins Strong* (Valley Forge, Pa.: Judson Press, 1981), 22.
18. One of the most fruitful disciplines I have ever undertaken has been to present a biographical study to the Bethlehem Conference for Pastors once a year. This has forced me to do more reading than I would have without this commitment. These are now being published in the series called The Swans Are Not Silent. See John Piper, *The Legacy of Sovereign Joy: God's Triumphant Grace in the Lives of Augustine, Luther, and Calvin* (Wheaton, Ill.: Crossway Books, 2000); *The Hidden Smile of God: The Fruit of Affliction in the Lives of John Bunyan, William Cowper, and David Brainerd* (Wheaton, Ill.: Crossway Books, 2001); *The Roots of Endurance: Invincible Perseverance in the Lives of John Newton, Charles Simeon, and William Wilberforce* (Wheaton, Ill.: Crossway Books, 2002). I would encourage all pastors to consider presenting to their people an inspiring biographical study of some great Christian at least once a year.

Our beloved brother Paul, according to the wisdom given him,
wrote to you, as also in all his letters . . .
in which are some things hard to understand,
which the untaught and unstable distort,
as they do also the rest of the Scriptures,
to their own destruction.

2 PETER 3:15–16 NASB

God is no fonder of intellectual slackers than of any other slackers.
If you are thinking of becoming a Christian, I warn you that you are em-
barking on something which is going to take the whole of you, brains
and all. But fortunately, it works the other way around. Anyone who is
honestly trying to be a Christian will soon find his intelligence being
sharpened: one of the reasons why it needs no special education to be a
Christian is that Christianity is an education itself.

C. S. LEWIS

14

BROTHERS, SHOW YOUR PEOPLE WHY GOD INSPIRED HARD TEXTS

THE IMPLICATIONS are huge that God has made a book so crucial in the preservation and declaration of saving truth. These implications become more remarkable because the book has some
parts that are really difficult to understand. What does it mean for
life and culture and history and worship that God has given

Christianity a book with some mind-straining texts and then built the church on it?

These thoughts were inspired as I was preaching through Romans and came to Romans 3:1–8. My brain almost broke trying to understand the complexity of that paragraph. So I stepped back and asked, "What was unleashed in the world by the fact that Christianity not only declares salvation through faith in Jesus but also builds its arguments and fixes its message in a book, the Bible, and in letters like the Letter to the Romans, and in paragraphs like Romans 3:1–8?"

Someone might say: "The problem is us. The Biblical writers are not perplexing. We are dull. If we were more spiritual, and more docile, we would not find God's word so difficult." Well, that is half true. I am dull. But that is not the only problem. The apostle Peter said in his second letter, "Our beloved brother Paul, according to the wisdom given him, wrote to you, as also in all his letters . . . in which are some things *hard to understand,* which the untaught and unstable distort, as they do also the rest of the Scriptures, to their own destruction" (2 Pet. 3:15–16 NASB).

Note four simple and obvious things: (1) Paul wrote with wisdom "given to him," and Peter means wisdom given by God (as 1 Cor. 2:13 says). (2) Therefore, Peter says, Paul's writings are in the category of the "other Scriptures"; the apostles' writings are in the same category as the inspired Old Testament Scriptures. (3) Nevertheless, some of what he wrote was "hard to understand." God, the perfect communicator (because He is perfect in every way) does not make everything easy when He guides a writer what to write. (4) This is an apostle talking, not John Piper. So I feel in good company when I say that some paragraphs in Paul are hard to understand.

And I go on now to ask, "What does it mean that God should inspire such difficult paragraphs in His book? What did God unleash in the world by building His Church on the foundation of writings like these?"

I'll mention four things and then balance them with the less complex side of the gospel. Four things: desperation, supplication, cogitation, and education.

1. *Desperation* (A sense of utter dependence on God's enablement)

I see this in 1 Corinthians 2:14, "The natural person does not accept the things of the Spirit of God, for they are folly to him, and he is not able to understand them because they are spiritually appraised." The natural person (all of us without the Spirit's work in our lives) should feel desperation before the revelation of God. He needs God's help. Well, the same thing is true of spiritual—yet finite and fallible and sinful—people like me, when I meet difficult texts of God's Word. I should feel desperation, a desperate dependence on God's help. That is what God wants us to feel. That is something He has unleashed by inspiring difficult texts.

2. *Supplication* (Prayer to God for help)

This follows from desperation. If you feel dependent on God to help you see the meaning of a text, then you will cry to Him for help. I see this in Psalm 119:18, "Open my eyes, that I may behold wondrous things out of your law." Seven times in one psalm the psalmist prays, "Teach me your statutes" (119:12, 26, 64, 68, 124, 135, 171). Or as Psalm 25:5 says, "Lead me in your truth and teach me." By inspiring some things hard to understand, God has unleashed in the world desperation which leads to supplication—the crying out to God for help.

3. *Cogitation* (Thinking hard about Biblical texts)

You might think, "No, no, you are confused, John. You just said that God wants us to *pray* for His help in understanding, not to *think* our way through to a solution." But the answer to that concern is, "No, praying and thinking are not alternatives." We saw this in chapter 11 from 2 Timothy 2:7, where Paul says to Timothy, "*Think over* what I say, for *the Lord* will give you understanding in everything." Yes, it is *the Lord* who gives understanding. But He does it through our God-given thinking and the efforts we make, *with prayer,* to think hard about what the Bible says. So when God inspired texts like Romans 3:1–8, He unleashed in the world an impulse toward hard thinking.

So alongside desperation and supplication there is cogitation. Which leads finally to . . .

4. *Education* (Training young people and adults to pray earnestly, read well, and think hard)

If God has inspired a book as the foundation of the Christian faith, there is a massive impulse unleashed in the world to teach people how to read. And if God ordained for some of that precious, sacred, God-breathed book to be hard to understand, then God unleashed in the world not only an impulse to teach people how to read but also how to think about what they read—how to read hard things and understand them and how to use the mind in a rigorous way.

Paul said to Timothy in 2 Timothy 2:2, "What you have heard from me in the presence of many witnesses entrust to faithful men who will be able to teach others also." Impart understanding to others, Timothy, in a way that will enable them to teach others also. In other words, the writings of the apostles—especially the hard ones—unleash generation after generation of education. Education is helping people understand something that they don't already understand. Or, more accurately, education is helping people (young or old) *learn how* to get an understanding that they didn't already have. Education is cultivating the life of the mind so that it knows how to grow in true understanding. That impulse was unleashed by God's inspiring a book with complex demanding paragraphs in it.

The personal, cultural, and historical impact of these impulses is enormous over the last two thousand years.

- Wherever Christianity has spread, the Bible has spread, and with it the impulse to translate it into other languages—with all the intellectual disciplines that go with effective translation.
- And with that goes the impulse to cultivate a literate people who can read the new translation. And with every new generation, there is the ongoing impulse to teach young people how to read, so they have direct access to God's Word.
- And with that goes the impulse to found schools as well as churches.
- And in time, since translating and reading the Bible involve thinking hard about many issues, there arises the impulse for higher learning, and colleges and universities follow in the wake of a culture founded on meeting God through His Word in a book.
- And in all of this there is the impulse to write down insights into these more difficult things, and so a commitment to scholarship emerges.
- And over time there is the impulse to preserve these treasures of insight, and so libraries emerge and various means of copying and then printing.
- And since accuracy matters so much in handling sacred texts and passing on precious insights, a discipline of exactness and carefulness in our work is unleashed over the centuries. And so on.

That is some of what God unleashed on the world by inspiring a Bible with hard passages in it like Romans 3:1–8.

Now I said earlier that I wanted to balance this with another kind of impulse from the Bible that flows from the less complex side of the gospel. How shall we do this? Perhaps it would help to do it like this: Consider that *God is love* (1 John 4:8, 16), and that *God is God* (Isa. 45:22; 46:9). In the truth that God is God is implied that God is who He is in all His glorious attributes and self-sufficiency. But in the truth that God is love is implied that all of this glory is moving our way for our everlasting enjoyment.

Now those two truths from the Bible have unleashed different impulses in the world. And we will see that a balance is introduced here, lest we make of Christianity an elitist affair, which it definitely is not.

- That *God is love* unleashes the impulse of simplicity, and that *God is God* unleashes the impulse of complexity.
- That *God is love* unleashes the impulse of accessibility, and that *God is God* unleashes the impulse of profundity.
- That *God is love* encourages a focus on the basics, and that *God is God* encourages a focus on comprehensiveness. One says, "Believe in the Lord Jesus, and you will be saved" (Acts 16:31). The other says, "I did not shrink from declaring to you the whole counsel of God" (Acts 20:27).
- That *God is love* impels us to be sure that the truth gets to *all* people, and that *God is God* impels us to be sure that what gets to all people is the *truth*.
- That *God is love* unleashes the impulse toward fellowship, and that *God is God* unleashes the impulse toward scholarship.
- That *God is love* tends to create extroverts and evangelists, and that *God is God* tends to create contemplatives and poets.

- That *God is love* helps foster a folk ethos, and that *God is God* helps foster fine ethos. The folk ethos revels in the intimacy of God and sings softly,

> Lord, You are more precious than silver.
>   Lord, you are more costly than gold.
> Lord, you are more beautiful than diamonds,
>   Nothing I desire compares with you.
>   ("Lord You Are," by Lynn Deshazo)

And the fine ethos revels in the transcendent majesty of God and sings with profound exultation:

> Far, far above thy thought
> His counsel shall appear,
> When fully He the work hath wrought
> That caused thy needless fear.
> Leave to his sovereign will
> To choose and to command:
> With wonder filled, thou then shalt own
> How wise, how strong His hand.
> ("Give to the Winds Thy Fears," by Paul Gerhardt)

Perhaps someone says at this point, "I don't like this separation between God is love and God is God, between folk and fine, evangelists and mystics, fellowship and scholarship, accessibility and profundity, simplicity and complexity." My response is: "Well, GOOD!" Because, in my mind, every one of these things is precious, and both sides of all these pairs are indispensable in the ministry and mission of Christ in the world.

My prayer for my people and for the pastors who read this book and for myself is that when we see these different impulses in Christianity, we will embrace both of them. If we lean toward one side (as all of us do), may we be respectful and affirming of those toward the other side. And may we not only be respectful of those at home on the other side, but may we be glad about it because of the fuller manifestation of God in His church and in the world. And may we rejoice that even the cause of evangelism and missions will advance when we make plain these differing impulses in Christianity, because this will help remove caricatures or stereotypes, and open the way for people to see all that God is for them in Christ, and to believe on Him.

Brothers, it is worth it! Show your people why God inspired hard texts.

> Keep a close watch on yourself and on the teaching.
> Persist in this, for by so doing
> you will save both yourself and your hearers.
>
> 1 TIMOTHY 4:16

> I endure everything for the sake of the elect,
> that they also may obtain the salvation that is
> in Christ Jesus with eternal glory.
>
> 2 TIMOTHY 2:10

> What is at stake on Sunday morning
> is not merely the upbuilding of the church,
> but its eternal salvation.
>
> JOHN PIPER

15

BROTHERS, SAVE THE SAINTS

I USED TO SAY my goal as a pastor-teacher was to glorify God by the salvation of sinners and the upbuilding of the body of Christ—winning the lost and edifying the saints. But there was an erroneous assumption behind this goal. The assumption was that my only role in saving people was to preach the gospel to the lost and pray for them. Then after they were converted and joined the church, my instrumentality in their salvation was over, and I was simply God's agent in their relative degree of edification or sanctification.

My error was in thinking that the salvation of only the lost depended on my preaching but not the salvation of the church.

For a time, therefore, it seemed strange to me that the Puritan pastors preached to their flocks as though the people's eternal lives depended on it. Why did Richard Sibbes, who died in 1635, and who was known as "the sweet dropper," plead so earnestly with the saints to "keep grace in exercise"? His answer: because "it is not sleepy habits, but grace in exercise, that preserveth us."[1]

The Puritans believed that without perseverance in the obedience of faith the result would be eternal destruction, not lesser sanctification. Therefore, since preaching and the pastoral ministry in general are a great means to the saints' perseverance, the goal of a pastor is not merely to edify the saints but to *save* the saints. What is at stake on Sunday morning is not merely the upbuilding of the church but its eternal salvation. It is not hard to see why the Puritans were so serious.

But it was not Sibbes and Baxter and Boston and Edwards and Spurgeon who caused me to change my goal. It was the apostle Paul. He wrote to Timothy, "Keep a close watch on yourself and on the teaching. Persist in this, for by so doing you will save both yourself and your hearers" (1 Tim. 4:16). The "hearers" Paul has in mind are not people outside the church (as verse 12 [NASB] shows, "Show yourself an example of those who believe"). Our salvation and the salvation of those who hear us week after week depend in large measure on our faithful attention to personal holiness and sound teaching. More is at stake in our work than greater or lesser progress in sanctification. The salvation of our believing hearers is on the line.

1. Richard Sibbes, *The Bruised Reed* (Edinburgh: The Banner of Truth Trust, 1998; original, 1630), 104.

In 2 Timothy 2:10, Paul recounts his suffering for the gospel and says, "I endure everything for the sake of the elect, that they also may obtain the salvation that is in Christ Jesus with eternal glory." The salvation of the elect is not automatic. It happens through God-appointed means. "I endure . . . that they also may obtain the salvation." "When God appoints" means, they are indispensable. Moreover, when Paul says he suffers for the salvation of the elect, he does not mean only people who are not yet converted. For he states in Colossians 1:24: "I rejoice in my sufferings for your sake, and in my flesh I am filling up what is lacking in Christ's afflictions for the sake of his body, that is, the church." Not only that, he says in the near context (2 Tim. 2:12): "If we endure, we will also reign with him; if we deny him, he also will deny us." The "we" here includes Paul. If Paul denies Christ, Christ will deny him. The salvation of the elect depends on their not denying Christ and on their enduring in faith and obedience.

Since Paul's pastoral labor is a means of helping the elect endure, therefore he sees all his labor as instrumental in their salvation. Is it any wonder that Paul groaned under "the daily pressure" of his "anxiety for all the churches" (2 Cor. 11:28)?

In that beautiful passage of 2 Corinthians where Paul teaches that God comforts us in order that we may comfort others, he goes beyond comfort and says, "If we are afflicted, it is for your comfort *and salvation*" (2 Cor. 1:6). Again it is the *salvation* of church members for which Paul suffers and labors.

One example of how Paul's pastoral labor leads to the salvation of the elect is found in 2 Corinthians 7. The Corinthian believers had fallen into sin. Paul wrote them a letter that grieved them deeply. But Paul rejoices because their grief produced repentance: "For godly grief produces a repentance that *leads to salvation* without regret" (v. 10).

What then was Paul's goal in this tough pastoral letter to the saints? It was repentance *unto salvation*. Paul's admonitions had caused the wavering believers to sober up and to work out their "own salvation with fear and trembling" (Phil. 2:12). He had brought back a wandering sinner from the error of his ways and thus will "save his soul" (James 5:19–20). The eternal life of the elect hangs on the effectiveness of pastoral labors. Oh, how earnest we should be in attending to ourselves and the soundness and helpfulness of our teaching!

It is the job of a pastor to labor so that none of his brothers and sisters is destroyed. Paul's pastoral heart seemed about to break as he saw the failure of love in the church at Rome (Rom. 14:15). The strong were flaunting their freedom to eat foods which for the weak would have been sin (v. 14). It is astonishing what Paul saw at stake here: "By what you eat, do not destroy the one for whom Christ died" (v. 15)! "Do not, for the sake of food, *destroy* the work of God" (v. 20).

The same admonition was given to the Corinthian believers who tended to flaunt their indifference to meat offered to idols. "Take care," Paul told them, "that this right of yours does not somehow become a stumbling block to the weak. . . . And so by your knowledge this weak person is *destroyed*, the brother for whom Christ died" (1 Cor. 8:9, 11).

It is unlikely that we should weaken this word "destroy" (*apollumi*). Its opposite is salvation, as 1 Corinthians 1:18 and 2 Corinthians 2:15 make clear. If a brother is destroyed, he is lost. The reference is to destruction beyond death, because Paul uses the same word when he says, "If Christ has not been raised . . . then those also who have fallen asleep in Christ have perished [that is, have been destroyed—in hell]" (1 Cor. 15:17–18).

Superficial appearances to the contrary, this does not imply that true saints can lose their salvation. Nor does it imply that Christ did not die for His elect in a way that is effectual in securing their eternal salvation. It does imply that one can be called a "brother" on the basis of appearances but in the end prove not to be a brother because of failing to persevere in faith. Such people are described in 1 John 2:19, "They went out from us, but they were not of us; for if they had been of us, they would have continued with us. But they went out, that it might become plain that they all are not of us." Such people would have been charitably called "brothers for whom Christ died" before they went out. But in the end they proved that they were not.

What is at stake in pastoral admonition and in preaching is not merely the church's progress in sanctification but its perseverance in final salvation.

But what a mistake it would be if we drew the conclusion: Let us then preach only messages which show the simple plan of salvation week after week. This is most emphatically not the way to tend the flock over which "the Holy Spirit has made you overseers" (Acts 20:28).

When Peter said, "Like newborn infants, long for the pure spiritual milk, that by it you may grow up to salvation" (1 Pet. 2:2), he did not mean by the word *milk* what Hebrews 5:12 means when it uses "milk" in contrast to "meat." What he meant was that the saints should hunger for the Word of God's grace (1 Pet. 1:25) as much as a baby hungers for milk. For only by feeding on the Word can you grow, and only by growing can you persevere and attain final salvation. A steady diet of gospel messages which do not help the saints grow out of infancy not only stunts their character but also jeopardizes their final salvation.

We must remember this: there is no standing still in the Christian life. Either we are advancing toward salvation, or we are drifting away to destruction. Drifting is mortal danger. "Therefore we must pay much closer attention to what we have heard, *lest we drift* away from it" (Heb. 2:1). If we do not point our people to the inexhaustible riches of Christ so as to stir them up to go forward into more of God, if we do not unfold "the whole counsel of God" (Acts 20:27), then we encourage drifting downstream where they will make shipwreck of their faith (1 Tim. 1:19).

There are two possibilities in Hebrews 2:1–3: Either we give heed to the Word of the Lord (vv. 1, 3), or we drift away from it. There is no sitting still in the river of indifference. Its current runs downstream to the falls. Therefore, verse 3 asks, "How shall we escape [God's just retribution] if we neglect such a great salvation?" Neglecting our great salvation means not giving heed to what has been revealed by the Son (Heb. 1:2), not setting our attention on Jesus (Heb. 3:1; 12:2). The result will be drifting away from the Word and therefore away from salvation. "Take care, brothers, lest there be in any of you an evil, unbelieving heart, leading you to fall away from the living God" (Heb. 3:12). "For we have become partakers of Christ, if we hold fast the beginning of our assurance firm until the end" (Heb. 3:14 NASB). The Son "became the source of eternal salvation to all who [go on obeying—present tense, continuous action] him" (Heb. 5:9).

Some readers will see this stress on the necessity of a change in obedience to Christ as "justification by works." But that would be a misinterpretation of what I am saying. That is why I wrote chapter 4 and put it near the front of this book, "Brothers, Live and Preach Justification by Faith." Obedience is the evidence of faith that alone unites us to Christ who is our justifying righteousness. Nothing I have said here contradicts that truth.

So I say again, the way to save yourself and your hearers (1 Tim. 4:16) is not to arrest the growth of your people by a meatless diet of "salvation messages." This had sent the "Hebrews" straight backward toward destruction (Heb. 5:11–14). The way to save the saints is to feed them all the Scriptures, for it is the Scriptures "which are able to make you wise *for salvation*" (2 Tim. 3:15).

One final word on eternal security. It is a community project. And that is why the pastoral ministry is so utterly serious, and why our preaching must not be playful but earnest. We preach so that saints might persevere in faith to glory. We preach not only for their growth, but because if they don't grow, they perish. If you rejoice in the sovereignty of God in salvation, then you rest in the sure word of Christ: "My sheep hear my voice, and I know them, and they follow me. I give them eternal life, and they will never perish" (John 10:27–28).

The elect will love the Word of God, the elect will grow, the elect will repent, and the elect will most assuredly be saved (Rom. 8:29–30). But they will not be saved apart from faithful teaching. God has ordained that there be pastor-teachers not only for the purpose of edification but also for the purpose of salvation.[2] Oh, that our preaching might have the flavor of eternity in it. For eternity is at stake every week.

2. For an elaboration of the view advocated in this chapter, see Thomas R. Schreiner and Ardel B. Caneday, *The Race Set Before Us: A Biblical Theology of Perseverance and Assurance* (Downers Grove, Ill.: InterVarsity Press, 2001).

> Remember that you were at that time separated from Christ,
> alienated from the commonwealth of Israel
> and strangers to the covenants of promise,
> having no hope and without God in the world.
>
> EPHESIANS 2:12

> The keener the memory of our awful rescue,
> the more naturally we pity those in a similar plight.
> The more deeply we feel how undeserved and free
> was the grace that plucked us from the flames,
> the freer will be our benevolence to sinners.
>
> JOHN PIPER

> When the heart no longer feels the truth of hell,
> the gospel passes from *good* news to just news.
> The intensity of joy is blunted
> and the heart-spring of love is dried up.
>
> JOHN PIPER

16

BROTHERS, WE MUST FEEL THE TRUTH OF HELL

IS NOT OUR most painful failure in the pastorate the inability to weep over the unbelievers in our neighborhoods and the carnal members of our churches? A great hindrance to our ministry is the gulf between our Biblical understanding and the corresponding passions of our hearts. The glorious and horrible truths which thunder through the Bible cause only a faint echo of fear and ecstasy in our hearts. We take a megaton of truth upon our lips and speak it with an ounce of passion. Do we believe in our hearts what we espouse with our lips?

I know for myself that in order to be a true shepherd and not a hireling, in order to grieve over the straying lambs, and in order to summon with tears the wild goats, I must believe in my heart certain terrible and wonderful things. If I am to love with the meek, humble, tender, self-effacing heart of Christ, I must *feel* the awful and glorious truths of Scripture. Specifically:

- I must *feel* the truth of hell—that it exists and is terrible and horrible beyond imaginings forever and ever. "These will go away into eternal punishment" (Matt. 25:46). Even if I try to make the "lake of fire" (Rev. 20:15) or the "fiery furnace" (Matt. 13:42) a symbol, I am confronted with the terrifying thought that symbols are not overstatements but understatements of reality. Jesus did not choose these pictures to tell us that hell is easier than burning.[1]

- I must *feel* the truth that once I was as close to hell as I am to the chair I am sitting on—even closer. Its darkness, like vapor, had entered my soul and was luring me down. Its heat had already seared the skin of my conscience. Its views were my views. I was a son of hell (Matt. 23:15), a child of the Devil (John 8:44) and of wrath (Eph. 2:3). I belonged

---

1. Every pastor should be concerned in our day about the open commitment, as well as secret leanings, of so many Christian scholars and leaders toward annihilationism—the belief that hell does not involve eternal conscience misery but is the cessation of existence. I have tried to answer the arguments for annihilationism in John Piper, *Let the Nations Be Glad: The Supremacy of God in Missions* (Grand Rapids, Mich.: Baker Book House, 2003), chapter 4. See also Ajith Fernando, *Crucial Questions about Hell* (Wheaton, Ill.: Crossway Books, 1991); Larry Dixon, *The Other Side of the Good News: Confronting the Contemporary Challenges to Jesus' Teaching on Hell* (Scotland: Christian Focus, 2003); Edward William Fudge and Robert A. Peterson, *Two Views of Hell: A Biblical & Theological Dialogue* (Downers Grove, Ill.: InterVarsity Press, 2000); Robert A. Peterson, *Hell on Trial: The Case for Eternal Punishment* (Phillipsburg, N.J.: Presbyterian and Reformed Publishing Co., 1995). For some excellent audio messages on this issue by Sinclair Ferguson, visit www.desiringGOD.org and take note of the album of cassettes titled "Universalism and the Reality of Eternal Punishment."

to the viper's brood (Matt. 3:7), without hope and without God (Eph. 2:12). I must believe that just as a rock climber, having slipped, hangs over the deadly cliff by his fingertips, so I once hung over hell and was a heartbeat away from eternal torment. I say it slowly, *eternal torment!*

- I must *feel* the truth that God's wrath was on my head (John 3:36); His face was against me (Ps. 34:16); He hated me in my sins (Ps. 5:5); His curse and fury were my portion (Gal. 3:10). Hell was not forced on God by Satan. It was His design and appointment for people like me (Matt. 25:41).

- I must *feel* in my heart that all the righteousness in the universe was on the side of God and against me. In the balances of justice, I was lighter than air. I had not one fraction of a right to appeal my sentence of condemnation. My mouth was stopped (Rom. 3:19). I was corrupt and guilty through and through, and God was perfectly righteous in His sentence (Ps. 51:4; Rom. 3:4).

Brothers, you have heard it said, "Do not think such negative thoughts, do not preach such negative things, do not look back. Speak of the blessed love of God and look to the new creation." But I say to you, on the authority of Scripture, *remember, remember, remember* the horrid condition of being separated from Christ, without hope and without God, on the brink of hell. "Remember that you were at that time separated from Christ, alienated from the commonwealth of Israel and strangers to the covenants of promise, having no hope and without God in the world" (Eph. 2:12).

If I do not believe in my heart these awful truths—believe them so that they are real in my feelings—then the blessed love of God in Christ will scarcely shine at all. The sweetness of the air of redemption will be hardly detectable. The infinite marvel of my new life will be commonplace. The wonder that to me, a child of hell, all things are given for an inheritance will not strike me speechless with trembling humility and lowly gratitude. The whole affair of salvation will seem ho-hum, and my entrance into paradise will seem as a matter of course. When the heart no longer feels the truth of hell, the gospel passes from *good* news to simply news. The intensity of joy is blunted and the heart-spring of love is dried up.

But if I remember these horrible things and do believe them in my heart; if I let every remaining sin and every moment of indifference to spiritual things remind me of the smell of hell lingering in the remnants of my corruption; if I let my knees become weak as on the day when I tottered on the cliff of my doom; if I recall that, apart from absolutely free grace, I would be the most hardened sinner and now in the torments of hell; if all this I remember and believe in my heart, then, oh, what a contrition, what a lowliness, what a meekness will be effected in my heart.

Then the gulf between my Biblical understanding and the passions of my heart will be taken away, and love will abound.

To whom can I return evil for evil as the Great Physician carries me from the crematorium of the universe into His intensive-care room alive, alive, alive? What disease will I be able to look on with scoffing? Where is the lowest sinner over whom I could feel one millimeter of superiority? Instead I become a broken-hearted leaper for joy. Tears for all my wickedness (yes, clean, middle-class, nice-boy wickedness of pride and unbelief and indifference and ingratitude and impurity of mind and worldliness of goals). Yet leaping with joy for the free and inexhaustible mercy of God.

We may remember Jonathan Edwards as the preacher of "Sinners in the Hands of an Angry God," but we may not remember the powerful practical effect of Edwards' vision of hell. What becomes of a person who has seen it and fled to the arms of Jesus for rescue? Edwards answers,

> A truly Christian love, either to God or men, is a humble brokenhearted love. The desire of the saints, however earnest, are humble desires: their hope is an humble hope; and their joy, even when it is unspeakable, and full of glory, is a humble, broken-hearted joy, and leaves the Christian more poor in spirit, and more like a little child, and more disposed to an universal lowliness of behavior.[2]

A broken, leaping heart will love like Jesus. And the power of the love will be proportionate to the felt fearfulness of our nearness to destruction. The keener the memory of our awful rescue, the more naturally we pity those in a similar plight. The more deeply we feel how *un*deserved and free was the grace that plucked us from the flames, the freer will be our benevolence to sinners.

We do not love as passionately as we ought because our belief in these things is not real. So our pride is not broken and our demeanor not lowly. And we do not look with aching and longing on the crowds that pass us in the airport or the straying members of our flock. John Newton, the author of "Amazing Grace," is a model of such compassion:

> Whoever . . . has tasted of the love of Christ, and has known, by his own experience, the need and the worth of redemption, is enabled, Yea, he is constrained, to love his fellow creatures. He loves them at first sight; and, if the providence of God commits a dispensation of the gospel,

---

2. Jonathan Edwards, *Treatise Concerning the Religious Affections*, in *The Works of Jonathan Edwards*, vol. 2, ed. John E. Smith (New Haven, Conn.: Yale University Press, 1959), 339–40.

and care of souls to him, he will feel the warmest emotions of friendship and tenderness, while he beseeches them by the tender mercies of God, and even while he warns them by his terrors.[3]

Brothers, we need to feel the truth of hell and the nearness of our own escape. Otherwise the gospel will be vapid, and we will be unable to count others better than ourselves *in all lowliness* (Phil. 2:3). Then who will tell our people of these things? Who else in their lives will love them enough to warn them with tenderness and tears?

3. John Newton, *The Works of the Rev. John Newton*, vol. 5 (Edinburgh: The Banner of Truth Trust, 1985), 132.

> The most powerful and painful acts of radical obedience,
> beginning with remorse for sin,
> must be motivated by an awakened taste for pleasure in God.
>
> JOHN PIPER

> The pain of remorse
> must grow in the soil of pleasure.
>
> JOHN PIPER

> God and His way of holiness must become your joy
> before you can weep over not having them.
> We must taste the pleasure of knowing God
> before we will experience the God-honoring pain of remorse for sin.
>
> JOHN PIPER

17

BROTHERS, LEAD THEM TO REPENTANCE THROUGH THEIR PLEASURE

THE FIRST SPIRITUAL step on the Calvary road of radical obedience to Jesus is repentance. Repentance includes remorse for inward corruption and sin. Repentance is not only remorse. It is a change of mind and heart about sin and righteousness and about Christ. It is a turning from the broken cisterns of the world to the fountain of life.

But part of that change of mind is remorse for failure to love God and be holy.

One of the great aims of our ministry is to lead people onto the Calvary road of radical obedience to Jesus. The reason this is so crucial is that Jesus said people see our good deeds and give glory to our Father in heaven (Matt. 5:16). If the glory of God is paramount in our preaching, then the aim of radical, life-offering obedience to Jesus is essential. It makes visible the value and beauty of all that God is for us in Christ.

We are committed to magnifying God in the obedience of our people because God is. This, David says, is why God leads us in righteousness: "He leads me in paths of righteousness *for his name's sake*" (Ps. 23:3). "*For your name's sake* you lead me and guide me" (Ps. 31:3). God upholds His glory by leading us in the path of obedience. Therefore we should join him in this God-exalting aim of preaching and ministry. When our people cast fear to the wind and spend themselves and risk their lives and fortune in the cause of God's truth, and in love for other people, then God is revealed for who He really is: infinitely valuable and satisfying—so much so that His people don't need the fleeting pleasures of sin in order to be content.

So we preach for radical obedience precisely out of a passion for the supremacy of God in our people and our world. Without this kind of obedience, the glory of God scarcely shines forth at all from the church in the world.

Now, if remorse for sin is the first spiritual step on this road of God-exalting obedience and love, the urgent questions for pastors become: How can I bring people to this place of remorse that yields life-transformation and God-exaltation? How can I make the people sad about their sin?

What I want to argue is that the most powerful and painful acts of radical obedience, beginning with remorse for sin, must be motivated by an awakened taste for pleasure in God, and that the preaching that kindles this must constantly portray God as supremely and everlastingly satisfying. It seems paradoxical at first that the pain of remorse must grow in the soil of pleasure. But to see what I mean, come with me on the path of discovery that I made a few years ago at an all-night prayer meeting at our church.

During this night of prayer, I was given the assignment to lead one of the hours with the focus on repentance and contrition. As I prepared for this, I made a startling discovery. I reread some portions of David Brainerd's diary. You recall that Brainerd was the young missionary to some tribes of American Indians in the eighteenth century. He died at age twenty-nine and his life has been preserved for us by Jonathan Edwards, who assembled his diary and journal.

I recalled that he had seen great repentance and contrition among the Indians at several times in his preaching. On August 9, 1745, he preached to the Indians of Crossweeksung, New Jersey, and made this observation:

> There were many tears among them while I was discoursing publicly, but no considerable cry: Yet some were much affected with a few words spoken to them in a powerful manner, which caused the persons to cry out in anguish of soul, although I spoke not a word of terror, but on the contrary, set before them the fullness and all-sufficiency of Christ's merits, and his willingness to save all that come to him; and thereupon pressed them to come without delay.[1]

He had said earlier on August 6:

1. Jonathan Edwards, *The Life of David Brainerd*, ed. by Norman Pettit, *The Works of Jonathan Edwards*, vol. 7 (New Haven, Conn.: Yale University Press, 1985), 310. For a more accessible version of Brainerd's diary, see *The Life and Diary of David Brainerd, ed. by Jonathan Edwards with a Biographical Sketch of the Life and Work of Jonathan Edwards* by Philip E. Howard Jr. (Grand Rapids, Mich.: Baker Book House, 1989).

It was surprising to see how their hearts seemed to be
pierced with the tender and melting invitations of the
Gospel, when there was not a word of terror spoken to
them.[2]

Again on November 30 he preached on Luke 16:19–26 concerning the rich man and Lazarus.

The Word made powerful impressions upon many in
the assembly, especially while I discoursed of the blessed-
ness of Lazarus "in Abraham's bosom" [Luke 16:22].
This, I could perceive, affected them much more than
what I spoke of the rich man's misery and torments. And
thus it has been usually with them. . . . They have almost
always appeared much more affected with the comfortable
than the dreadful truths of God's Word. And that which
has distressed many of them under convictions, is that
they found they wanted, and could not obtain, the happiness of the godly.[3]

This points to something remarkable about the spiritual cause of
true evangelical contrition, which is the beginning of all radical obedience. But before we analyze what that spiritual cause is, let's consider a Biblical example similar to Brainerd's experience with the
Indians.

The same dynamic seems to occur in Luke 5:1–10. After teaching the crowds from a boat off land in the lake of Gennesaret,
Jesus told the fishermen to push out into the deep and let down
their nets for a catch (v. 4). Simon protested, "Master, we toiled all
night and took nothing! But at your word I will let down the
nets." When the nets went down, they filled with so much fish that

2. Edwards, *The Life of David Brainerd*, 307.
3. Ibid., 342.

they started to break. Both boats were filled and started to sink from the catch.

Peter's response was remarkable, unlike our modern self-esteeming response to grace. Verses 8–10: "But when Simon Peter saw it, he fell down at Jesus' knees, saying, 'Depart from me, for I am a sinful man, O Lord.' For they and all that were with him were astonished at the catch of fish which they had taken." What is remarkable here is that a miracle of grace, not a word of judgment, broke Peter's heart and brought him to contrite repentance. It was the same with the Indians of Crossweeksung and the fisherman of Galilee.

Now why is that? Genuine evangelical contrition—as opposed to legalistic, fearful sadness simply owing to threats—is a sorrow for not having holiness. But now you have to be careful here. It is possible to weep over not having holiness *not* because you love God and want to enjoy all that He is for you in Christ but because you fear the punishment that comes for not having holiness. Many a criminal will weep when his sentence is read, not because he has come to love righteousness, but because his freedom to do more unrighteousness is being taken away. That kind of weeping is not true evangelical repentance. And it does not lead to radical Christian obedience.

The only true sorrow for not having holiness comes from a love for holiness, not just from a fear of the consequences of not having it. Or a more precise way to say it is this: true remorse over not having holiness is remorse over not enjoying God and living by the impulses of that joy. To cry over the punishment one is about to receive for wrongdoing is no sign of hating wrong but only hating pain. For crying and contrition to be real and evangelical, it must come from the brokenhearted feelings you have for lacking a life of joy in God, not just from the fearful feelings of being threatened with pain.

But now think what this means. This was the startling discovery I made in preparing for the night of prayer. If crying over something you don't have is going to show the preciousness of that "something" in itself, then you must really have some delight in it. And the more you delight in it, the more you feel distressed over not having it. This means that true evangelical contrition, true repentance, must be preceded by a falling in love with the all-satisfying God. To weep at not having holiness, you must long for holiness as a precious experience and reflection of God. To weep over not possessing it, it must be attractive to you for what it really is.

So you see how strange this seems at first: God and His way of holiness must become your joy before you can weep over not having them. You must fall in love before estrangement truly hurts. We must taste the pleasure of knowing God before we will experience the God-honoring pain of remorse for sin.

Now consider what this means for preaching. What kind of preaching is needed to produce true evangelical repentance? Brainerd found that words of winsome attractiveness produced more brokenheartedness in the Indians than did the words of warning. Warning has value in stirring us up to take the glories of holiness and heaven seriously so that we come to see them for what they are and delight in them. But it is the delight in them that causes the true grief when we fall short. No one cries over missing what they don't want to have.

Peter saw in the miracle of Jesus a treasure of hope and joy that was so wonderful he was overwhelmed with how out of sync his life was with such a treasure. If this much power and this much goodness is there in Jesus for those who trust Him, then oh! how different would be my life if I truly believed. How radical would be my obedience! What abandon would I feel in my living for such a Christ! What freedom from petty grievances and from fleeting pleasures of sin would I enjoy!

So the discovery I made was that true remorse and contrition and repentance are born from falling in love with all that God is for us in Jesus. Until God is our treasure, we will not grieve over our falling short of being satisfied in Him and begin living in a way that shows that satisfaction.

So preaching that aims to produce true evangelical remorse and contrition must devote itself to making God and His holiness look alluringly attractive and satisfying, so that, by the grace of regeneration and illumination, people will come to love it so much that they feel intense remorse over falling short of it. In other words, we must preach for joy in the glory of God if we would produce true grief over falling short of the glory of God. Evangelical repentance is grounded in an appealing sight of the holiness of God. That is why I say, brothers, pursue their repentance through their pleasure.

> Repent and be baptized.
>
> ACTS 2:38
>
> You were buried with him in baptism,
> in which you were also raised with him
> through faith in the working of God,
> who raised him from the dead.
>
> COLOSSIANS 2:12
>
> Baptism . . . saves you,
> not as a removal of dirt from the body
> but as an appeal to God for a good conscience,
> through the resurrection of Jesus Christ.
>
> 1 PETER 3:21
>
> And they shall not teach, each one his neighbor
> and each one his brother, saying, "Know the Lord,"
> for they shall all know me,
> from the least of them to the greatest.
>
> HEBREWS 8:11

18

BROTHERS, MAGNIFY THE MEANING OF BAPTISM

I RECALL A beautiful day in 1973. Professor Leonhard Goppelt had invited his university seminar on baptism to a retreat south of Munich in the foothills of the Bavarian Alps. He was Lutheran, and I was the lone American and the lone Baptist. We met in a monastery and for several hours debated the issue of infant baptism versus believer baptism.[1] It was a two-man show: sort of a David

1. It may sound unusual to say "believer baptism" rather than "believer's baptism." Nevertheless I use this term because Paul Jewett makes a good case for it when he says,

and Goliath affair. Only there were no Baptist Israelites cheering me on. Nor did Professor Goppelt fall. But to this day I believe the flight of my stones was true and that only the impervious power of a seventeenth-century tradition protected the bastion of paedobaptism.

I know there are non-Baptists reading this book. I am glad. I have no desire to be contentious. Most of my dead heroes baptized infants. I do not elevate the time or mode of baptism to a primary doctrine. It might be helpful, before I go on with my story, to describe a way of talking about our differences.

Take the Westminster Confession of Faith, for example, which I love as a magnificent statement of truths that are most precious to me. There are two distinctives of baptism in this document that set it off from the Baptist understanding. These are found in the key statements in paragraph 28: "Baptism is rightly administered by pouring, or sprinkling water upon the person" (28.3).[2] "The infants of one, or both, believing parents, are to be baptized" (28.4).[3]

On the first distinctive of mode, many of us would define *baptism* as "the immersion of the believer in water in the name of the Father and the Son and the Holy Spirit." If this is true, then it implies that the Westminster Confession is mistaken when it says, "Baptism is *rightly* administered by pouring, or sprinkling water upon the person." I take "rightly" to mean "properly" and "fittingly" and "appropriately." This implies that Baptists may describe pouring and sprinkling as "improper," "unfitting," and "inappropriate." And many would infer, then, that one should be properly, fittingly, appropriately (that is, rightly) baptized.

"Strictly, it should be written 'believer baptism,' without an 's', since it refers to baptism administered to believers, just as 'infant baptism' refers to baptism administered to infants. Hence the use of 'believer baptism' rather than 'believers' baptism' in this study." Paul Jewett, *Infant Baptism and the Covenant of Grace* (Grand Rapids, Mich.: Wm. B. Eerdmans Publishing Co., 1978), 226.

2. Philip Schaff, *The Creeds of Christendom* (Grand Rapids, Mich.: Baker Book House, 1977), 662.

3. Ibid., 662–63.

The second distinctive of the Westminster view is the assertion that infants of believers *"are to be baptized"* (28.4). Baptists would say the opposite: "Infants are *not* to be baptized." To baptize them would contradict our definition of baptism as "the immersion of the *believer* in water." So here again Baptists would view the Westminster Confession as mistaken on this point.

We need not go beyond this and say that the mistake is reprehensible or a sign of willful blindness. We may indeed respect the historic, theological arguments for administering the "sign of the covenant" to the children of believers as a God-honoring effort to see unity between the Old and New Covenant people of God. Therefore we need not view those who hold this view with moral or spiritual suspicion. Each of us has blind spots, which others see more clearly than we ourselves, and some of them are more owing to circumstantial factors than to willful or recalcitrant attitudes toward God and Scripture.

Therefore, when we share essential, deep, and wonderful truths with Presbyterian/Reformed brothers and sisters we may pursue partnerships and alliances in worship and ministry. In each situation participants will agree among themselves how the baptism question is to be handled so as not to compromise the conscience of anyone.

Now back to my story.

I have come to see that my little "battle of Bavaria" was fought at the wrong level. After coming to Bethlehem Baptist Church, Minneapolis, in 1980, I taught more membership classes than I can count. Almost every time there have been Lutherans or Catholics or Presbyterians, or the like, who were "baptized" (try not to take offense at the quotation marks) as infants but want to join our church. Little by little my understanding of why I embrace believer baptism has been refined. And now I see that I never got to the root of it in Bavaria.

Here's how my thought has progressed. There have been three stages—not unlike childhood, adolescence, and (I hope) maturity.

First, I saw that every baptism recorded in the Bible was the baptism of a person who had professed faith in Christ. Nowhere in Scripture is there any instance of an infant being baptized. The "household baptisms" (mentioned in Acts 16:15, 33 and 1 Cor. 1:16) are exceptions to this only if one *assumes* that the "household" included infants. But, in fact, Luke steers us away from this assumption, for example in the case the Philippian jailer (Acts 16:32) by saying that Paul first "spoke the word of the Lord . . . to all who were in his [the jailer's] house," and then baptized them. This looks like Luke's way of showing that a person needs to hear and believe "the word of the Lord" in order to be baptized. This is at least as plausible as the assumption that unmentioned infants were in the jailer's household.

Besides the absence of infant baptism in Scripture, and the pointer from Luke that hearing the word of the Lord seems to be a prerequisite for baptism, I also noticed—as every Baptist schoolboy knows—that the order of Peter's command was, "*Repent* and be baptized" (Acts 2:38). I saw no reason to reverse the order.

But I gradually came to see that these observations were only suggestive, not compelling. The fact that no infant baptisms are recorded does not prove there weren't any. And that Peter said, "*Repent,* and be baptized," to an adult audience does not rule out the possibility of his saying something different about the infants of believers. So I grew up to my second stage and decided, "I had better move beyond the examples of baptism to the teaching about baptism in order to make a more mature case for believer baptism." Perhaps the meaning of Luke's narrative would be clarified by the exposition of Paul and Peter.

Of course Romans 6:1–11 came to mind. "Do you not know that all of us who have been baptized into Christ Jesus were baptized into his death? We were buried therefore with him by baptism into death, in order that, just as Christ was raised from the dead by the glory of the Father, we too might walk in newness of life" (vv. 3–4). But this was Professor Goppelt's favorite weapon, because it contains not a word about faith or about any conscious response to God until verse 11; and there the response came *after* baptism. So he used Romans 6 as a defense that the *essential* meaning of baptism does not involve prior faith. I think most would agree that this text is not decisive for either view—except that it points toward immersion as the normal mode in the early church (we were buried with Him through baptism).

But Colossians 2:12 and 1 Peter 3:21 seemed to me to be problematic for the paedobaptist view. Paul compares baptism with circumcision (probably) and then says, "You were buried with him in baptism, in which you were also raised with him through faith in the working of God, who raised him from the dead" (RSV). This says clearly: *in baptism* we are raised *through faith*. It seems, therefore, that Paul is saying that baptism is an expression of the faith of the person being baptized. I did not see how an infant could properly receive this ordinance as an expression of his or her faith.

Then 1 Peter 3:21 says, "Baptism . . . saves you, not as a removal of dirt from the body but as an appeal to God for a good conscience, through the resurrection of Jesus Christ." This text frightens many Baptists away because it seems to come close to the Roman Catholic notion that the rite, in and of itself, saves (baptismal regeneration). But in fleeing from this text, we throw away a powerful argument for believer baptism. For as J. D. G. Dunn says, "1 Peter 3:21 is the nearest approach to a definition of baptism that the NT affords."[4]

According to Peter, baptism is "an appeal to God." That is, baptism is the cry of faith to God. In *that* sense and to *that* degree, it is

---

4. James D. G. Dunn, *Baptism in the Holy Spirit* (London: SCM Press Ltd., 1970), 219.

part of God's means of salvation.[5] This should not scare us off any more than the sentence, "If you confess with your mouth that Jesus is Lord . . . you will be saved" (Rom. 10:9). The movement of the lips in the air and the movement of the body in water save only in the sense that they give expression to the single justifying act, namely, faith (Rom. 3:28). Baptism is the outward appeal of faith to God in the heart.

So it seemed to me that Colossians 2:12 and 1 Peter 3:21 were compelling against baptizing infants who could not yet believe in Christ or appeal to God.

But that is where my "Bavarian battle" stopped. Since then I have been shown by a long succession of arguments in my church membership classes that even these texts leave open the remote possibility that an infant can be baptized on the strength of its parents' faith and in hope of its own eventual "confirmation." The argument says it is possible that these passages from Colossians and 1 Peter have relevance only for the missionary setting where adults are being converted and baptized. If Paul and Peter had addressed the issue of infants born into Christian homes, maybe they would have sounded like good Presbyterians.

I doubt it. For there is now a third stage of reasoning in favor of believer baptism. There is a grand Biblical and Baptist response to the Heidelberg Catechism's answer to question 74 as to whether infants are to be baptized. The Catechism answers:

> Yes; for since they, as well as their parents, belong to
> the covenant and people of God, and both redemption
> from sin and the Holy Ghost, who works faith, are

---

5. "Baptism now saves you—not the outward physical ceremony of baptism but the inward spiritual reality which baptism represents." Wayne Grudem, *1 Peter*, Tyndale New Testament Commentaries (Grand Rapids, Mich.: Wm. B. Eerdmans; Leicester, England: Inter-Varsity Press, 1988), 163. For an excellent defense of believer baptism, see Wayne Grudem, *Systematic Theology: An Introduction to Biblical Doctrine* (Grand Rapids, Mich.: Zondervan; Leicester, England: Inter-Varsity Press, 1994), 966–84.

through the blood of Christ promised to them no less than to their parents, they also are to be baptized as a sign of the covenant, to be engrafted into the Christian church and distinguished from the children of unbelievers, as was done in the Old Testament by circumcision, in place of which in the New Testament baptism is appointed.[6]

In other words, the justification of infant baptism in the Reformed churches hangs on the fact that baptism is the New Testament counterpart of circumcision.

There is in fact an important continuity between the signs of circumcision and baptism, but the Presbyterian representatives of Reformed theology seem to have undervalued the *dis*continuity. This is the root difference between Baptists and Presbyterians on baptism. I am a Baptist because I believe that on this score we honor both the continuity *and* discontinuity between Israel and the church and between their respective covenant signs.

The continuity is expressed like this: Just as circumcision was administered to all the physical sons of Abraham who made up the physical Israel, so baptism should be administered to all the spiritual sons of Abraham who make up the spiritual Israel, the church. Consider the difference between the "old covenant" people of God and the "new covenant" people of God as Jeremiah and the author of Hebrews describe them. Both these Biblical writers say that under the new covenant one will not have to look at other members of the covenant and say, "Know the Lord," for to be a covenant member *is* to know the Lord.[7] This implies that entry into the old covenant people of God was by physical birth, and entry into the new covenant people of God is by spiritual birth. It would seem to

---

6. Schaff, *The Creeds of Christendom*, 331.
7. Hebrews 8:11 (Jer. 31:34): "And they shall not teach, each one his neighbor and each one his brother, saying, 'Know the Lord,' for they shall know me, from the least of them to the greatest."

follow, then, that the sign of the covenant would reflect this change and would be administered to those who give evidence of spiritual birth.[8]

But who are these spiritual sons of Abraham who constitute the people of God in our age? Galatians 3:7 says, "Know then that it is those of *faith* who are the sons of Abraham." The new thing, since Jesus has come, is that the covenant people of God are no longer a political, ethnic nation, but a body of believers.

John the Baptist inaugurated this change and introduced the new sign of baptism. By calling all *Jews* to repent and be baptized, John declared powerfully and offensively that physical descent does not make one part of God's family and that circumcision, which signifies a physical relationship, will now be replaced by baptism, which signifies a spiritual relationship. The apostle Paul picks up this new emphasis, especially in Romans 9, and says, "Not all are children of Abraham because they are his descendants . . . it is not the children of the flesh who are the children of God" (vv. 7–8).

Therefore an important change has occurred in redemptive history. There is discontinuity as well as continuity.

Calvin and some of his heirs have treated signs of the covenant as if no significant changes happened with the coming of Christ. But God is forming His people today differently from when he strove with an ethnic people called Israel. The visible people of God are no longer formed through natural birth but through new birth and its expression through faith in Christ.

With the coming of John the Baptist and Jesus and the apostles, the emphasis now is that the spiritual status of our parents does not determine our membership in the covenant community. The beneficiaries of the blessings of Abraham are those who have the

---

8. I want to thank my assistant, Justin Taylor, for helping me see and formulate this particular insight.

faith of Abraham. These are the ones who belong to the covenant community.

And these are the ones who should receive the sign of the covenant: believer baptism. So if I could go back and do Bavaria again, I would get to the root in a hurry. This is where our "defense and confirmation" will be won or lost. But the Lord brings us through childhood, adolescence, and maturity for a reason. Every stage of reasoning is useful. Know your audience, brothers, and magnify the meaning of baptism.

Why have I dwelt on this? Because my sense is that many pastors, in order not to be contentious on this issue, neglect it almost entirely and do not call people to "repent and be baptized." What I am doing here is trying to model a responsible and reasonable defense of one view of baptism in the context of amicable and respectful relationships with those who hold other views. I think we need to teach our people the meaning of baptism and obey the Lord's command to baptize converts (Matt. 28:19), without elevating the doctrine to a primary one that would unduly cut us off from shared worship and ministry with others who share more important things with us.

When through fiery trials thy pathways shall lie,
My grace, all sufficient, shall be thy supply;
The flame shall not hurt thee; I only design
Thy dross to consume, and thy gold to refine.
"HOW FIRM A FOUNDATION"

He whose heart is kind beyond all measure
Gives unto each day what He deems best—
Lovingly, its part of pain and pleasure,
Mingling toil with peace and rest.
"DAY BY DAY"
(KAROLINA WILHELMINA SANDELL–BERG)

Judge not the Lord by feeble sense,
But trust Him for His grace;
Behind a frowning providence
He hides a smiling face.
His purposes will ripen fast,
Unfolding every hour;
The bud may have a bitter taste,
But sweet will be the flower.
"GOD MOVES IN A MYSTERIOUS WAY"
(WILLIAM COWPER)

19

BROTHERS, OUR AFFLICTION IS FOR THEIR COMFORT

PASTORS AND their people must suffer. "Through many tribulations we must enter the kingdom of God" (Acts 14:22). "You yourselves know that we are destined for this" (1 Thess. 3:3). "The Lord disciplines the one he loves, and chastises *every* son he receives" (Heb. 12:6).

The afflictions suffered by the family of God are from the Heavenly Father for our good. Karolina Wilhelmina Sandell-Berg wrote the hymn, "Day by Day," in 1865, with the deeply Biblical words about God's sovereignty over our daily trials.

> He whose heart is kind beyond all measure
> Gives unto each day what He deems best—
> Lovingly, its part of pain and pleasure,
> Mingling toil with peace and rest.

This is a Biblical insight. Job and Paul have this in common: When struck by Satan, they felt the hand of *God*. Ultimately, their suffering was from the Lord, and they knew it.

The Lord said to Satan, "All that [Job] has is in your hand" (Job 1:12). But when the calamity struck, Job responded, "The LORD gave, and the LORD has taken away; blessed be the name of the LORD" (1:21). A second time the Lord said to Satan, "Behold, [Job] is in your hand; only spare his life" (2:6). But when the horrid disease came and Job's wife urged him to curse God, Job replied, "Shall we receive good from *God,* and shall we not receive evil?" (2:10). And the inspired writer adds: "In all this Job did not sin with his lips."

Even if Satan is sometimes involved as the nearer cause of our calamities, it is not sin to see God as the more distant, primary, and ultimate cause. Satan's design is the destruction of faith (Job 2:5; 1 Thess. 3:5), but God's design is the deep cure of our soul, as the hymn, "How Firm a Foundation," says so powerfully:

> When through fiery trials thy pathways shall lie,
> My grace, all sufficient, shall be thy supply;
> The flame shall not hurt thee; I only design
> Thy dross to consume, and thy gold to refine.

Like Job, Paul recognized his thorn in the flesh as a "messenger of Satan" (2 Cor. 12:7) but designed *by God* for a gracious purpose: "to keep me from being too elated [conceited]."

Satan does not have free rein in the world and even less so in the family of God. Therefore, in our struggle with suffering, it will never be a sufficient comfort to say, "It is of Satan and not of God." The only genuine comfort will come from acknowledging that the all-powerful God has done it and that He is infinitely wise and infinitely loving to those who trust Him. William Cowper, who knew the darkness of depression, put it this way in his hymn, "God Moves in a Mysterious Way,"

> Judge not the Lord by feeble sense,
> But trust Him for His grace;
> Behind a frowning providence
> He hides a smiling face.
> His purposes will ripen fast,
> Unfolding every hour;
> The bud may have a bitter taste,
> But sweet will be the flower.

God has made plain to us one of the purposes for which pastors must suffer. Paul tells us in 2 Corinthians 1:6: "If we are afflicted, it is *for your comfort and salvation.*" A sermon on this text would have as its main point: "The afflictions of a Christian minister are designed by God to achieve the comfort and salvation of his flock."

When Paul says to the Corinthians that his afflictions are for their comfort and salvation, he implies that there is a design and purpose in his sufferings. But whose design? Whose purpose? He does not design and plan his own afflictions. And Satan surely does not design them to comfort and save the church. Therefore, Paul must mean that God designs and purposes his pastoral afflictions for the good of the church.

God ordained the sufferings of Christ for the redemption of the church (Acts 2:23; 4:27–28), and He ordains the suffering of Christian ministers for the application of that redemption. "Now I rejoice in my sufferings for your sake, and in my flesh I am filling up what is lacking in Christ's afflictions for the sake of his body, that is, the church" (Col. 1:24). Christ's afflictions lack nothing in atoning worth. What they lack is a personal presentation in suffering human form to those for whom He died. This is what pastors and missionaries "complete."

This is a sobering thought but also a comforting one. On the one hand, it means that the fabric of a pastor's life will be laced with dark threads of pain. But on the other hand, it means that every affliction he must endure is designed not only for his own good but for the good of his flock. Our suffering is not in vain; God never wastes the gift of pain (Phil. 1:29). It is given to His ministers as He knows best, and its design is the consolation and salvation of our people.

No pastoral suffering is senseless. No pastoral pain is pointless. No adversity is absurd or meaningless. Every heartache has its divine target in the consolation of the saints, even when we feel least useful.

How does a pastor's suffering achieve the consolation and salvation of his flock? The context of Paul's words suggests the following scenario: Circumstances conspire to crush a pastor's spirits—perhaps loss of health, loss of a loved one, defection of a friend, unresponsive people, slander, weariness, personal threats, overwork. Things become so bad that he even despairs of life itself. He cries out, "Why?" The answer comes back from 2 Corinthians 1:9: "That was to make us rely not on ourselves but on God who raises the dead." If, by grace, we manage a mustard seed of faith in

God's sovereign goodness through it all, we will discover unspeakable comfort.

God's first great design in all our trouble is that we might let go of self-confidence. When we do that, there is a temporary sense of falling. But by faith in God's mercy, we land, infinitely more secure, in the arms of our Father, who is utterly in control at the brink of life and death.

But has He brought us through this wrenching fall for ourselves only? No. "If we are afflicted, it is for *your* comfort." Now, as 2 Corinthians 1:4 says, we are able to "comfort those who are in any affliction, with the comfort with which we ourselves are comforted by God." Only one thing comforts in the end: "God who raises the dead."

All pastoral afflictions are graciously designed to make us rely on God and not ourselves. And therefore our afflictions prepare us to do the one thing most needful for our people—to point them away from ourselves to the All-sufficient God. In this alone is consolation and salvation. Therefore, "If we are afflicted, it is for your comfort and salvation."

At least twice again in 2 Corinthians, Paul delivers this sober message. In 2 Corinthians 4:8–12, he describes his ministerial miseries and interprets them like this: "We are . . . always carrying in the body the death of Jesus, so that the life of Jesus may also be manifested in our bodies. For we who live are always being given over to death for Jesus' sake, so that the life of Jesus also may be manifested in our mortal flesh. So *death is at work in us, but life in you.*"

This is another way of saying, "If we are afflicted, it is for your salvation."

When Paul endures "weaknesses, insults, hardships, persecutions, and calamities," and accepts them as God's gracious therapy, the power of Christ is perfected in his life (2 Cor. 12:7–10). And since it is Christ's power, not Paul's, that brings life to the church, we can see why he said, "Death is at work in us, but life in you" (2 Cor. 4:12). Paul's weakness and affliction minister life to the church. And so should ours.

Finally, Paul reminds us that this is the pattern of Christ: He brought life to the church through weakness and affliction; so should his ministers. "For though he was crucified through weakness, yet he liveth by the power of God. For we also are weak in him, but we shall live with him by the power of God toward you" (2 Cor. 13:4 KJV—the most literal).

This is a complicated sentence, but I think it means: A minister's life in Christ shares all the weaknesses (and more) that brought Christ to the cross. "We also are weak in him." But in our weakness God's power triumphs with two effects: (1) We share in Christ's resurrection life and triumph over death ("we shall live with him by the power of God"); (2) we love and serve the church in this weak power ("we shall live with him by the power of God *toward you*"). The main idea is repeated in 2 Corinthians 13:9, "We are glad when we are weak and you are strong."

The Christian pastor will not expect to comfort or save his people except by following the Calvary Road. "Though [Christ] was rich, yet for your sake he became poor, so that you by his poverty might become rich" (2 Cor. 8:9). Thus Paul describes himself "as poor, yet making many rich" (2 Cor. 6:10). Poor, that our people might be rich. Weak, that they might be strong. Afflicted for their comfort and for their salvation.

But note well: not a whiff of self-pity. For there is nothing we desire more than to "know [Christ] and the power of his resurrection, and . . . *share his sufferings, becoming like him in his death,* that by any means possible I may attain the resurrection from the dead" (Phil. 3:10–11).

142

We know that it is more blessed to give than to receive (Acts 20:35). Therefore, apart from all naïve and romantic idealizations, the Christian pastor says with Paul, "In all our affliction, I am overflowing with joy" (2 Cor. 7:4). For "if we are afflicted, it is for your comfort and salvation" (2 Cor. 1:6).

> The danger of formalism is real.
> But the danger of spontaneity is also great.
> If the heart is without passion
> it will produce lifeless, jargon-laden spontaneity.
> And if the heart is aflame,
> no form will quench it.
>
> JOHN PIPER

> There is no necessary contradiction between form and fire.
>
> JOHN PIPER

20

BROTHERS, LET THE RIVER RUN DEEP

I HAVE ALWAYS felt that the works of the famous British New Testament scholar, F. F. Bruce, are unnecessarily dry. In reading his memoirs, *In Retrospect,* I discovered one of the reasons why. He said, "I do not care to speak much—especially in public—about the things that mean most to me."[1] When you eliminate what means

---

1. F. F. Bruce, *In Retrospect: Remembrance of Things Past* (Grand Rapids, Mich.: Wm. B. Eerdmans Publishing Co., 1980), 304.

most to you from your writing and speaking, they will be dry. For myself, I would say just the opposite: "I do not care to speak much—especially in public—about the things that *don't* mean most to me."

This raises a question that is larger than the relative transparency of our souls. It raises the question about the way in which deep emotions can be expressed in public. What is the place of spontaneity and form in venting the passions of one's heart? This is more of a problem for me than for Bruce. That's one reason I moved from teaching in college to preaching in the church. I assume passion has a big place in the life of a preacher. So maybe my ruminations on how Jeremiah handles emotions in the Book of Lamentations will fit your soul too.

I will make two observations about "The Lamentations of Jeremiah" and then draw out some implications for the use of spontaneity and form in the expression of "what means most to us."

First, Lamentations is a deeply emotional book. Jeremiah writes about what means most to him, and he writes in agony. He feels all the upheaval of Jerusalem in ruins. There is weeping (1:2), desolation (1:4), mockery (1:7), groaning (1:8), hunger (1:11), grief (2:11), and the horrid loss of compassion as mothers boil their own children to eat them (2:20; 4:10). If there ever was intensity and fervor in the expression of passion from the heart, this is it.

The second observation, then, comes as a surprise: This seems to be the most formally crafted book in the Old Testament. Of the five chapters, chapters 1, 2, and 4 are each divided into twenty-two stanzas (the number of letters in the Hebrew alphabet), and each stanza begins with a different letter of the alphabet. They are three acrostics. Chapter 3 is even more tightly structured. Again there are twenty-two stanzas, but now each stanza has exactly three lines. The three lines in each stanza begin with the same letter, and each of the twenty-two stanzas begins with a different letter in alphabetical order. Chapter 5 is the only chapter that is not an acrostic. But it still has twenty-two lines in conformity with the acrostic pattern of chapters 1–4.

Now what do these two observations imply? First, they imply that genuine, heartfelt expression of our deepest emotions does *not* require spontaneity. Just think of all the mental work involved in finding all the right words to construct four alphabetical acrostics! What constraint, what limitation, what submission to form! Yet what passion and power and heart! There is no necessary contradiction between form and fire.

Chapter 3 of Lamentations is the most personal and most intense. Here first-person references abound: "Remember *my* affliction and *my* wanderings, the wormwood and the gall!" (3:19). Here the peak of hope is reached: "Great is your faithfulness!" (3:23). But here the author submits himself to the narrowest form in all the book.

After reading Lamentations, we can no longer believe that unpondered prayers are more powerful or real or passionate or heartfelt or genuine or alive than prayers that are thoughtfully and earnestly (and painfully?) poured out through a carefully crafted form. The danger of formalism is real. Prayers and sermons that are read from a manuscript are usually stiff and unnatural and artificial. But the danger of spontaneity is also great. If the heart is without passion, it will produce lifeless, jargon-laden spontaneity. And if the heart is aflame, no form will quench it.

But not only is spontaneity no necessary advantage and form no necessary hindrance to deep, personal expression of feeling, but even more, formed affection often strikes deeper. Deeper into reality and deeper into the hearer. Formed grief, while not heaving to and fro with uncontrollable sobs, has a peculiar profundity.

Imagine a man's response when he first hears that his wife and children have been taken captive by the enemy and slaughtered. He throws himself to the ground, cries out in torment, rips his clothes, and rubs his head in ashes, until his energy ebbs into a pitiable "No, no, no." Here is utter spontaneity, utterly real emotion, no studied design, no conscious constraints.

But picture this man a week later, when the services are over and the friends have departed, and he is alone with the weight of his loss. The excruciating pain of the first blast is gone, and now there is the throb and ache of an amputated soul. What does he do to express this deep and settling grief? Between the periodic heaving sobs he reaches for a form and begins to make his lamentation. Studied, crafted, pondered, full of power. When the time comes, he will read or recite this lamentation. But no one will say of this formed grief: "It is canned." On the contrary, it will strike deeper than the sobs. It will show more of what he has brought up from the depths.

Emotions are like a river flowing out of one's heart. Form is like the riverbanks. Without them the river runs shallow and dissipates on the plain. But banks make the river run deep. Why else have humans for centuries reached for poetry when we have deep affections to express? The creation of a form happens because someone feels a passion. How ironic, then, that we often fault form when the real evil is a dry spring.

Years ago I wrote a poem called "The Innkeeper," about the pain that the innkeeper may have experienced when Herod's soldiers came to kill the baby boys and started the slaughter at the innkeeper's place—"the price for housing the Messiah here." In the introduction I pondered why poets struggle to let deep emotion flow through narrow forms of art.

> Why this struggle? Why does the poet bind his heart
> with such a severe discipline of form? Why strain to give
> shape to suffering? Because Reality has contours. God is
> who He is, not what we wish or try to make Him be. His

Son, Jesus Christ, is the great granite Fact. His hard sacrifice makes it evident that our spontaneity needs Calvary-like discipline. Perhaps the innkeeper paid dearly for housing the Son of God. Should it not be costly to penetrate and portray this pain?[2]

Many pastors are not known for expressing deep emotions. This seems to me especially true in relation to the profoundest theological realities. This is not good, because we ought to experience the deepest emotions about the deepest things. And we ought to speak often, and publicly, about what means most to us, in a way that shows its value.

Brothers, we must let the river run deep. This is a plea for passion in the pulpit, passion in prayer, passion in conversation. It is not a plea for thin, whipped-up emotionalism. ("Let's all stand up and smile!") It is a plea for deep feelings in worthy forms from God-besotted hearts and minds.

2. John Piper, *The Innkeeper* (Wheaton, Ill.: Crossway Books, 1998), 3.

> For the legalist, morality serves the same function
> that immorality does for the antinomian or the progressive;
> namely, as the expression of self-reliance and self-assertion.
>
> JOHN PIPER

> Legalism is a more dangerous disease than alcoholism
> because it doesn't look like one.
> Alcoholism makes men fail;
> legalism helps them succeed in the world.
> Alcoholism makes men depend on the bottle;
> legalism makes them self-sufficient, depending on no one.
> Alcoholism destroys moral resolve;
> legalism gives it strength.
> Alcoholics don't feel welcome in the church;
> legalists love to hear their morality extolled in church.
>
> JOHN PIPER

21

BROTHERS, DON'T FIGHT FLESH TANKS WITH PEASHOOTER REGULATIONS

THE ISSUE OF total abstinence from alcohol in relation to church membership may not even be on your church's radar screen. But the Biblical principles involved in handling this issue are relevant for other matters of personal holiness and church purity. When I came to Bethlehem Baptist Church over two decades ago, this was one of the first controversies I had to deal with. We survived it and are the better for it. I think what I learned may be helpful.

Among Baptist and other congregationally governed churches, the local church constitution generally contains an affirmation of faith and a church covenant. The church covenant describes a core set of Biblical expectations relating to how members live; while the affirmation of faith describes a core of Biblical expectations relating to what members believe. As a general rule, therefore, the expectations of the church covenant, along with the affirmation of faith, function as prerequisites for church membership.

Many congregationally governed churches have a sentence in their church covenants which goes something like this: "We engage to abstain from the use and the sale of intoxicating liquors as a beverage." In principle, therefore, these churches exclude all persons except teetotalers from church membership. The leaders of the church may have to say to a candidate for membership, "Even though you trust Jesus Christ as your Savior, and aim with all your heart to live under His lordship, and have been duly baptized according to His ordinance, and give hearty assent to our affirmation of faith, nevertheless you cannot be a member of this church because you use wine on some festive occasions, or when you visit relatives."

I am persuaded that such a regulation for church membership falls into the category of legalistic exclusivism and stands under the judgment of the apostolic word in Scripture. This is my persuasion even though I am a total abstainer myself and believe total abstinence is a wise and biblically defensible way of life for our day.

In what follows I will try to show what legalism means and why the requirement of total abstinence for church membership falls into this category and is therefore wrong. Finally, I will make a practical proposal for how church covenants might be improved by being made more radical and less specific.

Since the New Testament does not use the term *legalism*, I will try to define it in a generally accepted way so that it will be clear that the issue is indeed treated in the New Testament. *Legalism* has at least two meanings, but both express a single root problem.

First, legalism means treating Biblical standards of conduct as regulations to be kept by our own power in order to earn God's favor. In other words, legalism is present whenever a person is trying to be ethical in his own strength, that is, without relying on the merciful help of God in Christ. Simply put, moral behavior that is not from faith is legalism (Rom. 14:23).

The legalist is usually a moral person. In fact, the majority of moral people in the Western world are legalists because their so-called Judeo-Christian morality, inherited from their forefathers, does not grow out of a humble, contrite reliance on the blood-bought, Spirit-wrought, merciful enabling of God. On the contrary, for the legalist, morality serves the same function that immorality does for the antinomian or the progressive—namely, as the expression of self-reliance and self-assertion. The reason some Pharisees tithed and fasted was the same reason some university students take off their clothes and lie around naked in the parks in Munich and Amsterdam.

The moral legalist is the elder brother of the immoral prodigal (Luke 15:11–32). They are blood brothers in God's sight because both reject the mercy of God in Christ as a means to righteousness and use either morality or immorality as a means of expressing their independence and self-sufficiency and self-determination. And it is clear from the New Testament that both will result in a tragic loss of eternal life, if there is no repentance.

So the first meaning of legalism is the terrible mistake of treating Biblical standards of conduct as regulations to be kept by our own power in order to show our moral prowess and earn God's favor. It is a danger that all of us must guard against every day.

The second meaning of legalism is this: the erecting of specific requirements of conduct beyond the teaching of Scripture and making adherence to them the means by which a person is qualified for membership in a local church. This is where unbiblical exclusivism arises.

There is no getting around the fact that the universal church does not include everyone, and the local church does not include every Christian. We do exclude people from membership because we believe membership should imply commitment to the lordship of Christ the head of the church (hence, the exclusion of non-Christians), and because local churches understand that lordship in particular and important ways (hence, the exclusion of some Christians with whom we disagree). But exclusion of people from local church membership should never be taken lightly. It is a serious matter.

Schools and clubs and societies can set up any human regulations they wish in order to keep certain people out and preserve, by rule, a particular atmosphere. But the church is not man's institution. It belongs to Christ. He is the head of the body, and He alone should set the entrance requirements.

These two uses of the term *legalism* have a common root. On the one hand, *legalism* means treating Biblical standards of conduct as regulations to be kept by our own power in order to earn God's favor. On the other hand, it means erecting specific requirements of conduct beyond the teaching of Scripture and making adherence to them the means by which a person is qualified for local church membership.

In the first case, we use our own power to make *ourselves* moral. In the second case, we use our own power to make the *church* moral. In the first case, we fail to rely on the power of God for our own sanctification. In the second case, we fail to rely on the power of God for the sanctification of others.

Therefore, what unites these two forms of legalism at the root is unbelief—unbelief in regard to ourselves, that it is God who is in us "to will and to work for his good pleasure" (Phil. 2:13); and unbelief in relation to others, that God will make His will known and incline them to do it. As Paul says in Philippians 3:15, "Let those of us who are mature think this way, and if in anything you think otherwise, God will reveal that also to you." He confidently entrusts the purification of the church to God.

Wherever happy confidence in the sovereign power of God for our own lives and the lives of others grows weak, legalism creeps in. We inevitably try to compensate for loss of dynamic faith by increased moral resolve and the addition of man-made regulations. But wherever joyful confidence in the power of God is waning, the flesh is waxing. Which means that the morality we had hoped would save ourselves and the regulations we hoped would purify our church fall victim to the massive power of the flesh and become its instruments of self-reliance and self-sufficiency.

It seems beyond doubt that God hates legalism as much as He hates alcoholism. And I believe it is a literal understatement that legalism has brought more people to eternal ruin than alcohol has, though the devastations of alcohol are huge.

Let us not be deceived by outward appearances. Satan "disguises himself as an angel of light" (2 Cor. 11:14). He keeps his deadliest diseases most sanitary. He clothes his captains in religious garments and houses his weapons in temples. Legalism is a more dangerous disease than alcoholism because it doesn't look like one. Alcoholism makes men fail; legalism helps them succeed in the world. Alcoholism makes men depend on the bottle; legalism makes them self-sufficient, depending on no one. Alcoholism destroys moral resolve; legalism gives it strength. Alcoholics don't feel welcome in the church; legalists love to hear their morality extolled in church.

Therefore, what we need in the church is not front-end regulations to try to keep ourselves pure. We need to preach and pray and believe that neither circumcision nor uncircumcision, neither teeto-talism nor social drinking, neither legalism nor alcoholism is of any avail with God, but only a new heart.

The enemy is sending against us every day the Sherman tank of the flesh with its cannons of self-reliance and self-sufficiency. If we try to defend ourselves or our church with peashooter regulations, we will be defeated even in our apparent success. The only defense is to be "rooted and built up in [Christ] and established in the faith" (Col. 2:7); "strengthened with all power, according to his glorious might, for all endurance and patience with joy" (Col. 1:11); "hold-ing fast to the Head, from whom the whole body, nourished and knit together . . . grows with a growth that is from God" (Col. 2:19).

From God! From God! And *not* from ourselves.

The seedbed of all these thoughts has been Colossians 2:16–23. This was the key passage that gave me guidance at the beginning of my ministry to make my way through this controversy. It seems to me that these verses put total abstinence as a requirement for church membership in the category of legalism and thus show it to be wrong. Paul's teaching here may be summed up under five points:

1. *"Let no one pass judgment on you in questions of food and drink"* (Col. 2:16).

The consumption of food and drink is in itself no basis for judg-ing a person's standing with God or standing in God's family. To be sure, Paul had to deal with the abuse of food and drink, the prob-lem of eating meat offered to idols, and the problem of drunkenness (1 Cor. 8; 11:21; Rom. 14). But his approach to these abuses was never to forbid food or drink. It was always to forbid what de-stroyed God's temple and injured faith (which may at times include food or drink!). He taught the principle of *love* but did not deter-mine its application with regulations in matters of food and drink.

A church covenant requiring total abstinence goes too far in limiting the principle of love.

2. *"Let no one disqualify you, insisting on asceticism and worship of angels"* (Col. 2:18).

The false teaching at Colossae had two parts: It called for angel worship on the one hand and strict ascetic regulations on the other. Both of these were erected as requirements for those who wanted to qualify for "fullness" of life (2:10) or full participation in the spiritual community. Paul denounced both requirements. The Colossian believers' theology was wrong; their ascetic regulations regarding food and drink were useless because all the fullness of deity dwells in Christ. And these are only shadows of reality and lead to being puffed up.

3. *The source of life and purity and growth is not through religious visions and regulations about food and drink, but through "holding fast to the Head [Christ], from whom the whole body, nourished and knit together through its joints and ligaments, grows with a growth that is from God"* (Col. 2:19).

The only hope for spiritual growth and health in the body of Christ is personal cleaving to Christ the head, not exclusive regulations.

4. *"If with Christ you died to the elemental spirits of the world, why, as if you were still alive in the world, do you submit to regulations—'Do not handle, Do not taste, Do not touch' (referring to things that all perish as they are used)—according to human precepts and teachings?"* (Col. 2:20–22).

A church which erects regulations about food and drink as a means of judging or excluding does not yet know what it means to die with Christ and be freed from the powers of the world. This is what I meant earlier when I said that whenever authentic, joyful confidence in Christ diminishes, regulations are brought in to preserve what the power of Christ once created. If you erect enough regulations and build a big enough endowment, an institution can endure for decades after the spiritual dynamic that brought it into existence is gone.

5. *"These [regulations] have indeed an appearance of wisdom in promoting self-made religion and asceticism and severity to the body, but they are of no value in stopping the indulgence of the flesh"* (Col. 2:23).

Total abstinence as an entrance requirement may secure a church membership with one common attitude toward alcohol, but it is of no help in making us a pure people who do not live according to the flesh. On the contrary, by imposing a restriction which the New Testament never imposes, this entrance requirement, in principle, involves us in a legalism that has its roots in unbelief. It is the sign of a faded power and joy and heart righteousness that once was created by the power of Christ but cannot be preserved by laws.

I conclude, therefore, that the apostle Paul would not approve of contemporary church covenants which make total abstinence a requirement for local church membership. As a practical alternative to the total abstinence clause, I would suggest substituting a sentence like this: "We engage to abstain from all drugs, food, drink, and practices which bring unwarranted harm to the body or jeopardize our own or another's faith." This is a more radical commitment, but it provides a Biblical latitude for the freedom of conscience in Christ.

> What we suffer from today is humility in the wrong place.
> Modesty has moved from the organ of ambition.
> Modesty has settled upon the organ of conviction;
> where it was never meant to be.
> A man was meant to be doubtful about himself,
> but undoubting about the truth;
> this has been exactly reversed.
>
> G. K. CHESTERTON

> Relativism no longer means:
> your claim to truth is no more valid than mine;
> but now means:
> you may not claim to speak the truth.
>
> JOHN PIPER

22

BROTHERS, DON'T CONFUSE UNCERTAINTY WITH HUMILITY

FROM TIME TO TIME pastors are drawn into controversy for the love of truth and the good of the church and the glory of God. It is a necessary and painful place to be. Much of the New Testament is the fruit of controversy. So we are in good company when it is necessary. But the price is high, and in these days of truth-minimizing pluralism and relativism the accusation of arrogance is inevitable.

So in recent years I have had to think much about pride and humility. For example, I have been drawn into the controversy surrounding Open Theism, which denies that God foreknows all that shall come to pass.[1] One of the most common criticisms applied to brothers in this controversy is that they are arrogant or that their view is arrogant. For example, words like the following have been published in reference to some of us who have spoken publicly and written on this issue:

> A group of authoritarian Calvinist pastors and scholars, who reject the pluralism and irenicism of other Calvinists and the pietist commitments of the Baptist General Conference, are engaging in a narrow, *arrogant* theological discourse. . . . The outrageous arrogance of these defenders of Calvin's honor is breathtaking.

But the strategy of labeling someone as proud or haughty is much bigger than our little conflict. "Arrogance" is the condemnation of choice in the political and religious arena for anyone who breaks the rules of relativism. If you say of anybody's view of God that it is wrong and harmful, you will be accused of arrogance. If you say that Christians should share Christ with their Jewish friends in the hope that they would believe on Jesus and be saved, you will be accused of arrogance. If you say to a straying church member

---

1. For a helpful discussion and critical response to Open Theism, see Bruce A. Ware, *God's Lesser Glory: The Diminished God of Open Theism* (Wheaton, Ill.: Crossway Books, 2000). For the nature of the controversy I have been involved in, see John Piper with Justin Taylor, *Resolution on the Foreknowledge of God: Reasons and Rationale* (Minneapolis, Minn.: Desiring God Ministries, 2000), available at DGM: 1-888-DGM-4700. See also John M. Frame, *No Other God: A Response to Open Theism* (Phillipsburg, N.J.: Presbyterian and Reformed Publishing Co., 2001); *Beyond the Bounds: Open Theism and the Undermining of Biblical Christianity*, ed. by John Piper, Justin Taylor, and Paul Kjoss Helseth (Wheaton, Ill.: Crossway, forthcoming).

enmeshed in sin, "Repent and come back," you may be accused of judgmentalism and arrogance.

So we have here an issue that touches our pastoral life everywhere we act or speak on the basis of Biblical conviction. And the issue is serious not only because it touches all we do but also because the charge is so serious. God hates pride, the root sin of all sin.

> For the LORD of hosts will have a day of reckoning
> against everyone who is proud and lofty and against
> everyone who is lifted up, that he may be abased. . . .
> Against all the lofty mountains, against all the hills that
> are lifted up, against every high tower, against every forti-
> fied wall, against all the ships of Tarshish and against all
> the beautiful craft. The pride of man will be humbled and
> the loftiness of men will be abased; and the LORD alone
> will be exalted in that day (Isa. 2:12, 14–17 NASB).

On the other hand, wonderful promises and commendations are held out to the humble. "Blessed are the poor in spirit, for theirs is the kingdom of heaven" (Matt. 5:3). "God opposes the proud, but gives grace to the humble" (James 4:6). "Whoever exalts himself shall be humbled; and whoever humbles himself shall be exalted" (Matt. 23:12).

It seems to me, therefore, that what we pastors need to do is carefully ponder what pride and humility really are, not so much to defend ourselves from calumny—which almost always backfires—but rather to test ourselves and make sure that we are fighting against every whiff of pride in our own souls.

What is humility and its opposite, pride?

In 1908, the British writer G. K. Chesterton described the embryo of today's full-grown relativistic culture. One mark of that culture is the hijacking of the word *arrogance* to refer to *conviction*, and the word *humility* to refer to *uncertainty*. Chesterton saw it coming:

What we suffer from today is humility in the wrong place. Modesty has moved from the organ of ambition. Modesty has settled upon the organ of conviction; where it was never meant to be. A man was meant to be doubtful about himself, but undoubting about the truth; this has been exactly reversed. Nowadays the part of a man that a man does assert is exactly the part he ought not to assert—himself. The part he doubts is exactly the part he ought not to doubt—the Divine Reason. . . . We are on the road to producing a race of man too mentally modest to believe in the multiplication table.[2]

So, if humility is not the abandonment of conviction or the embrace of agnosticism and relativism, what is it? God has told us at least six things about humility.

1. *Humility begins with a sense of subordination to God in Christ.*

"A disciple is not above his teacher, nor a servant above his master" (Matt. 10:24). "Humble yourselves . . . under the mighty hand of God" (1 Pet. 5:6).

There is the fact: God is above. We are beneath. We are not worthy to untie His shoes. The distance between God and us is infinite. His greatness, His power, His wisdom, His justice, His truth, His holiness, His mercy and grace are as high above ours as the heavens are above the earth.

Besides the fact that God is above and we are beneath, there is the heartfelt *sense* of the fact. Besides truth there is the sinking in and the *feeling* of the truth. That is as crucial here as knowing the truth. Do we feel this distance between God above and us beneath?

---

2. G. K. Chesterton, *Orthodoxy* (Garden City, N.Y.: Doubleday and Co., 1957; original, 1908), 31–32.

Are we really humbled by it, or do we paradoxically even take pride in knowing that we have seen that it exists. Oh, how subtle is the creeping contamination of pride!

2. *Humility does not feel a right to better treatment than Jesus got.*

"If they have called the master of the house Beelzebul, how much more will they malign those of his household" (Matt. 10:25).

Therefore humility does not return evil for evil. Humility does not build a life based on its perceived rights. "Christ also suffered for you, leaving you an example, for you to follow in His steps. . . . While suffering, He uttered no threats, but handed [His cause] over to Him who judges righteously" (1 Pet. 2:21–23 JP).

Much of our anger and resentment in relationships comes from the expectation that we have a right to be treated well. But, as George Otis once said to a gathering in Manila, "Jesus never promised His disciples a fair fight." We must assume mistreatment, and not be indignant when we get it. This is what humility would look like. Peter (1 Pet. 2:21–23) and Paul (Rom. 12:19) give us great moral assistance in this difficult task by reminding us that God will settle all accounts justly and that temporary injustice will not be swept under the rug of the universe. It will be dealt with—on the cross or in hell. We need not avenge ourselves. We can leave it to God.

3. *Humility asserts truth not to bolster the ego with control or with triumphs in debate, but as service to Christ and love to the adversary.*

"Love . . . rejoices in the truth" (1 Cor. 13:6 NKJV). "What I [Jesus] tell you in the darkness, speak in the light. . . . Do not fear" (Matt. 10:27–28 NASB). "We do not preach ourselves but Christ Jesus as Lord, and ourselves as your bond-servants for Jesus' sake" (2 Cor. 4:5 NASB).

If truth is precious, to speak it is a necessary part of love. And if truth is an instrument for salvation and sanctification and preservation and freedom and joy, then speaking the truth is an essential part of love. "You will know the truth, and the truth will set you free" (John 8:32). "Sanctify them in the truth; your word is truth" (John 17:17). "[People] perish, because they did not receive the love of the truth so as to be saved" (2 Thess. 2:10 NASB).

Therefore, speaking the truth is service to Christ and love to others, even if they consider themselves your adversaries. This is clearest in the case of evangelism where you are accused of arrogance for telling the gospel to Muslims or Jews or Buddhists. This has always been true in missionary settings and is true now in the less-than-tolerant American public square, where relativism no longer means: Your claim to truth is no more valid than mine; but now means: You may not claim to speak the truth. If you do, you are at best arrogant and, at worst, the nourisher of hate crimes.

For example, I wrote an editorial for the Minneapolis *StarTribune* (October 2, 1999) arguing that it was a loving thing for Christians to speak the gospel of Jesus Christ to Jewish people because "whoever has the Son has life; whoever does not have the Son of God does not have life" (1 John 5:12). Several clergy wrote to the paper and said, "Unfortunately, *arrogant* is the right word to describe any attempts at proselytizing—in this case the effort of Christians to 'win over' their Jewish brothers and sisters. Thoughtful Christians will disassociate themselves from any such effort."

We must help one another stand against this kind of intimidation. In the name of humility, it attempts to call into question the heart of the gospel—that Jesus Christ is the only way of salvation: We must remind each other that to tell this gospel is not arrogant but loving.

4. *Humility knows it is dependent on grace for all knowing, believing, living, and acting.*

"For by grace you have been saved through faith. And this is not your own doing; it is the gift of God, not a result of works, so that no one may boast" (Eph. 2:8–9). "What do you have that you did not receive? If then you received it, why do you boast as if you did not receive it?" (1 Cor. 4:7). "Of his own will he brought us forth by the word of truth, that we should be a kind of firstfruits of his creation. . . . Receive with meekness the implanted word, which is able to save your souls" (James 1:18, 21).

Perhaps the clearest connection in the Bible between embracing the sovereignty of God and escaping from arrogance is found in James 4:13–16. Here James says that what we believe about the overarching providence of God in the nitty-gritty of our daily planning governs whether we are "arrogant."

> Come now, you who say, "Today or tomorrow we shall go to such and such a city, and spend a year there and engage in business and make a profit." Yet you do not know what your life will be like tomorrow. You are just a vapor that appears for a little while and then vanishes away. Instead, you ought to say, "If the Lord wills, we shall live and also do this or that." But as it is, you boast in your arrogance; all such boasting is evil (James 4:13–16 NASB).

Therefore, humility does the opposite. It submits moment by moment to the sovereign rule of God over our daily lives and rests quietly in the tough and tender decrees of God's loving wisdom.

5. *Humility knows it is fallible and so considers criticism and learns from it, but it also knows that God has made provision for unshakable human conviction and that He calls us to persuade others.*

"We see in a mirror dimly, but then face to face; now I know in part, but then I will know fully just as I also have been fully known"

(1 Cor. 13:12 NASB). "A wise man is he who listens to counsel" (Prov. 12:15). "Therefore, knowing the fear of the Lord, *we persuade* others" (2 Cor. 5:11). "These things speak and exhort and reprove *with all authority.* Let no one disregard you" (Titus 2:15 NASB).

We do not know everything. And what we know, we do not know with perfect balance and comprehensive completeness. But God has revealed Himself in Christ and in His Word. He means for us to humble ourselves under the objectivity of this revelation and embrace with conviction what He has said. By the blood of the Lamb and by the word of our testimony, we may conquer the devil, if we love not our lives even unto death (Rev. 12:11).

At the bottom of all these marks of humility is this: True humility senses that humility is a gift beyond our reach. If humility is the product of reaching, then we will instinctively feel proud about our successful reach. Humility is the gift that receives all things as gift. It is the fruit not of our achievement but of the Holy Spirit (Gal. 5:22). It is the fruit of the gospel, knowing and feeling that we are desperate sinners and that Christ is a great and undeserved Savior.

Brothers, for the sake of the truth, and for the good of your people, and for the glory of God in the world, don't confuse timid uncertainty with truthful humility.

> Provide yourselves with moneybags that do not grow old,
> with a treasure in the heavens that does not fail.
>
> LUKE 12:33

> There is no room for a preaching devoid
> of ethical directness and social passion,
> in a day when heaven's trumpets sound
> and the Son of God goes forth to war.
>
> JAMES STEWART

> If you want to be a conduit for God's grace,
> you don't have to be lined with gold.
> Copper will do.
>
> JOHN PIPER

23

BROTHERS, TELL THEM COPPER WILL DO

WE WILL NEVER persuade our people that the parable of the rich fool (Luke 12:13–21) applies to them unless we apply it to ourselves. God called the man a fool because, when his fields produced a surplus, he built bigger barns and took his ease.

What should he have done with the God-given surplus? Verse 33 answers: "Sell your possessions, and give to the needy." Instead of increasing his own ease and security, he should have used his extra possessions to alleviate suffering.

"Fool" is what God calls a person who uses his excess money to increase his own comforts. And Luke adds, "So is the one who lays up treasure for himself and is not rich toward God" (v. 21). Does this mean the man should have made God rich and not himself? How can you make God rich? He already owns everything—the cattle on a thousand hills (Ps. 50:10) and our own souls (Luke 12:20)!

There is another possible meaning. Luke 12:33 says, "Provide yourselves with moneybags that do not grow old, with a treasure in the heavens that does not fail." So maybe "rich toward God" does not mean "make God rich" but "make yourself rich with God." It does not say, "Provide God with a purse." It says, "Provide yourselves with purses." Provide yourselves with treasure in heaven that does not fail. Seek real security!

Being "rich toward God" means looking Godward for heavenly wealth. It means "taking your ease" in Him, finding your security in Him. And it means using your money in a way that enlarges the barn of your joy in heaven, not the barn of your comfort on earth. God gives us money on earth in order that we may invest it for dividends in heaven.

The person who thinks the money he makes is meant mainly to increase his comforts on earth is a fool, Jesus says. Wise people know that all their money belongs to God and should be used to show that God, and not money, is their treasure, their comfort, their joy, and their security.

How do we use our money to show that God is our treasure? How do we show that we are "rich toward God"? Luke 12:21 says it is by not laying up treasures for ourselves. And verse 33 says it is by giving alms.

But does not the Old Testament promise that God will prosper the faithful? Indeed! God increases our yield so that by giving we can prove that our yield is not our God. God does not prosper a man's business so that man can move from a Buick to a BMW. God prospers a business so that hundreds of unreached peoples can be reached with the gospel. He prospers a business so that 20 percent of the world's population can move a step back from the precipice of starvation.

Brothers, many of our people have barely begun to grasp this. Too many are more shaped by the consumer culture than by the economics of Christ. They still operate on the simple rule: If you earned it, you deserve it. It's yours; use it for your own material comfort.

They have been taken in by the half-truth that says we glorify God with money by enjoying thankfully all luxuries He enables us to buy. The true half is this: we *should* give thanks for every good thing God gives us. That does glorify Him. The false half is the subtle implication that God can be glorified in this way by every decent purchase we make.

If this were true, Jesus would not say, "Sell your possessions, and give to the needy" (Luke 12:33). He would not say, "Do not seek what you are to eat and what you are to drink" (Luke 12:29). John the Baptist would not have said, "Whoever has two tunics is to share with him who has none" (Luke 3:11). The Son of Man would not have walked around with no place to lay His head (Luke 9:58). And Zacchaeus would not have given half of his goods to the poor (Luke 19:8).

God is not glorified when we keep for ourselves (no matter how thankfully) what we ought to be using to alleviate the misery of unevangelized and uneducated and unhoused and unfed millions.

The evidence that many of our people are not rich toward God is how little they give and how much they own. Over the years God has prospered them. And by an almost irresistible law of consumer culture, they have bought bigger (and more) houses, newer (and more) cars, fancier (and more) clothes, and all manner of trinkets and gadgets and containers and devices and equipment to make life more fun.

Very few of our people have said to themselves: we will live at a level of joyful, wartime simplicity and use the rest of what we earn to alleviate misery. But surely that is what Jesus wants. I do not see how we can read the New Testament, then look at two billion un-evangelized people, and still build another barn for ourselves. We can only justify the exorbitance of our lifestyle by ignoring the lostness of the unreached and the misery of the poor.

Brothers, we are leaders, and the burden of change lies most heavily on us. The place to start is our own lives. Is it the thrill of your life to live in such a sacrificial way that all can see that *God* is your treasure, not things? Are your home and clothes and cars and recreation the mark of a wartime lifestyle? Is your giving to the church pacesetting (not that your people will know what you give, but God does)? Does your burden for the unreached and the poor stab your people's love for luxury and comfort?

I do not say that we should become professional economists, just prophets. James Stewart of Scotland said thirty years ago:

> It is the function of economists, not the pulpit, to work out plans of reconstruction. But it is emphatically the function of the pulpit to stab men broad awake to the terrible pity of Jesus, to expose their hearts to constraint of that divine compassion which haloes the oppressed and the suffering and flames in judgment against every social wrong. . . . There is no room for a preaching devoid of ethical directness and social passion, in a day when heaven's trumpets sound and the Son of God goes forth to war.[1]

---

1. James Stewart, *Heralds of God* (Grand Rapids, Mich.: Baker Book House, 1972), 97.

What should a pastor say to his people concerning the purchase and ownership of two homes in a world where twenty-four thousand people starve to death every day and mission agencies cannot penetrate unreached peoples for lack of funds?

First, you may want to quote Amos 3:15: "I will strike the winter house with the summer house, and the houses of ivory shall perish, and the great houses shall come to an end." Then you may read Luke 3:11: "Whoever has two tunics is to share with him who has none."

Then you might tell about Bob and Myrna Gemmer of St. Petersburg, Florida, who caught a vision for the housing needs of the poor. They sold their second home in Ohio and used the funds to build houses for several families in Immokalee, Florida.

Then you will ask, "Is it wrong to own a second home that sits empty part of the year?" And you will answer, "Maybe and maybe not." You will not make it easy by creating a law. Laws can be obeyed under constraint with no change of heart. Prophets want new hearts for God, not just new real-estate arrangements. You will empathize with their uncertainty and share your own struggle to discover the way of love. You will not presume to have a simple answer to every lifestyle question. You will acknowledge that your own lifestyle, if it's in America, is lavishly comfortable in comparison with most people in the world.

But you will help them decide. You will say, "Does your house signify or encourage life at a level of luxury enjoyed in heedless unconcern for the needs of others? Or is it a simple, oft-used retreat for needed rest and prayer and meditation that sends people back to the city with a passion to deny themselves for the evangelization of the unreached and the pursuit of justice for the suffering oppressed?" You will leave the arrow lodged in their conscience and challenge them to seek a lifestyle in sync with the gospel.

Ephesians 4:28 says, "Let the thief no longer steal, but rather let him labor, doing honest work with his own hands, so that he may have something to share with anyone in need." So there are three levels of how to live with things: (1) you can steal to get, (2) or you can work to get, (3) or you can work to get in order to give.

Many of us live on level two. Almost all of the forces of our culture urge us to live on level two. But the Bible is unrelenting in pushing us to level three.

As Paul said, "God is able to make all grace abound to you, so that having all sufficiency in all things at all times, you may abound in every good work" (2 Cor. 9:8). So why does God bless our people with abundance? So they can have enough to live on and then use the rest for all manner of good works that alleviate spiritual and physical misery. Enough for us; abundance for others.

You will have to make clear to the business people in your congregation that you are not against multimillion-dollar industries. Nor are you necessarily against their six-digit salaries. The problem arises when they endorse the professional status quo that says a six-digit salary should have a six-digit lifestyle. It shouldn't. Perhaps it should have a $40,000 lifestyle and support two families on a new mission field.

The problem is not with earning a lot. The problem is the constant accumulation of luxuries that are soon felt to be needs. If you want to be a conduit for God's grace, you don't have to be lined with gold. Copper will do.

But, brothers, it must begin with us. We have to stop accumulating. We have to stop building barns. We have to show that the greatest thing to do with money is to use it to provide treasure in heaven, not on earth. We have to be "rich toward God." So bore the gold out of your own conduit. And tell them copper will do.

> "The LORD gave
> and the LORD has taken away;
> blessed be the name of the LORD."
>
> JOB 1:21
>
> Rejoice with those who rejoice, weep with those who weep.
>
> ROMANS 12:15
>
> Whom have I in heaven but You?
> And besides You, I desire nothing on earth.
> My flesh and my heart may fail,
> but God is the strength of my heart and my portion forever.
>
> PSALM 73:25–26 NASB
>
> God is the only sure and stable thing in the universe.
>
> JOHN PIPER

24

BROTHERS, HELP YOUR PEOPLE HOLD ON AND MINISTER IN CALAMITY

AT ABOUT 11:30 A.M. on Tuesday, April 20, 1999, the anniversary of Adolph Hitler's birth, two students of Columbine High School in Littleton, a suburb of Denver, Colorado, entered the cafeteria and opened fire on students with guns and with homemade bombs. They moved through the school and into the library where, after killing thirteen, they killed themselves. Even more stunning to our nation, on the morning of September 11, 2001, terrorists flew two commercial jets into the World Trade Center Towers in New York and one into the Pentagon. Over three thousand people died in the attacks. The entire nation trembled, wept, and raged.

What should a pastor do in times like these when the entire nation is talking about life and death and evil and loss and pain? I was on a month's writing leave when Columbine happened. Since I was not there to preach to the people, I decided to write to the elders. I asked them, "What shall we say about this calamity in order to honor God and minister to people for their good?" In answer, I wrote a fifteen-point response to Columbine that I sent to the elders within days of April 20, 1999.

When the September 11 calamity occurred, I was with the staff listening to the radio. As we got on our faces to seek the Lord for our nation and our people, we conceived a three-service response. We called the threefold service (Tuesday, Wednesday, and Sunday) "A Service of Sorrow, Self-Humbling, and Steady Hope in Our Savior and King, Jesus Christ." In addition, I took the 15-point response to Columbine and added six more points and put it on our web site for the people to use in ministering to one another. What follows is that response which, I pray, will help you and sustain and strengthen your people in calamity.

1. *Pray. Ask God for His help for you and for those you want to minister to. Ask Him for wisdom and compassion and strength and a word fitly chosen. Ask that those who are suffering would look to God as their help and hope and healing and strength. Ask that He would make your mouth a fountain of life.*

James 1:5: "If any of you lacks wisdom, let him ask God, who gives generously to all without reproach, and it will be given him."

Deuteronomy 32:2: "May my teaching drop as the rain, my speech distill as the dew, like gentle rain upon the tender grass, and like showers upon the herb."

Proverbs 13:14: "The teaching of the wise is a fountain of life, that one may turn away from the snares of death."

2. *Feel and express empathy with those most hurt by this great evil and loss; weep with those who weep.*

Ecclesiastes 3:1, 4, 5: "For everything there is a season, and a time for every matter under heaven: . . . a time to weep, and a time to laugh; a time to mourn, and a time to dance . . . a time to embrace, and a time to refrain from embracing."

Romans 12:15: "Rejoice with those who rejoice, *weep with those who weep.*"

3. *Feel and express compassion because of the tragic circumstances of so many loved ones and friends who have lost more than they could ever estimate.*

John 11:33–35: "When Jesus saw her weeping, and the Jews who had come with her also weeping, he was deeply moved in his spirit and greatly troubled. And he said, 'Where have you laid him?' They said to him, 'Lord, come and see.' *Jesus wept.*"

Luke 19:41–44: "*When he drew near and saw the city, he wept over it*, saying, 'Would that you, even you, had known on this day the things that make for peace! But now they are hidden from your eyes. For the days will come upon you, when your enemies will set up a barricade around you and surround you and hem you in on every side and tear you down to the ground, you and your children within you. And they will not leave one stone upon another in you, because you did not know the time of your visitation.'"

Luke 7:11–17: "Soon afterward he went to a town called Nain, and his disciples and a great crowd went with him. As he drew near to the gate of the town, behold, *a man who had died was being carried out, the only son of his mother, and she was a widow, and a considerable crowd from the town was with her. And when the Lord saw her, he had compassion on her* and said to her, 'Do not weep.' Then he came up and touched the bier, and the bearers stood still. And he said, 'Young man, I say to you, arise.' And the dead man sat up and began to speak, and Jesus gave him to his mother. Fear seized them all, and they glorified God, saying, 'A great prophet has arisen among us!' and 'God has visited his people!' And this report about him spread through the whole of Judea and all the surrounding country."

4. *Take time and touch, if you can, and give tender care to the wounded in body and soul.*

Matthew 8:14–15: "And when Jesus entered Peter's house, he saw his mother-in-law lying sick with a fever. *He touched her hand,* and the fever left her, and she rose and began to serve him.

Mark 1:40–41: "And a leper came to him, imploring him, and kneeling said to him, 'If you will, you can make me clean.' Moved with pity, *he stretched out his hand and touched him* and said to him, 'I will; be clean.'"

Luke 10:30–37: "Jesus replied, 'A man was going down from Jerusalem to Jericho, and he fell among robbers, who stripped him and beat him and departed, leaving him half dead. Now by chance a priest was going down that road, and when he saw him he passed by on the other side. So likewise a Levite, when he came to the place and saw him, passed by on the other side. But a Samaritan, as he journeyed, came to where he was, and when he saw him, *he had compassion. He went to him and bound up his wounds, pouring on oil and wine. Then he set him on his own animal and brought him to an inn and took care of him. And the next day he took out two denarii and gave them to the innkeeper, saying, "Take care of him, and whatever more you spend, I will repay you when I come back."* Which of these three, do you think, proved to be a neighbor to the man who fell among the robbers?' He said, 'The one who showed him mercy.' And Jesus said to him, 'You go, and do likewise.'"

5. *Hold out the promise that God will sustain and help those who cast themselves on Him for mercy and trust in His grace. He will*

strengthen you for the impossible days ahead in spite of all darkness.

Psalm 34:18: "The LORD is *near to the brokenhearted* and *saves the crushed in spirit."*

Isaiah 41:10: "Fear not, for I am with you; be not dismayed, for I am your God; *I will strengthen you, I will help you, I will uphold you* with my righteous right hand."

Psalm 23:4: "Even though I walk through the valley of the shadow of death, I will fear no evil, *for you are with me; your rod and your staff, they comfort me."*

2 Corinthians 1:3–4: "Blessed be the God and Father of our Lord Jesus Christ, the *Father of mercies and God of all comfort,* who *comforts us in all our affliction* so that we may be able to comfort those who are in any affliction, with the comfort with which we ourselves are comforted by God."

2 Corinthians 1:8–9: "We do not want you to be unaware, brothers, of the affliction we experienced in Asia. For we were so burdened beyond our strength that we despaired of life itself. Indeed, we felt that we had received the sentence of death. *But that was to make us rely not on ourselves, but on God who raises the dead."*

6. *Affirm that Jesus Christ tasted hostility from men and knew what it was to be unjustly tortured and abandoned, and to endure overwhelming loss, and then be killed, so that He is now a sympathetic mediator for us with God.*

Hebrews 4:15–16: "*For we do not have a high priest who is unable to sympathize with our weaknesses,* but one who in every respect has been tempted [or "tested" which makes the application larger!] as we are, yet without sin. Let us then with confidence draw near to the throne of grace, so that we may receive mercy and find grace to help in time of need."

Isaiah 53:3–6: "He was despised and *rejected* by men; a *man of sorrows, and acquainted with grief;* and as one from whom men hide their face he was despised, and we esteemed him not. *Surely he has borne our griefs and carried our sorrows; yet we esteemed him stricken, smitten by God, and afflicted. But he was wounded for our transgressions; he was crushed for our iniquities; upon him was the chastisement that brought us peace*, and with his stripes we are healed. All we like sheep have gone astray; we have turned every one to his own way; and the LORD has laid on him the iniquity of us all."

7. *Declare that this murder was a great evil, and that God's wrath is greatly kindled by the wanton destruction of human life created in His image.*

Exodus 20:13: "You shall not murder."

Genesis 9:5–6: "For your lifeblood I will require a reckoning: from every beast I will require it and from man. From his fellow man I will require a reckoning for the life of man. Whoever sheds the blood of man, by man shall his blood be shed, for God made man in his own image."

Deuteronomy 29:24–25: "All the nations will say, 'Why has the LORD done thus to this land? Why this great outburst of anger?' Then men will say, 'Because they forsook the covenant of the LORD, the God of their fathers, which he made with them when he brought them out of the land of Egypt.'"

8. *Acknowledge that God has permitted a great outbreak of sin against His revealed will, and that we do not know all the reasons why He would permit such a thing now, when it was in His power to stop it.*

Deuteronomy 29:29: "The secret things belong to the LORD our God, but the things that are revealed belong to us and to our children forever, that we may do all the words of this law."

Romans 11:33–36: "Oh, the depth of the riches and wisdom and knowledge of God! How unsearchable are his judgments and how inscrutable his ways! 'For who has known the mind of the Lord, or who has been his counselor?' 'Or who has given a gift to him that he might be repaid?' For from him and through him and to him are all things. To him be glory forever. Amen."

9. *Express the truth that Satan is a massive reality in the universe that conspires with our own sin and flesh and the world to hurt people and to move people to hurt others, but stress that Satan is within and under the control of God.*

Job 1:6, 12, 21–22; 2:6–10: "Now there was a day when the sons of God came to present themselves before the LORD, and Satan also came among them. . . . And the LORD said to Satan, 'Behold, all that he has is in your hand. Only against him do not stretch out your hand.' So Satan went out from the presence of the LORD. . . [After losing all his possessions and his ten children Job says] 'Naked I came from my mother's womb, and naked shall I return. *The LORD gave, and the LORD has taken away*; blessed be the name of the LORD. In all this Job did not sin or charge God with wrong. . . . [After a second meeting in heaven] the LORD said to Satan, 'Behold, he is in your hand; only spare his life.' So Satan went out from the presence of the LORD and struck Job with loathsome sores from the sole of his foot to the crown of his head. . . . Then his wife said to him, 'Do you still hold fast your integrity? Curse God and die!' But he said to her, 'You speak as one of the foolish women would speak. *Shall we receive good from God, and shall we not receive evil?*'"

Job 42:2, 11: "I know that you can do all things, and that no purpose of yours can be thwarted. . . . Then came to him all his brothers and sisters and all who had known him before, and ate bread with him in his house. And they showed sympathy and comforted him for all the evil that *the LORD had brought upon him*."

Luke 22:31–32: "Simon, Simon, behold, Satan demanded to have you, that he might sift you like wheat, but I have prayed for you that your faith may not fail. And when you have turned again, strengthen your brothers."

2 Corinthians 12:7–9: "So to keep me from being too elated by the surpassing greatness of the revelations, a thorn was given me in the flesh, *a messenger of Satan* to harass me, to keep me from being too elated. Three times I pleaded with the Lord about this, that it should leave me. But he said to me, 'My grace is sufficient for you, for my power is made perfect in weakness.' Therefore I will boast all the more gladly of my weaknesses, so that the power of Christ may rest upon me."

Compare the following two perspectives on the cause of Jesus' death.

Luke 22:3–4: "*Satan entered into Judas* called Iscariot, who was of the number of the twelve. He went away and conferred with the chief priests and officers how he might betray him to them."

Acts 4:27–28: "Truly in this city there were gathered together against your holy servant Jesus, whom you anointed, both Herod and Pontius Pilate, along with the Gentiles and the peoples of Israel, to do *whatever your hand and your plan had predestined to occur.*"

10. *Express that these terrorists rebelled against the revealed will of God and did not love God or trust Him or find in God their refuge and strength and treasure, but scorned His ways and His Person.*

2 Thessalonians 3:1–2: "Finally, brothers, pray for us . . . that we may be delivered from *wicked and evil men. For not all have faith.*"

Galatians 5:6: "For in Christ Jesus neither circumcision nor un-circumcision counts for anything, but only *faith working through love.*"

Galatians 5:16: "Walk by the Spirit, and you will not gratify the desires of the flesh."

James 4:1–4: "What causes quarrels and what causes fights among you? Is it not this, that your passions are at war within you? You desire and do not have, so you murder. You covet and cannot obtain, so you fight and quarrel. You do not have, because you do not ask. You ask and do not receive, because you ask wrongly, to spend it on your passions. You adulterous people! Do you not know that friendship with the world is enmity with God? Therefore whoever wishes to be a friend of the world makes himself an enemy of God."

11. *Since rebellion against God was at the root of this act of murder, let us all fear such rebellion in our own hearts, and turn from it, and embrace the grace of God in Christ, and renounce the very impulses that caused this tragedy.*

Proverbs 3:5–6: "*Trust in the* LORD *with all your heart, and do not lean on your own understanding. In all your ways acknowledge him, and he will make straight your paths.*"

Psalm 9:10: "And those who know your name put their *trust* in you, for you, O LORD, have not forsaken those who seek you."

Psalm 56:3: "When I am afraid, I put my *trust* in you."

12. *Point the living to the momentous issues of sin and repentance in our own hearts and the urgent need to get right with God through His merciful provision of forgiveness in Christ, so that a worse fate than death will not overtake us.*

Luke 13:1–5: "There were some present at that very time who told him about the Galileans whose blood Pilate had mingled with their sacrifices. And he answered them, 'Do you think that these Galileans were worse sinners than all the other Galileans, because they suffered in this way? No, I tell you; but unless you repent, you will all likewise perish. Or those eighteen on whom the tower in Siloam fell and killed them: do you think that they were worse offenders than all the others who lived in Jerusalem? No, I tell you; but unless you repent, you will all likewise perish.'"

Revelation 9:18–21: "By these three plagues [as a judgment of God] a third of mankind was killed, by the fire and smoke and sulfur coming out of their mouths. . . . The rest of mankind, who were not killed by these plagues, did not repent of the works of their hands nor give up worshiping demons and the idols . . . nor did they repent of their murders or of their sorceries or of their sexual immorality or their thefts."

Revelation 16:8–9: "The fourth angel poured out his bowl on the sun, and it was allowed to scorch people with fire. They were scorched by the fierce heat, and they cursed the name of God who had power over these plagues. They did not repent and give him glory."

13. *Remember that even those who trust in Christ may be cut down like these thousands who were in New York and Washington, but that does not mean they have been abandoned by God or not loved by God even in those agonizing hours of suffering. God's love conquers even through calamity.*

Romans 8:35–39: "Who shall separate us from the love of Christ? Shall tribulation, or distress, or persecution, or famine, or nakedness, or danger, or sword? As it is written, 'For your sake we are being killed all the day long; we are regarded as sheep to be slaughtered.' No, in all these things we are more than conquerors through him who loved us. For I am sure that neither death nor life, nor angels nor rulers, nor things present nor things to come, nor powers, nor height nor depth, nor anything else in all creation, will be able to separate us from the love of God in Christ Jesus our Lord."

14. *Mingle heart-wrenching weeping with unbreakable confidence in the goodness and sovereignty of God who rules over and through the sin and the plans of rebellious people.*

Lamentations 3:32–33: "For if he cause grief, he will have compassion according to the abundance of his steadfast love. For he does not willingly afflict or grieve the children of men."

Genesis 45:7: [Joseph said to his brothers who sinfully sold him into Egypt] "God sent me before you to preserve for you a remnant on earth, and to keep alive for you many survivors."

Genesis 50:20: [Joseph says to his fearing brothers] "As for you, you meant evil against me, but God meant it for good, to bring it about that many people should be kept alive, as they are today."[1]

15. *Trust God for his ability to do the humanly impossible, and bring you through this nightmare and, in some inscrutable way, bring good out of it.*

Romans 8:28: "And we know that for those who love God all things work together for good, for those who are called according to his purpose."

Lamentations 3:21-24: "This I call to my mind, and therefore I have hope. The steadfast love of the LORD never ceases; his mercies never come to an end; they are new every morning; great is your faithfulness. 'The LORD is my portion,' says my soul, 'Therefore I have hope in him.'"

2 Corinthians 1:8-9: "For we do not want you to be ignorant, brothers, of the affliction we experienced in Asia. For we were so utterly burdened beyond our strength that we despaired of life itself. Indeed, we felt that we had received the sentence of death. But that was to make us rely *not on ourselves but on God who raises the dead.*"

2 Corinthians 4:17: "This slight momentary affliction is preparing for us an eternal weight of glory far beyond all comparison."

16. *Explain, when the time is right and they have the wherewithal to think clearly, that one of the mysteries of God's greatness is that He ordains that some things come to pass which He forbids and disapproves.*

The clearest example is his ordaining that his Son be killed.

---

[1]Other texts on the absolute sovereignty of God over all things: Ephesians 1:11; Isaiah 46:9-10; Lamentations 3:37; Amos 3:6; Proverbs 16:33; Exodus 4:11; 1 Samuel 2:6-7; 2 Samuel 12:15-18; John 9:2-3; James 4:15; 1 Peter 3:17; 4:19; Matthew 10:29.

Acts 4:27–28: "Truly in this city there were gathered together against your holy servant Jesus, whom you anointed, both Herod and Pontius Pilate, along with the Gentiles and the peoples of Israel, to do whatever your hand and your purpose predestined to take place."[2]

17. *Express your personal cherishing of the sovereignty of God as the ground of all your hope as you face the human impossibilities of life. The very fulfillment of the New Covenant promises of our salvation and preservation hang on God's sovereignty over rebellious human wills.*

Mark 10:24–26: "The disciples were amazed at his words. But Jesus said to them again, 'Children, how difficult it is to enter the kingdom of God! It is easier for a camel to go through the eye of a needle than for a rich person to enter the kingdom of God.' They were exceedingly astonished, and said to him, 'Then who can be saved?' Looking at them, Jesus said, *'With man it is impossible, but not with God. For all things are possible with God.'*"

Jeremiah 32:40: "I will make with them an everlasting covenant, that I will not turn away from doing good to them. And I will put the fear of me in their hearts, that they may not turn from me."

Hebrews 13:20–21: "Now the God of peace, who brought again from the dead our Lord Jesus, the great Shepherd of the sheep, by the blood of the eternal covenant, equip you with everything good that you may do his will, *working in us that which is pleasing in his sight,* through Jesus Christ, to whom be the glory forever and ever. Amen."

18. *Count God your only lasting treasure, because He is the only sure and stable thing in the universe.*

[2]See the Appendix titled "Are There Two Wills in God? Divine Election and God's Desire for All to Be Saved," in *The Pleasures of God* (Sisters, Oreg.: Multnomah Press, 2000), 313–40, also in *Still Sovereign: Contemporary Perspectives on Election, Foreknowledge, and Grace,* ed. by Thomas R. Schreiner and Bruce A. Ware (Grand Rapids, Mich.: Baker Books, 2000), 107–31.

Psalm 73:25–26: "Whom have I in heaven but you? And there is nothing on earth I desire besides you. My flesh and my heart may fail, but God is the strength of my heart and my portion forever."

19. *Remind everyone that to live is Christ and to die is gain.*

Philippians 1:21, 23: "For to me, to live is Christ and to die is gain. . . . I am hard-pressed between the two. My desire is to depart and be with Christ, for that is far better."

2 Corinthians 5:7–9: "We walk by faith, not by sight. Yes, we are of good courage, and we would rather be away from the body and at home with the Lord. So whether we are at home or away, we make it our aim to please him."

20. *Pray that God would incline their hearts to his word, open their eyes to his wonders, unite their hearts to fear him, and satisfy them with his love.*

Psalm 119:36: "Incline my heart to your testimonies, and not to selfish gain!"

Psalm 119:18: "Open my eyes, that I may behold wondrous things out of your law."

Psalm 86:11: "Unite my heart to fear your name."

Psalm 90:14: "Satisfy us in the morning with your steadfast love, that we may rejoice and be glad all our days."

21. *At the right time sound the trumpet that all this good news is meant by God to free us for radical, sacrificial service for the salvation of men and the glory of Christ. Help them see that one message of all this misery is to show us that life is short and fragile and followed by eternity, and small, man-centered ambitions are tragic.*

Acts 20:24: "But I do not account my life of any value nor as precious to myself, if only I may finish my course and the ministry that I received from the Lord Jesus, to testify to the gospel of the grace of God."

Titus 2:14: "[Christ] gave himself for us to redeem us from all

lawlessness, and to purify for himself a people for his own possession who are *zealous for good works.*"

Philippians 1:21: "To live is Christ."

———————————

There are precious and painful moments in the life of every
church and every nation when people are ready to let the precious
truth of God's sovereign mercy sink into their souls. Before those
moments, and during them, brothers, help your people hold on and
minister in calamity.

> Go therefore and make disciples of all nations.
>
> MATTHEW 28:19

> There are three possibilities with the Great Commission.
> You can go. You can send. Or you can be disobedient.
> Ignoring the cause is not a Christian option.
>
> JOHN PIPER

> This gospel of the kingdom shall be preached in the whole world
> as a testimony to all the nations,
> and then the end will come.
>
> MATTHEW 24:14 NASB

> If we love God's fame
> and are committed to magnifying His name above all things,
> we cannot be indifferent to world missions.
>
> JOHN PIPER

25

BROTHERS, GIVE THEM GOD'S PASSION FOR MISSIONS

I BEAR WITNESS to the grace of God in my life for giving me a passion for world missions—that is, a passion for the supremacy of God in all things for the joy of all peoples. All peoples! As Psalm 67:4 says, "Let the nations be glad and sing for joy!" God has been good to me in opening my eyes to the supremacy of God and the joy of the nations through world missions.

He put me into the family of an evangelist, Bill Piper, who led his children in prayer for missionaries during every family prayer time and is spending the last chapter of his fruitful life in his eighties managing Bible correspondence courses among forty nations. Then God sent me to a college with the heritage of alumni like Jim Elliot and Billy Graham.

Then He sent me to a seminary which was starting one of the first graduate level schools of world missions in those days and put me in classes with the likes of Ralph Winter. Then He sent me overseas to do my graduate work in a different culture and a different language. Then He sent me to teach at Bethel College and become a part of the Baptist General Conference with its world missions vision. And then in 1980, He sent me to Bethlehem Baptist Church, with its one-hundred-year-old history of sending missionaries like Ola Hanson in 1890 to the unreached peoples of the world like the Kachin of Burma.

And in 1983, God opened my eyes during a missions conference to see the connection between my vision of Christian hedonism (see chapter 7) and world evangelization. And in the early '90s He put it in the heart of our elders to give me time to put into writing what I had learned in the years since that experience in 1983. The book is titled *Let the Nations Be Glad*[1] from Psalm 67:4, "Let the nations be glad and sing for joy; for You will judge the peoples with uprightness and guide the nations on the earth" (NASB).

All of this I call the grace of God in my life.

From time to time in the life of the church, it becomes crucial that pastors rehearse the essential truths about missions that feed a passion for God's supremacy among the nations. Why do we care so

---

1. John Piper, *Let the Nations Be Glad: The Supremacy of God in Missions* (Grand Rapids, Mich.: Baker Book House, 1993; revised edition to be released in 2003).

much about missions? The people need to hear this. And what is it anyway? Many Christians are oblivious of the most glorious story in world history, the spread of Christianity through the blood and tears and joy of world missions.

There are seven truths we have seen over the years that define and ignite our passion for world missions at Bethlehem. I think they might be helpful for you to ponder. If the church around the world were set on fire by these things, it would, as Peter says in 2 Peter 3:12, "Hasten the coming of the day of God" and the end of history as we know it.

1. *We discovered that God is passionately committed to His fame. God's ultimate goal is that His name be known and praised and enjoyed by all the peoples of the earth.*

"This gospel of the *kingdom* shall be preached in the whole world" (Matt. 24:14 NASB). The gospel is about the kingdom of God. It is about the reign of God. It is about the triumph of King Jesus over sin and death and judgment and Satan and guilt and fear. It is good news—not that we reign as kings but that our God reigns. "How lovely on the mountains are the feet of him who brings good news . . . who announces salvation, and says to Zion, 'Your God reigns!'" (Isa. 52:7 NASB). It's the gospel of God's reign.

And the aim of preaching this "gospel of the kingdom" is that the nations might know King Jesus and admire Him and honor Him and love Him and trust Him and follow Him and make Him shine in their affections. We have come to see that God is passionately committed to upholding and displaying His name, His reputation, in the world.

Over and over we read this in the Bible—that God does what He does so "that [His] name might be proclaimed in all the earth" (Rom. 9:17). The central command of missions is Isaiah 12:4, "Make known his deeds among the peoples, proclaim that his name is exalted."

God is passionately committed to His fame (see chapter 2, "Brothers, God Loves His Glory"). This is His highest priority: that He be known and admired and trusted and enjoyed as an infinitely glorious King. This is the "good news of the kingdom." This is the goal of missions. As Paul said in Romans 15:9, "That the nations might *glorify God* for His mercy"(JP).

That is discovery number one. Some of us saw more clearly than ever in 1983 that if we loved God's fame and were committed to magnifying His name above all things, we could not be indifferent to world missions.

2. *We discovered that God's purpose to be known and praised and enjoyed among all the nations cannot fail. It is an absolutely certain promise. It is going to happen.*

Jesus said, "This gospel of the kingdom *shall* be preached in the whole world as a testimony to all the nations, and then the end will come" (Matt. 24:14 NASB). This is an absolute promise. It *will* happen. The ground of this certainty is the sovereignty of Jesus: "All authority in heaven and on earth has been given to me. Go therefore . . ." (Matt. 28:18). Nothing can stop Him: "I will build my church and the gates of hell shall not prevail against it" (Matt. 16:18).

From this discovery we saw that if we as a church are disobedient, it is not ultimately the cause of God and the cause of world missions that will lose; *we* will lose. God's counsel will stand, and He will accomplish all His purpose (Isa. 46:10). His triumph is never in question, only our participation in it—or our incalculable loss. We can be drunk with private concerns and indifferent to the great enterprise of world evangelization, but God will simply pass over us and do His great work while we shrivel up in our little land of comfort.

3. *We discovered that the missionary task is focused on reaching unreached peoples, not just people—people groups, not just individuals—and is therefore finishable.*

Again, Jesus said, "This gospel of the kingdom shall be preached in the whole world as a testimony to all the nations, and *then* the end will come" (Matt. 24:14 NASB). With the help of Ralph Winter and others, our eyes were opened to the Biblical truth that "nations" in the Bible are not political-geographic states like America, Argentina, China, Germany, Uganda, etc. "Nations" means ethnic groupings with cultural and language distinctions that make it hard for the gospel to spread naturally from one group to the other.[2] "Nations" are groups like the "Amorites, and the Hittites, and the Perizzites, and the Canaanites, and the Hivites, and the Jebusites" (Exod. 23:23), Ojibwe, Niguhr, Berber, Fulani. The task of missions was not only to win individuals but to reach all these different groups in the world.

That's why Revelation 5:9 became as important for us as Matthew 28:19–20, "Worthy are You to take the book and to break its seals; for You were slain, and purchased for God with Your blood men from every tribe and tongue and people and nation" (NASB). That is the task of missions: not just reaching more and more people but more and more peoples—tribes, tongues, peoples, nations.

This discovery gave us a sense of clarified and refined direction for our prayers and our mobilizing efforts. The task was not primarily to try to keep up with or gain on the population growth rate in the world—as wonderful as that would be. The task is to make steady headway in reaching more and more "nations," people groups. Which means that the task is finishable, because while the number of individual people keeps growing and changing, the number of people groups (by and large) does not. That was the third

2. For an exegetical and theological defense of this, see ibid., 167–218.

thing we discovered: the missionary task is focused on reaching unreached peoples, not just people.

4. *We discovered that the scarcity of Paul-type missionaries has been obscured by the quantity of Timothy-type missionaries.*

I'll explain these terms. There seem to be two kinds of missionaries needed in the world. There is the Timothy-type missionary and the Paul-type missionary. We call Timothy a missionary because he left home (Lystra, Acts 16:1), joined a traveling team of missionaries, crossed cultures, and ended up overseeing the younger church in Ephesus (1 Tim. 1:3) far from his homeland. But we have come to distinguish this Timothy-type missionary from the Paul-type missionary because Timothy stayed and ministered on the "mission field" long after there was a church planted with its own elders (Acts 20:17) and its own outreach (Acts 19:10).

Paul (the Paul-type missionary), on the other hand, was driven by a passion to make God's name known among all the unreached peoples of the world. He never stayed in a place long, once the church was established. He said in Romans 15:20, "I make it my ambition to preach the gospel, not where Christ has already been named" (Rom. 15:20). That is what we call "frontier missions" or "pioneer missions." That is a Paul-type missionary.

For me, back in 1983, it proved to be a stunning revelation that perhaps 90 percent of our missionary force from North America are Timothy-type missionaries working with established churches among reached peoples, and only 10 percent are Paul-type missionaries, even though hundreds of people groups, some would say several thousand, remain unreached—that is, there is no indigenous evangelizing movement among them at all.

From this discovery I came to feel that one of my callings as a pastor is to pray and preach and write for the mobilizing of more and more Paul-type missionaries, while not hindering the obedience of those, like Timothy, who are called to stay in the mission field of "Ephesus."

5. *We discovered that domestic ministries are the goal of frontier missions, and frontier missions is the establishment of domestic ministries.*

By domestic ministries I mean the call to live out the love and justice of Jesus in our own culture: taking up, for example, the issues of evangelism, poverty, medical care, unemployment, hunger, abortion, unwed mothers, runaway kids, pornography, family disintegration, child abuse, divorce, hygiene, education at all levels, drug abuse and alcoholism, environmental concerns, crime, prison reform, moral abuses in the media and business and politics, etc. In general, being salt and light at all levels of society in our own culture.

Sometimes people championed these causes but had a spirit of indifference or even hostility to frontier missions. They felt that these important causes would be neglected or threatened by a focus on frontier missions. They said that the needs are great at home, which, of course, is true. But then we discovered the real relationship between domestic ministries and frontier missions.

Frontier missions is the effort of the church to penetrate an unreached people with the "gospel of the kingdom" and establish there an ongoing indigenous church which will apply the love and justice of Christ to that culture. This means that the aim of frontier missions is to build a new base of operations for domestic ministries. The goal of a missionary is to help start an indigenous church that will do in its own culture all the soul-saving, life-changing, suffering-alleviating, need-meeting, culture-transforming domestic ministries that the American church ought to be doing here.

This was a stunning discovery for some of us. Frontier missions is the transportation and adaptation of domestic ministries to people groups where they don't exist because Christ is not known. The surprising conclusion we found was that frontier missions is the (exporting) servant of domestic ministries. And domestic ministries here are the training ground and breeding ground for frontier missionaries.

The great irony we found, in all the emotional turmoil of those days, was that the people who ought to have the greatest burden for frontier missions are the people who have the biggest heart for domestic ministries. The same love of Christ and the same sense of justice that burdens a person for evangelism and housing and unemployment and hunger and health care in their own cities will also burden a person for these same needs in people groups where no Christian impulse for transformation exists at all.

In fact, in more recent days we see the domestic ministries and frontier missions merging in utterly unforeseen ways as the unreached peoples move to Minneapolis. The move from domestic ministry to frontier missions does not have to be a geographic move, though it is still a cultural one. For us, as I write this, the move to an unreached Muslim people group is about fifty yards.

6. *We have come to see that God ordains suffering as the price and the means of finishing the Great Commission.*

It is no fluke that my books, *Let the Nations Be Glad* (1993), *Future Grace* (1995), and *Desiring God* (1996) all have chapters on suffering. I have seen more clearly than ever in recent years that suffering is not only a *result* of trying to penetrate unreached peoples, but a *means* of penetrating them. Five verses before Matthew 24:14, Jesus said, "They will deliver you to tribulation, and will kill you, and you will be hated by all nations because of My name" (v. 9 NASB). This is the price of missions, and it is going to be paid.

Even more important was the discovery that suffering is not just the price but the means God ordains to finish the work. In Colossians

1:24, Paul says, "I rejoice in my sufferings for your sake, and in my flesh I do my share on behalf of His body (which is the church) in filling up what is lacking in Christ's afflictions" (NASB). The sufferings of Paul complete what is lacking in the afflictions of Christ; that is, they become a present, visible demonstration of the kind of love Christ has for the unreached peoples of the world.[3] Our suffering becomes an extension and presentation of Christ's suffering for those for whom He died. Suffering is not an accidental result of obedience. It is an ordained means of penetrating the peoples and the hearts of the lost.

Josef Tson, the Romanian pastor who risked his life teaching and preaching under the communists until he was exiled in 1981, has written a book on *Suffering, Martyrdom, and Rewards in Heaven.* He says in conclusion, "Suffering and martyrdom have to be seen as part of God's plan; they are His instruments by which He achieves His purposes in history and by which He will accomplish His final purpose with man."[4] That is what I have been learning from the Bible and from history in these recent years.

I do not hide this from my people. They know that when I pray and preach and write to win them for the greatest cause in the world, I am calling them to suffer and perhaps to die for Christ. We have spoken too casually and too long about "interesting cross-cultural experiences." The time is here to get Biblical and get real: "Behold, I am sending you out as sheep in the midst of wolves" (Matt. 10:16). "They will put some of you to death, and you will be hated by all because of My name. Yet not a hair of your head will perish" (Luke 21:16–18 NASB).

> 7. *Finally, we have discovered that God is most glorified in us when we are so satisfied in Him that we accept suffering*

---

3. Ibid., 93–96.
4. Josef Tson, *Suffering, Martyrdom, and Rewards in Heaven* (New York: University Press of America, 1997), 423.

and death for His sake in order to extend our joy to the unreached peoples of the earth.

Another way to say it is that worshiping God—being satisfied in God and cherishing God and admiring God—is the fuel and the goal of missions. Missions comes from being satisfied with all that God is for us in Christ and aims at helping others be satisfied with all that God is for them in Christ.

The clearest, most powerful evidence that God is worthy of that admiration and delight is when His people say in the midst of suffering, "This slight momentary affliction is preparing for us an eternal weight of glory beyond all comparison" (2 Cor. 4:17). "I consider that the sufferings of this present time are not worth comparing with the glory that is to be revealed to us" (Rom. 8:18). "I count all things to be loss in view of the surpassing value of knowing Christ Jesus my Lord" (Phil. 3:8 NASB).

When people talk like that, missions is in the making. So get radical with your people. Don't let them settle down and be comfortable, middle-class Americans. Call them to a wartime lifestyle and a world missions orientation. Tell them there are three possibilities. They can be goers, senders, or disobedient. But to ignore the cause is not a Christian option. Speak the words of Jesus to them: "As the Father has sent me, even so I am sending you" (John 20:21). Remind them of the radical challenge of Hebrews 13:12–14 that Jesus suffered outside the gate. So let's go with Him outside the camp, bearing reproach for Him. For here we have no lasting city, but we seek a city that is to come. Brothers, give them a passion for world missions.

26

BROTHERS, SEVER THE ROOT OF RACISM

THE ISSUE OF racial prejudice and snubbing and suspicion and mistreatment is not a social issue; it is a blood-of-Jesus issue. When you get the conviction and the courage to say something about it to your people, tell them you are not becoming a social-gospeler but a lover of the blood-bought blessings of the cross of Christ. I will come back to this in a minute and show you the Bible texts that I have in mind. But first some background.

It doesn't matter whether your church is in Mississippi or Minnesota, your people are tinged by racism—to put it softly. Time passes swiftly, memories are long, and we have not come very far in the heart. Only eighty-one years ago, as I write this, in Duluth, Minnesota, a mob of ten thousand white people dragged three black prisoners from the city jail before any trial and lynched them on city lampposts.[1] That was one generation ago in northern Minnesota, not the deep dark ages or pre-Civil War South.

Moreover, there are probably more vicious white supremacists all over America today than there were in 1968 when Martin Luther King was killed in Memphis, Tennessee. The Ku Klux Klan has no corner on hate. In 1963, in St. Augustine, Florida, the police beat and jailed nonviolent demonstrators with ruthless precision and stood idly by while the Klan bombed and strafed African-American homes and fired shotguns into black nightclubs. I will spare you the details of the horrific abductions and beatings and tortures that every black person in this country knows about.

But I won't spare you the reminder of June 6, 1998, outside Jasper, Texas, when James Byrd, a forty-nine-year-old African-American, was beaten and chained by his ankles to the back of a 1982 pickup truck and dragged two miles until his head came off. Many things have changed, but some deep things haven't changed. These events are the blood-red tip of a deep, partially subconscious, iceberg in American culture. It affects all of us. But few in the majority culture feel it or admit it. That is the privilege of being the majority. Your color and your ways are assumed. Whiteness is not an issue for us, we say, so why should blackness be an issue? We are naïve at best.

---

1. Michael Fedo, "The 1920 Duluth Lynchings, an Untold Chapter of Minnesota History," in *Minnesota Spokesman-Recorder*, 22–28 February 2001, 8b.

I am aware that the issue of race relations in America is bigger than black and white. And even the category "black-white" is an oversimplification in view of infinite shadings and transracial families and the influx into America of thousands of blacks who do not have three hundred years of painful heritage to deal with in this land. But I cannot minimize the unique evil and pain that still colors the relations of Anglo-Americans and African-Americans. What I have to say applies more broadly, but I am glad to be heard as addressing the African-American issue primarily.

Brothers, what about tackling this issue first in your own heart with some reading and some serious Biblical meditation on the meaning of race and God's will for His church in this regard? For example, read the biography of Martin Luther King by Stephen Oates, *Let the Trumpet Sound*,[2] and make it the jumping-off place for addressing your people on the Sunday before Martin Luther King Day. And when you jump off, jump into the Bible.

Yes, I know King is a hot potato for many of you. For some of you this might cost you your job. But perhaps you should risk it. You might start with something like this: It is remarkable how distance in time makes our heroes look better. This is one reason some Christians stumble over Martin Luther King Day but not over Presidents' Day. King is too close, and his warts can still be seen at the distance of three or four decades.

But George Washington stands over two hundred years away from us, and, through the haze of time, we do not see so clearly that his Anglican faith was largely a social convention and that he seems never to have taken communion. John Adams, the second president, was skeptical of traditional Christianity. Thomas Jefferson, the third

---

2. Stephen Oates, *Let the Trumpet Sound: The Life of Martin Luther King, Jr.* (New York: Penguin Books, 1982).

president, scoffed at the notion of the Trinity and the deity of Christ.[3] And James Madison, the fourth president, drifted toward the deism typical of men of his standing in Virginia in the early 1800s.[4] But from a distance we don't feel the same indignation about the flaws of our heroes that we feel when they are so close that their sins feel threatening.

From a distance we can make distinctions. We can say: This was an admirable trait but not that. This we will celebrate, and that we will deplore. I suggest we do that with Martin Luther King. He was a sinner, as he well knew, especially when he was caught in some of his inexcusable behavior.[5] But this should not prevent us from reminding our people about the truth and vision he so eloquently proclaimed.

King spoke with a prophetic message that rings within my ears even today with great power. One of the most compelling things he wrote was "Letter from Birmingham Jail." It was Tuesday, April 16, 1963. King had been arrested on Good Friday, April 11, in a peaceful demonstration against the deeply discriminatory practices characteristic of most southern cities in those days. The *Birmingham News* carried a letter by eight Christian and Jewish clergyman of Alabama (all white), criticizing King for his activities and calling for more patience. Oates describes King's "Letter" as "the most eloquent and learned expression of the goals and philosophy of the nonviolent movement ever written."[6]

We pastors need to hear—and help our people hear—the power and insight with which King spoke in the sixties, enraging thousands and inspiring thousands:

---

3. Jefferson even edited his own account of the Gospels—with every reference to the supernatural activity of God (like the virgin birth, healings, resurrection, etc.) neatly trimmed out with scissors. See Thomas Jefferson, *The Jefferson Bible: The Life and Morals of Jesus of Nazareth* (Boston, Mass.: Beacon Press, 1991), orig. 1816.

4. Mark Noll, *A History of Christianity in the United States and Canada* (Grand Rapids, Mich.: Eerdmans Publishing Co., 1992), 133–35, 404.

5. Oates, *Let the Trumpet Sound*, 322.

6. Ibid., 222.

Perhaps it is easy for those who have never felt the stinging darts of segregation to say, "Wait." But when you have seen vicious mobs lynch your mothers and fathers at will and drown your sisters and brothers at whim; when you have seen hate-filled policemen curse, kick, and even kill your black brothers and sisters; when you see the vast majority of your twenty million Negro brothers smothering in an airtight cage of poverty in the midst of an affluent society; when you suddenly find your tongue twisted and your speech stammering as you seek to explain to your six-year-old daughter why she cannot go to the public amusement park that has just been advertised on television, and see tears welling up in her eyes when she's told that Funtown is closed to colored children, and see ominous clouds of inferiority beginning to form in her little mental sky, and see her beginning to distort her personality by developing an unconscious bitterness toward white people; when you have to concoct an answer for a five-year-old son who is asking, "Daddy, why do white people treat colored people so mean?"; when you take a cross-country drive and find it necessary to sleep night after night in the uncomfortable corners of your automobile because no motel will accept you; when you are humiliated day in and day out by nagging signs reading "white" and "colored"; when your first name becomes "Nigger," your middle name becomes "Boy" (however old you are) and your last name becomes "John," and your wife and mother are never given the respected title "Mrs."; when you are harried by day and haunted by night by the fact that you are a Negro, living constantly at tiptoe stance, never quite knowing what to expect next, and are plagued with inner fears and outer resentments; when you are forever fighting a degenerating sense of "nobodiness"—then you will understand why we find it difficult to wait. There comes a time when the cup of endurance runs over, and men are no longer willing to be plunged into the abyss of despair. I hope, sirs, you can understand our legitimate and unavoidable impatience.[7]

The depth of his commitment becomes clearer when he responds to the charge that he was an extremist:

Was not Jesus an extremist for love: "Love your enemies, bless them that curse you, do good to them that hate you, and pray for them which despitefully use you, and persecute you"? Was not Amos an extremist for justice: "Let justice roll down like waters and righteousness like an ever-flowing stream"? Was not Paul an extremist for the Christian gospel: "I bear in my body the marks of the Lord Jesus"? Was not Martin Luther an extremist: "Here I stand; I cannot do otherwise, so help me God"? And John Bunyan: "I will stay in jail to the end of my days before I make a butchery of my conscience." And Abraham Lincoln: "Thus this nation cannot survive half slave and half free." And Thomas Jefferson: "We hold these truths to be self-evident, that all men are created equal. . . ." So the question is not whether we will be extremist, but what kind of extremist we will be. Will we be extremists for hate or for love?[8]

---

7. Martin Luther King Jr., "Letter from Birmingham Jail," with an introduction by Paul Chaim Schenck [no place, no date], 8–9. The letter may be read on many Internet Web sites by simply entering the title in your search engine.
8. Ibid., 14.

Then he delivered a powerful call to the church, which rings as true today as it did forty years ago. Every pastor in America needs to hear it and let it shape the church.

There was a time when the church was very powerful—in the time when the early Christians rejoiced at being deemed worthy to suffer for what they believed. In those days the church was not merely a thermometer that recorded the ideas and principles of popular opinion; it was a thermostat that transformed the mores of society. . . . But the judgment of God is upon the church [today] as never before. If today's church does not recapture the sacrificial spirit of the early church, it will lose its authenticity, forfeit the loyalty of millions, and be dismissed as an irrelevant social club with no meaning for the twentieth century.[9]

There's the question for us: are our churches thermometers registering the racial attitudes and actions of the world; or are they thermostats raising the warmth of commitment to racial understanding and love and demonstrable harmony? Most of the Christians in the majority white culture never even think about the issue. That is not a sign of peace but of obliviousness.

I was seventeen when, on August 28, 1963, King stood before the Lincoln Memorial and gave his most memorable speech:

I have a dream that one day on the red hills of Georgia the sons of former slaves and the sons of former slave-owners will be able to sit down together at the table of brotherhood. . . . I have a dream that my four children will one day live in a nation where they will be judged not by the color of their skin but by the content of their character.[10]

9. Ibid., 17.
10. You can type any of these distinctive phrases into your favorite Internet search engine to find the whole copy of the speech on many internet sites.

Whatever you think of his life and strategy of nonviolent action, Martin Luther King articulated and symbolized a great dream, and it is not yet realized. And one of our jobs in the pastoral ministry is to enlarge that dream up to a full-blown Biblical vision of God's purpose for the world and then call the church consciously to be a part of it. The Biblical vision is much bigger than how black and white people relate to each other. King knew that. It's about people from every race and every language and every tribe uniting in Jesus Christ with a passion for the supremacy of God in all things. But whether we believe that God gives the power and grace to realize that vision globally is tested in the daily and weekly life of the church—and especially in its attitudes and actions toward the different ethnic groups closest to home.

So God has convicted me in recent years that I need to do a lot more than in previous years to address the matter of race relations in our church. Some years ago a twenty-three-member team at our church took over a year to draw up a vision statement for our church that included six fresh initiatives. Number three reads like this:

> Against the rising spirit of indifference, alienation and
> hostility in our land, we will embrace the supremacy of
> God's love to take new steps personally and corporately
> toward racial reconciliation, expressed visibly in our com-
> munity and in our church.[11]

If this is going to happen in our churches, the root of racism in our hearts that we are often unaware of must be severed. This takes us pastors finally to the Word of God, which carries the authority and power to change people beyond anything Martin Luther

---

11. Initiative 3 in the Vision Statement of Bethlehem Baptist Church. You can see the entire document at www.bbcmpls.org under "Vision Statement."

King Jr. or any champion could have. But we must preach it and teach it and live it.

I said at the beginning that the issue of racial prejudice and snubbing and suspicion and mistreatment is not a social issue; it is a blood-of-Jesus issue. I could base that on many passages where love is rooted in the death and resurrection of Jesus. But there are two passages in particular that explicitly relate the death of Jesus to racial harmony in Christ.

The first is Ephesians 2:11–12. It begins with a description of the alienation between Jews and Gentiles, specifically Jewish Christians and Gentiles.

> Therefore remember that at one time you Gentiles in the flesh, called "the uncircumcision" by what is called the circumcision, which is made in the flesh by hands— remember that you were at that time separated from Christ, alienated from the commonwealth of Israel and strangers to the covenants of promise, having no hope and without God in the world.

Then in verses 19–22 the text ends with a description of the reconciliation between Jewish Christians and Gentile Christians.

> So then you are no longer strangers and aliens, but you are fellow citizens with the saints, and are of God's household, having been built on the foundation of the apostles and prophets, Christ Jesus Himself being the corner stone, in whom the whole building, being fitted together, is growing into a holy temple in the Lord, in whom you also are being built together into a dwelling of God in the Spirit (NASB).

That is what God is aiming at in our salvation: a new people (one new man, v. 15) that is so free from enmity and so united in truth and peace that God Himself is there for our joy and for His glory forever. That's the aim of reconciliation: a place for God to live among us and make Himself known and enjoyed forever and ever.

Keep in mind here that the divide between Jews and Gentiles was not small or simple or shallow. It was huge and complex and deep. It was, first, *religious*. The Jews knew the one true God, and Christian Jews knew His Son, the Messiah, Jesus Christ. Then the divide was *cultural or social* with lots of ceremonies and practices like circumcision and dietary regulations and rules of cleanliness and so on. These were all designed to set the Jews apart from the nations for a period of redemptive history to make clear the radical holiness of God. Then the divide was *racial*. This was a bloodline going back to Jacob, not Esau, and Isaac, not Ishmael, and Abraham, not any other father. So the divide here was as big or bigger than any divide that we face today between black and white or red and white or Asian and African-American.

So here is the question: What happened between verses 11–12 that describes the alienation and separation between Jews and Gentiles and verses 19–22 that describes the full reconciliation and unity?

Here you could preach for weeks. Ephesians 2:13–18 is so rich and thick with doctrine that it would take many sermons to unpack it all. So I will make one main point that I think is the most essential thing. What happened between the alienation of verses 11–12 and the reconciliation of verses 19–22 was that Jesus Christ, the Son of God, died, and He died by design. Yes, He rose and is alive. But the emphasis here falls on His death. Where do we see it? We see it in the word *blood* in verse 13b: "You who formerly were far off have been brought near by the *blood* of Christ." We see it in the word *flesh* in verse 15, "abolishing in His *flesh* the enmity" (NASB). And we see it in the word *cross* in verse 16, "and might reconcile them both in one body to God through the *cross*" (NASB).

The point is that God aims to create one new people in Christ who are reconciled to each other across racial lines. Not strangers. Not aliens. No enmity. Not far off. Fellow citizens of one Christian "city of God." One temple for a habitation of God. And He did this at the cost of His Son's life. We love to dwell on our reconciliation with God through the death of His Son. And well we should. It is precious beyond measure to have peace with God.

But let us also dwell on this: that God ordained the death of His Son to reconcile alien people groups to each other in one body in Christ. This too was the design of the death of Christ. Think on this: Christ died to take enmity and anger and disgust and jealousy and self-pity and fear and envy and hatred and malice and indifference away from your heart toward all other persons who are in Christ by faith—whatever the race.

If we want the meaning and the worth and the beauty and the power of the cross of Christ to be seen and loved in our churches, and if the design of the death of His Son is not only to reconcile us to God but to reconcile alienated ethnic groups to each other in Christ, then will we not display and magnify the cross of Christ better by more and deeper and sweeter ethnic diversity and unity in our worship and life?

The second text is Revelation 5:9–10. Again this is a glimpse into the purposes of God in the death of His Son, the Lamb of God, Jesus Christ:

> And they sang a new song, saying, "Worthy are You [referring to the slain and risen Lamb of God] to take the book [that is, the book of history in the last days] and to

207

break its seals; for You were slain, and purchased for God
with Your blood men from every tribe and tongue and
people and nation. You have made them to be a kingdom
and priests to our God; and they will reign upon the
earth" (NASB).

The implications here for racial and ethnic harmony in the
church are staggering when you let it sink in. The price of God's securing ethnic diversity in the "priesthood," and the "kingdom" is
the death of His Son. The design of the atonement is racial diversity
in the company of the redeemed. Applying and pursuing this is not
merely a "social issue." It is a blood-of-Jesus issue. That is what it
cost. And that is how important it is.

Not only that, we can up the ante even more. Notice that in
Revelation 5:9 this diversity was purchased "for God." "You . . .
purchased *for God* . . . men from every tribe" (NASB). The issue is
not only a blood-of-Jesus issue, it is a glory-of-God issue. Blood-
bought racial diversity and harmony is for the glory of God through
Christ. It is all aiming at the all-satisfying, everlasting, God-
centered, Christ-exalting experience of many-colored worship.

If the pursuit of ethnic diversity and harmony in the company
of the redeemed cost the Father and the Son such a price, should
we expect that it will cost us nothing? Or that it will be easy? No,
the devil, who hates the glory of God and despises the aims of the
cross, will not relent without a fierce battle. To join God in pursuing racial diversity and racial harmony will be costly for you
and your church—so costly that many will try it for a while and
then give up and walk away from the effort to easier things.

But some will persevere and be found doing their duty when the
Master comes. Be among that number, brothers. There is an old
African-American prayer chant that calls us to "a mighty long journey."

> It's a mighty long journey,
> But I'm on my way;
> It's a mighty long journey,
> But I'm on my way.[12]

That's where we are in the American church—on a journey toward the perfect experience of Revelation 5:9–10. And we want as much of it now as we can, don't we? So the world will see the glory of God and the worth of Christ. So, brothers, read and study and pray and preach and take the risks necessary to sever the root of racism.

---

12. Quoted in Timothy George and Robert Smith Jr., *A Mighty Long Journey: Reflections on Racial Reconciliation* (Nashville, Tenn.: Broadman & Holman, 2000), 1.

> For you formed my inward parts;
> you knitted me together in my mother's womb.
>
> PSALM 139:13
>
>
> Give justice to the weak and the fatherless;
> maintain the right of the afflicted and the destitute.
> Rescue the weak and the needy;
> deliver them from the hand of the wicked.
>
> PSALM 82:3–4
>
>
> No person shall . . . be deprived of life . . .
> without due process of law.
>
> AMENDMENT V, U. S. CONSTITUTION
>
>
> Pastors should put their lives and ministries on the line
> in the issue of abortion.
>
> JOHN PIPER

27

BROTHERS, BLOW THE TRUMPET FOR THE UNBORN

MANY PASTORS surpass me in their courage and consistency. I praise God for them. I will happily honor their superior rewards in the last day. But oh, how I long to be among them. So when it comes to abortion, I try. So much more could be done. I agonize over what more I should do, and this is not the only such issue! But for fifteen awakened years I have done what I can.

I preach on the horrific sin and injustice of abortion and on the glory of the cause of life at least once a year in our church. I try to encourage the Sanctity of Human Life Task Force in our church in other ways. I call our people to dream of ways of being sacrificially involved in the pro-life efforts to make abortion unthinkable in our country. I glorify adoption and fan the flames of its spread in our church. I offer precious blood-bought forgiveness and hope to all the women and men in the congregation who have experienced or encouraged abortion. I speak and pray at pro-life gatherings outside abortion clinics and support crisis pregnancy centers with my presence and my money. In past days I have joined peaceful protests and been arrested numerous times and spent one night in jail. I have made my case for life before angry crowds, and before judges, and over lunch with an abortionist. I will say more about him in a moment.

The point is this: I believe pastors should put their lives and ministries on the line in this issue. The cowardice of some pastors when it comes to preaching against abortion appalls me. Many treat the dismemberment of unborn humans as an untouchable issue on the par with partisan politics. Some have bought into the incredible notion that they can be *personally* pro-life but publicly pro-choice or noncommittal. In response to this attitude our church sponsored an ad in the Minneapolis *StarTribune* with these simple words: "I am personally pro-life, but politically pro-choice"— Pontius Pilate.

The law of our land is immoral and unjust. That should be declared from tens of thousands of pulpits in America. When the American Medical Association was formed in 1847, abortion was commonly practiced "before quickening." But through the efforts of the AMA and antiobscenity crusaders and (ironically) feminists, abortion became illegal everywhere in the U.S. by 1900.

The key reversal of this legal situation came on January 22, 1973, when the Supreme Court in *Roe v. Wade* made the following rulings.[1]

- That no state may make laws regulating abortion during the first three months of pregnancy except to provide that they be done by licensed physicians.
- That laws regulating abortion between the third month and the time of viability are constitutional only insofar as they are aimed at safeguarding the health of mothers.
- That laws relating to the time from viability (6 months) until the end of the pregnancy may not prevent abortion if it is "to preserve the life or health of the mother."
- That the "health" of the mother includes "all factors— physical, emotional, psychological, familial and the woman's age—relevant to the well-being of the patient."

Then on July 1, 1976, the court extended its original decision to affirm:

- That abortions may be performed on minor daughters without the knowledge or consent of their parents.
- That women (whether married or unmarried) may obtain abortions without the knowledge or consent of the baby's father.[2]

In effect, therefore, the law of our land today is that any abortion is legal until birth if the mother can give reason that the pregnancy or the child will be an excessive burden or stress on her well-being. Since that ruling we have killed on average 1.5 million babies every year.

1. For a social history of abortion before *Roe v. Wade,* see Marvin Olasky, *Abortion Rites: A Social History of Abortion in America* (Wheaton, Ill.: Crossway Books, 1992).
2. These facts can be verified on the internet at www.mdrtl.org/Law.html.

In response to this we should point out that even pro-choice people know that the unborn are human beings and as such should be given the right to life, even on the grounds of the U.S. Constitution ("No person shall . . . be deprived of life, liberty, or property, without due process of law," Amendment V), and even more because of the Word of God. How do we know they know this?

1. In Minnesota they know that the Fetal Homicide Law makes a person guilty of manslaughter, or worse, if he kills the baby in a mother's womb. There is an exception clause for abortion. What does this mean? It means that if the mother chooses to have the baby killed it is legal. If she doesn't, it is illegal. Nothing in the essence of the unborn determines the right to life. Only the will of the mother. They know it is the essence of totalitarian rule: the will of the strong determines the rights of the weak.

2. They know there is a lethal inconsistency between doing fetal surgery on babies in the womb to save them while their cousin, at a similar stage of development, is being killed just down the hall.

3. They know that a baby can live on its own at twenty-three or twenty-four weeks. Yet they say it may be legally killed even at and beyond this age if the mother will be distressed by its live birth more than its abortion. Facts like this give an opportunity for a prophetic voice in your community. One example is a letter I wrote to the Minneapolis *StarTribune* (which they would not print):

   Dear Editor,
   Are you aware of the fact that the same day the Senate Health and Human Services Committee approved the

unconditional permission to terminate the lives of twenty-four-week-old fetuses, the neonatology unit at Abbot Northwestern was caring for a twenty-two-and-a-half week-old (500 gram) preemie with good chances of healthy life?

Now that is news and calls for profound reflection. Instead, your lead editorial the morning after (Feb. 26) glossed over this critical issue and endorsed abortion because it is "one of the most personal decisions a woman can make" and because "the abortion decision is undeniably sensitive." This level of reflection is unworthy of major editorials in good newspapers.

I assume you mean by "personal decision" not: having deep personal implications, but: having deep personal implications for only one person, the mother.

But abortion is emphatically not a "personal" decision in that limited sense. There is another person, namely, the unborn child. If you deny this, you must give an account of what that little preemie is at Abbot Northwestern. Abortion is a decision about competing human rights: the right not to be pregnant and the right not to be killed.

I assume you approve of the Committee's action. But I also assume you would not approve of the mother's right to strangle the preemie at Abbot before its twenty-fifth week of life. If so you owe your readers an explanation of your simple endorsement of abortion because it is "personal" and "sensitive."

In fact I challenge you to publish two photographs side by side: one of this "child" outside the womb and another of a "fetus" inside the womb both at twenty-three or twenty-four weeks, with a caption that says something like: "We at the Star Tribune regard the termination of the preemie as manslaughter and the termination of the fetus as the personal choice of the mother."

I have read in your pages how you disdain the use of pictures because abortion is too complex for simplistic solutions. But I also remember how you approved the possible televising of an execution as one of the most effective ways of turning the heart of America against capital punishment (a similarly complex issue).

We both know that if America watched repeated termination of twenty-three-week-old fetuses on television (or saw the procedure truthfully documented in your paper), the sentiment of our society would profoundly change. (The Alan Guttmacher Institute estimated over nine thousand abortions after twenty-one weeks in 1987.)

Words fail to describe the barbarity of an unconditional right to take the life of a human being as fully developed as twenty-three weeks. You could never successfully defend it in the public presence of the act itself.

You can do so only in the moral fog of phrases like: Abortion must be left to the woman because it is "undeniably sensitive." This is not compelling. There are many sensitive situations where the state prescribes limits for how we express our feelings where others are concerned. And there is another concern. If you are willing, you may meet this "other person" face-to-face in dozens of hospitals around the country.

Sincerely yours,
John Piper

4. Those who argue that "viability" is the point where babies should get rights of protection know that a baby's living without an umbilical cord is not the criterion of human

personhood and the condition of the right to life. They all acknowledge this because their own living on a respirator or dialysis machine would not jeopardize our own personhood. The source of food and oxygen does not determine personhood.

5. They know that the size of a human is irrelevant to human personhood. They know this because they do not make a one-month-old postborn baby vulnerable to killing even though it is so much smaller than a five-year-old. Yet they act as if the littleness of the embryo makes it less human.

6. They know that developed reasoning powers are not the criterion of personhood. They know this because a one-month-old postborn baby does not have these powers either, yet its life is not in jeopardy because of that—except for some who advocate euthanasia for disabled babies.[3]

7. They know that we are human beings scientifically by virtue of our genetic makeup. The human code in the chromosomes is there from the start. We are utterly different from monkeys or rats or elephants as soon as the chromosomes meet.

---

3. For example Peter Singer, professor of bioethics at Princeton, who wrote in 1993, "Suppose that a newborn baby is diagnosed as a haemophiliac. The parents, daunted by the prospect of bringing up a child with this condition, are not anxious for him to live. Could euthanasia be defended here? . . . The total view makes it necessary to ask whether the death of the haemophiliac infant would lead to the creation of another being who would not otherwise have existed. In other words, if the haemophiliac child is killed, will his parents have another child whom they would not have if the haemophiliac child lives? If they would, is the second child likely to have a better life than the one killed? . . . When the death of a disabled infant will lead to the birth of another infant with better prospects of a happy life, the total amount of happiness will be greater if the disabled infant is killed. The loss of happy life for the first infant is outweighed by the gain of a happier life for the second. Therefore, if killing the haemophiliac infant has no adverse effect on others, it would, according to the total view, be right to kill him." *Practical Ethics,* 2nd ed. (New York: Cambridge University Press, 1993), 185–86.

8. They know that at eight weeks all the organs are present, the brain is functioning, the heart is pumping, the liver is making blood cells, the kidneys are cleaning the fluids. And there are clear fingerprints.[4] Yet almost all abortions happen later than this date.

9. They know that ultrasound has given a stunning window on the womb that shows the unborn at eight weeks sucking thumb, recoiling from pricking, responding to sound. They can see the amazing pictures in *Life* magazine by photographer Lennart Nilsson. Pictures do count even though they say they don't.

Add to these observations the vastly more important Word of God.

Psalm 139:13 says, "Thou didst form my inward parts, thou didst knit me together in my mother's womb" (RSV). The least we can draw out of this text is that the formation of the life of a person in the womb is the work of God, and it is not merely a mechanical process but a work on the analogy of weaving or knitting. The life of the unborn is the knitting of God, and what He is knitting is a human being in His own image, unlike any other creature in the universe.

Another relevant text is Job 31:13–15. Job is protesting that he has not rejected the plea of any of his servants, even though in that culture many thought that servants were nonpersons and only property. The thing to watch for here is how Job argues.

---

4. See especially Randy Alcorn's section, "Arguments Concerning Life, Humanity and Personhood," in *ProLife Answers to ProChoice Arguments,* expanded and updated (Sisters, Oreg.: Multnomah Publishers, 2000), 49–100. Also, Francis J. Beckwith, *Politically Correct Death: Answering Arguments for Abortion Rights* (Grand Rapids, Mich.: Baker Book House, 1994).

If I have rejected the cause of my manservant or my maidservant,
when they brought a complaint against me,
what then shall I do when God rises up?
When he makes inquiry, what shall I answer him?
Did not he who made me in the womb make him?
And did not one fashion us in the womb?

Verse 15 gives the reason Job would be without excuse if he treated his servant as less than a human equal. The issue isn't really that one may have been born free and the other born in slavery. The issue goes back before birth. When Job and his servants were being fashioned in the womb, the key person at work was God—the same God, shaping both the fetus-Job and the fetus of his servants. It is irrelevant that Job's mother was probably a freedwoman and the mother of the servant was probably a bondwoman. Why? Because mothers are not the main nurturers and fashioners during the time of gestation, God is, the same God for both slave and free. That's the premise of Job's argument.

So both Psalm 139 and Job 31 emphasize God as the primary workman—nurturer, fashioner, knitter, Creator—in this time of gestation. Why is that important? It's important because God is the only One who can create personhood. Mothers and fathers can contribute some impersonal egg and some impersonal sperm, but only God creates independent personhood. So when the Scripture emphasizes that God is the main nurturer and shaper in the womb, it is stressing that what is happening in the womb is the unique work of God, namely, the making of a person. From the Biblical point of view gestation is the unique work of God fashioning personhood.

We can argue till doomsday about when this little being becomes "whole" (as if personhood is quantifiable and divisible). But the Bible treats the unborn in the same way it treats babies that have been born (see Gen. 25:22; compare Luke 1:44 and 2:12; Exod. 21:22–25).[5] And we can at least say, with great confidence: what is happening in the womb is a unique person-forming work of God, and only God knows how deeply and mysteriously the creation of personhood is woven into the making of a body. Therefore it is arbitrary and unwarranted to assume that at some point in the knitting together of this person its destruction is not an assault on the prerogatives of God the Creator. Let me say that again positively: the destruction of conceived human life—whether embryonic, fetal, or viable—is an assault on the unique person-forming work of God. And therefore to the degree that we recognize even in fallen personhood a unique value, because of its potential to glorify God with conscious obedience and praise, to that degree will we shrink back with reverence and fear from assaulting or obstructing the divine work of God fashioning such a person in the womb.

I mentioned at the beginning of this chapter having lunch with an abortionist. He was doing abortions in a clinic about four blocks from our church. I went to lunch armed with my arguments that unborn children are human beings and therefore should not be killed. I was unprepared for what I heard. He said, almost incidentally, that the main driving force behind his involvement was his wife, because, for her and thousands of other women, he said, this is a root issue of women's rights. Will they govern their own bodies and their reproductive freedom or will others? More essentially, and even more surprisingly, he conceded my arguments immediately and said I didn't have to waste my time proving that the unborn were human beings. He said bluntly that he believed that. The issue was whether the taking of human life is warranted by the greater good of a woman's right's. I have found this position repeated in talking with

5. John Piper, "Exodus 21:22–25 and Abortion." See www.desiringGOD.org, Topic Index, Abortion.

other pro-choice professionals; when pressed they don't dispute that they are taking the life of human beings. They admit it is not ideal but the lesser of two evils, especially in view of the tragic situations into which so many of these children would be born.

So I switched my approach, and instead of trying to defend the humanity of the unborn, I simply spelled out my reasons for the unborn not to be aborted. Believe it or not, some of these doctors want to be Christian and Biblical and do not see their abortion practice as wrong. Here is my summary argument. It is the kind of thing you could preach from the Word of God to strengthen your people's conviction.

1. God commanded, "Thou shalt not kill" (Exod. 20:13 KJV).

I am aware that some killing is endorsed in the Bible. The word for "kill" in Exodus 20:13 is the Hebrew *rahaz*. It is used forty-three times in the Hebrew Old Testament. It always means violent, personal killing that is actually murder or is accused as murder. It is never used of killing in war or (with one possible exception, Num. 35:27) of killing in judicial execution. Rather a clear distinction is preserved between legal "putting to death" and illegal "murder." For example, Numbers 35:19 says, "The murderer shall certainly be put to death" (JP). The word *murderer* comes from *rahaz* which is forbidden in the Ten Commandments. The word "put to death" (a hiphil form of *mut*) is a general word that can describe legal executions.

When the Bible speaks of killing that is justifiable, it generally has in mind God's sharing some of His rights with the civil authority. When the state acts in its capacity as God's ordained preserver of justice and peace, it has the right to "bear the sword" as Romans 13:1–7 teaches. This right of the state is always to be exercised to punish evil, never to attack the innocent (Rom. 13:4). Therefore, "Thou shalt not kill" (KJV) stands as a clear and resounding indictment of the killing of innocent unborn children.

2. The destruction of conceived human life—whether embryonic, fetal, or viable—is an assault on the unique
   person-forming work of God.

See above where I have developed the textual basis for this from
Psalm 139:13 and Job 31:13–15.

3. Aborting unborn humans falls under the repeated Biblical
   ban against "shedding innocent blood."

The phrase "innocent blood" occurs about twenty times in the
Bible. The context is always one of condemning those who shed this
blood or warning people not to shed it. Innocent blood includes the
blood of children (Ps. 106:38). Jeremiah 22:3 puts it in a context
with refugees and widows and orphans: "Thus says the LORD: Do
justice and righteousness, and deliver from the hand of the oppres-
sor him who has been robbed. And do no wrong or violence to the
alien, the fatherless, and the widow, nor shed innocent blood in this
place." Surely the blood of the unborn is as innocent as any blood
that flows in the world.[6]

4. The Bible frequently expresses the high priority God puts
   on the protection and provision and vindication of the
   weakest and most helpless and most victimized members
   of the community.

---

6. When God orders the destruction of whole pagan cities including the children
(Num. 31:17; Deut. 2:34; 3:6; 13:15; Josh. 6:21; 10:28; 10:40; 1 Sam. 15:2–3), we are to
understand that this is owing to a particular period in the progress of redemptive history
when God was executing judgment on evil, pagan societies through the agency of the
Israelite army. The children were seen as part of the defiled society and were swept away
in the judgment not unlike the judgment of the flood or other natural disasters that God
brings upon societies from time to time. This is God's prerogative, not ours. All life is His,
and He gives and takes according to His wise and holy purposes. In the New Testament
the church does not have the role of the people of Israel in cleansing the promised land
(Deut. 9:5). In the full light of God's grace in Jesus Christ, we are, in fact, to do just the
opposite, namely, to lay our lives down in loving our enemies so that they might see the
truth of saving grace in our bodies (Matt. 5:12–13, 38–48; Col. 1:24; see chapter 19,
"Brothers, Our Affliction Is for Their Comfort").

Again and again we read of the sojourner and the widow and the orphan. These are the special care of God and should be the special care of his people. "Give justice to the weak and the fatherless; maintain the right of the afflicted and the destitute. Rescue the weak and the needy; deliver them from the hand of the wicked" (Ps. 82:3–4; see Exod. 22:21–24; Ps. 68:5; 94:5, 23).

5. By judging difficult and even tragic human life as a worse evil than taking life, abortionists contradict the widespread Biblical teaching that God loves to show His gracious power through suffering and not just by helping people avoid suffering.

This does not mean we should seek suffering for ourselves or for others. But it does mean that suffering is generally portrayed in the Bible as the necessary and God-ordained, though not God-pleasing, plight of this fallen world (Rom. 8:20–25; Ezek. 18:32). It is seen as the necessary portion of all who would enter the kingdom (Acts 14:22; 1 Thess. 3:3–4) and live lives of godliness (2 Tim. 3:12). This suffering is never viewed merely as a tragedy. It is also viewed as a means of growing deep with God and becoming strong in this life (Rom. 5:3–5; James 1:3–4; Heb. 12:3–11; 2 Cor. 1:9; 4:7–12; 12:7–10) and becoming something glorious in the life to come (2 Cor. 4:17; Rom. 8:18).

When abortionists argue that taking life is less evil than the difficulties that will accompany life, they are making themselves wiser than God who teaches us that His grace is capable of stupendous feats of love through the suffering of those who live.

6. It is a sin of presumption to justify abortion by taking comfort in the fact that all these little children will go to heaven or even be given full adult life in the resurrection.

This is a wonderful hope when the heart is broken with penitence and seeking forgiveness. But it is evil to justify killing by the happy outcome of eternity for the one killed. This same justification could be used to justify killing one-year-olds, or any heaven-bound believer for that matter. The Bible addresses the question: "Are we to continue in sin that grace may abound?" (Rom. 6:1). "And why not do evil that good may come?" (Rom. 3:8). In both cases the answer is a resounding no! It is presumption to step into God's place and try to make the assignments to heaven or to hell. Our duty is to obey God, not to play God.

7. The Bible commands us to rescue our neighbor who is being unjustly led away to death.

Rescue those who are being taken away to death; hold back those who are stumbling to the slaughter. If you say, ". . . We did not know this," does not he who weighs the heart perceive it? Does not he who keeps watch over your soul know it, and will he not repay man according to his work? (Prov. 24:11–12).

There is no significant scientific, medical, social, moral, or religious reason for putting the unborn in a class where this text does not apply to them. It is disobedience to this text to abort unborn children.

8. Aborting unborn children falls under Jesus' rebuke of those who spurned children as inconvenient and unworthy of the Savior's attention.

"Now they were bringing even infants to him that he might touch them. And when the disciples saw it, they rebuked them. But Jesus called them to him, saying, 'Let the children come to me, and do not hinder them, for to such belongs the kingdom of God'" (Luke 18:15–16). The word for *infant* in Luke 18:15 is the same word Luke uses for the unborn infant in Elizabeth's womb in Luke

1:41, 44. Even more forcefully, Mark says in Mark 9:36–37, "And he [Jesus] took a child, and put him in the midst of them, and taking him in his arms, he said to them, 'Whoever receives one such child in my name receives me, and whoever receives me, receives not me but him who sent me.'"

9. It is the right of God the Maker to give and to take human life. It is not our individual right to make this choice.

When Job heard that his children had all been killed in a collapsing house, he bowed to worship the Lord and said, "Naked I came from my mother's womb, and naked shall I return. *The LORD gave,* and *the LORD has taken away;* blessed be the name of the LORD" (Job 1:21).

When Job spoke of coming from his mother's womb, he said, "The LORD gave." And when Job spoke of dying, he said, "The LORD has taken away." Birth and death are the prerogatives of God. He is Giver and Taker in this awesome affair of life. We have no right to make individual choices about this matter. Our duty is to care for what He gives and use it to His glory.

10. Finally, saving faith in Jesus Christ brings forgiveness of sins and cleansing of conscience and help through life and hope for eternity. Surrounded by such omnipotent love, every follower of Jesus is free from the greed and fear that might lure a person to forsake these truths in order to gain money or avoid reproach.

"In him we have redemption through his blood, the forgiveness of our trespasses, according to the riches of his grace" (Eph. 1:7). "For God so loved the world that he gave his only Son, that whoever believes in him should not perish but have eternal life" (John 3:16). "Keep your life free from love of money, and be content with what you have; for he has said, 'I will never fail you nor forsake you.' Hence we can confidently say, 'The Lord is my helper, I will not be afraid; what can man do to me?'" (Heb. 13:5–6).

What then should you call your people to do? Here is what I have said to my flock:

First, submit yourselves to God. Draw near to Him. Live by the power of His grace. Let Him shape your desires rather than the world and the feisty, self-centered temperament of our culture. Let your life and your mouth bear witness to the real delights of knowing and trusting and obeying and being shaped and guided by the Creator of all things who loved us and gave Himself for us. Be a Christian—and a visible and audible one. The world needs you so badly.

Second, pray earnestly and regularly for awakening in the churches that will spill over in citywide and nationwide and worldwide evangelization of the lost and reformation of the life of the church.

Third, use your imagination to see what abortion really is! Fight against the kind of social stupor that gripped Nazi Germany, the feeling that the problem is so huge and so horrendous and so out of our control that it just can't be wrong. Use your imagination to see and feel what is really happening behind those sterile clinic doors. The children will not be saved, and God's work will not be reverenced without an act of sustained sympathetic imagination. Otherwise it is out of sight out of mind—just like Dachau, Buchenwald, Belsen, and Auschwitz. It just couldn't be happening. And so we act as if it isn't.

"If you say, 'Behold, we did not know this,' does not he who weighs the heart perceive it? Does not he who keeps watch over your soul know it, and will he not repay man according to his work?" (Prov. 24:12).

Fourth, support alternatives to abortion with your money and time and prayers. Find out about concrete opportunities that are available in our region for all kinds of involvement. Even better, create new pro-life ministries. Let's be a church of dreamers and entrepreneurs for justice.

Finally, use your democratic privileges of free speech and representation and demonstration to press for legal protection for the unborn. One of the strongest arguments against legal enactments to protect the unborn is the claim that legal constraints without widespread social consensus is tyranny. The argument loses much of its force when applied to the historical situation of slaves in this country. On March 6, 1857, the Supreme Court, in *Dred Scott v. Stanford*, ruled that no act of Congress or territorial legislature could make laws banning slavery. The fundamental argument was that slaves are not free and equal persons but the property of their masters.

The ruling is analogous to *Roe v. Wade* because today no state may make a law banning abortion to protect the unborn. The argument is similar—basically because the unborn are at the sovereign disposal of their mothers and do not have personal standing in their own right. There was no consensus in this country on the personhood and rights of slaves. We were split down the middle. But the issue was so fundamental that the states went to war, and in the end the Lincoln administration overturned the Dred Scott decision. And today, 130 years later, we look back with amazing consensus and marvel at the blindness of our forefathers.

Brothers, may we not dare to believe that by the grace of God and the perseverance of His people in prayer and piety and political action there could emerge in the coming decades a consensus for life and that the twenty-first century could look back on our generation with the same dismay that we look back on the slave laws of this land and on the concentration camps of World War II? Nationwide reformation has happened before—with Wilberforce in England and Lincoln in America. It can happen again. Will you put the trumpet to your lips or be silent?

> But the hour is coming, and is now here,
> when the true worshipers will worship the Father in spirit and truth,
> for the Father is seeking such people to worship him.
>
> JOHN 4:23

> The essence of praising Christ is prizing Christ.
>
> JOHN PIPER

> Christ is praised in death
> by being prized above life.
> And Christ is most glorified in life
> when we are most satisfied in Him even before death.
>
> JOHN PIPER

> God is mightily honored when a people know
> that they will die of hunger and thirst unless they have God.
>
> JOHN PIPER

28

BROTHERS, FOCUS ON THE ESSENCE OF WORSHIP, NOT THE FORM

FEW OF US have had or will have the luxury of escaping the "worship wars." The "wars" are usually waged over forms and styles, not over the essence of what worship is. But leading your people into the essence is all-important. So I want to call you to put your focus and energies in the most fruitful place for the glory of God. Focus on the essence, not the form. If you succeed in breeding a church that experiences the essence, they will probably survive the wars, and you will be able to lead them through to more peaceful waters.

The New Testament reveals a stunning silence about the outward forms of corporate worship and a radical intensification of worship as an inner, Godward experience of the heart. The silence about outward forms is obvious in the fact that the gathered life of the church is never called "worship" in the New Testament. Moreover, the main Old Testament word for worship (*proskuneō* in the Greek Old Testament) is virtually absent from the New Testament letters. Its usage clusters in the Gospels (26 times) and in the Book of Revelation (21 times). But in the Epistles of Paul it occurs only once, namely, in 1 Corinthians 14:25 where the unbeliever falls down at the power of prophecy and confesses God is in the assembly. It doesn't occur at all in the letters of Peter, James, or John.

The reason for this unusual spread is probably that the Old Testament idea, captured in the Greek word *proskuneō*, implied a physical falling down in reverence before a visible majesty. This happened as people came to the visible, incarnate Christ in the Gospels. And it happened in Revelation as the saints and angels and elders were actually in the presence of the visible, risen Christ. But in the age between the ascension and the second coming Christ is not visibly here to worship. Therefore, worship is radically internalized and delocalized.[1]

In addition, the intensification of worship as a nonlocal inner experience of the heart is seen in the words of Jesus from John 4 that the hour is coming and now is when worship will not be located in

1. Heinrich Greeven, in the *Theological Dictionary of the New Testament,* vol. 6, ed., Gerhard Kittel and Gerhard Friedrich (Grand Rapids, Mich.: Wm. B. Eerdmans Publishing Company, 1968), 765, concludes from this distribution of *proskuneō:* "This is, however, a further proof of the concreteness of the term. *Proskunēsis* demands visible majesty before which the worshipper bows. The Son of God was visible to all on earth (the Gospels) and the exalted Lord will again be visible to His own when faith gives way to sight (Revelation)."

Samaria or Jerusalem but will be "in spirit and truth" (John 4:21–23). Inner spiritual reality replaces geographic locality. "Neither on this mountain nor in Jerusalem" (v. 21) is replaced by "in spirit and truth." We see this inward intensification of worship again in Matthew 15:8–9 when Jesus says, "This people honors me with their lips, but their heart is far from me; in vain do they worship me." Worship that does not come from the heart is vain, empty. It is not authentic worship.

To confirm this and to see even more clearly how radically non-place and nonevent-oriented the New Testament view of worship is, consider what Paul does to some of the other words related to Old Testament worship. For example, the next most frequent word for worship in the Old Testament (after *proskuneō*) is the word *latreuō* (over 90 times, almost always translating the Hebrew *abad*) which is usually translated "serve" as in Exodus 23:24, "You shall not worship their gods, nor *serve* them" (NASB).

When Paul uses it for Christian worship, he goes out of his way to make sure that we know he means not a localized or outward form for worship practice but a nonlocalized, spiritual experience. In fact, he takes it so far as to treat virtually all of life as worship when lived in the right spirit. For example, in Romans 1:9 he says, "I *serve* [or worship] [God] *with my spirit* in the gospel of his Son." And in Philippians 3:3, Paul says that true Christians "worship [God] *in the Spirit* of God . . . and put no confidence in the flesh" (NASB). And in Romans 12:1, Paul urges Christians to "present your bodies as a living sacrifice, holy and acceptable to God, which is your *spiritual* worship."

So even when Paul uses an Old Testament word for worship, he takes pains to let us know that what he has in mind is not mainly a localized or external event of worship but an internal, spiritual experience—so much so that he sees all of life and ministry as an expression of that inner experience of worship.

You see the same thing if you take the New Testament use of the Old Testament language for temple "sacrifices" and "priestly service." The praise and thanks of the lips is called a sacrifice to God (Heb. 13:15). But so are good works in everyday life (Heb. 13:16). Paul calls his own ministry a "priestly service (of worship)," and he calls the converts themselves an "acceptable offering (in worship)" to God (Rom. 15:16; cf. Phil. 2:17). He even calls the money that the churches send him "a fragrant aroma and acceptable sacrifice to God (in worship)" (Phil. 4:18 JP). And his own death for Christ he calls a "drink offering" to God (2 Tim. 4:6).[2]

So you can see what is happening in the New Testament. Worship is being significantly deinstitutionalized, delocalized, de-externalized. The whole thrust is being taken off of ceremony and seasons and places and forms and is being shifted to what is happening in the heart—not just on Sunday but every day and all the time in all of life.

This is what it means when we read things like, "Whether you eat or drink, or whatever you do, do all to the glory of God" (1 Cor. 10:31). And "whatever you do in word or deed, do all in the name of the Lord Jesus, giving thanks through Him to God the Father" (Col. 3:17 NASB). This is the central New Testament action of worship: to act in a way that reflects the glory of God—to do a thing in the name of Jesus with thanks to God. But the New Testament uses those greatest of all worship sentences without any reference to Sunday worship services. They describe life.

I conclude that the essence of worship is not external, localized acts, but an inner, Godward experience that shows itself externally

2. The same thrust is seen in the imagery of the people of God (body of Christ) as the New Testament "Temple" where spiritual sacrifices are offered (1 Pet. 2:5) and where God dwells by His Spirit (Eph. 2:21–22) and where all the people are seen as the holy priesthood (1 Pet. 2:5, 9). Second Corinthians 6:16 shows that the New Covenant hope of God's presence is being fulfilled even now in the church as a people, not in any particular gathered meeting: "We are the temple of the living God; just as God said, 'I will dwell in them and walk among them; and I will be their God, and they shall be My people'" (NASB).

not primarily in church services (though they are important) but primarily in daily expressions of allegiance to God.

The fundamental reason for this is probably that the Old Testament was mainly a "come see" religion and the New Testament fulfillment is a "go tell" religion. In other words, while the focus was on the people Israel in one place, worship could be structured in fixed and formal ways. But once Jesus said, "Go make disciples of all nations"—all cultures, all languages, all temperaments—the issue of form almost vanished out of the New Testament. The New Testament is a missionary handbook. It is a book for all cultures. This is the fundamental reason for its sparing treatment of form in worship.

Now the crucial questions become: What is the essence of that inner experience which we call worship? If it is not essentially an outward act but an experience of the heart, what is that experience?

I take it as a given that worship—whether an inner act of the heart, or an outward act of the body, or of the congregation collectively—is *a magnifying of God*. That is, it is an act that shows how magnificent He is. It is an act that reveals or expresses how great and glorious He is. Worship is all about consciously reflecting the worth or value of God.

So the question I am asking is: What inner experience of the heart does that? If the essence of worship is not mere outward form but inner Godward experience, what experience reveals and expresses how great and glorious God is? To answer that question we go to Philippians 1:20–21.

Notice from verse 20 what Paul's mission in life is. He says it is "my earnest expectation and hope, that I will not be put to shame in anything, but that with all boldness, Christ will even now, as always, be exalted [this is the key word, "magnified," "shown to be great"] in my body, whether by life or by death" (NASB). In other words, Paul's passion is that what he does with his body, whether in life or death, will always be worship. In life and death his mission is to magnify Christ—to show that Christ is magnificent, to exalt Christ, and demonstrate that He is great. That's plain from verse 20, that Christ shall be "exalted in my body, whether by life or death."

The questions now become: Does Paul tell us what kind of inner experience exalts Christ in this way? Does he reveal the essence of worship? The answer is that he does, and he does so in the next verse (v. 21).

Notice the reference to "life" and "death" in verse 20, that Christ shall be "exalted in my body, whether by *life or death*" (NASB), and then notice the link with the corresponding words "live" and "die" in the next verse (21): "For to me to *live* is Christ, and to *die* is gain." So "life" and "death" in verse 20 correspond to "live" and "die" in verse 21. And the connection between the two verses is that verse 21 is the *basis* for how living and dying can exalt or magnify Christ. We know that because verse 21 begins with "for" or "because." My expectation and hope is that Christ will be exalted whether by my life or my death, *for (because)* to live is Christ and to die is gain.

Verse 21 describes the inner experience that exalts Christ and is the essence of worship. To see this let's take each pair separately, starting with "death" in verse 20 and "die" in verse 21. Boil down the verses to read: "*My expectation and hope is that Christ will be exalted in my body by death, for to me to die is gain.*" Christ will be exalted in my dying, if my dying is for me gain. Do you see it? The inner experience that magnifies Christ in dying is to experience death as gain.

Why is that? Verse 23 shows why dying is gain for Paul: "My desire is to depart and be with Christ, for that is far better." That is what death does: it takes us into more intimacy with Christ. We depart, and we are with Christ in such a way that it is "far better" than our experience of Him here. And that, Paul says, is gain. And when you experience death this way, Paul says, you exalt Christ. Experiencing Christ as gain in your dying magnifies Christ. It is the inner essence of worship in the hour of death.

We can now say that the inner essence of worship is cherishing Christ as gain, indeed as more gain than all that life can offer—family, career, retirement, fame, food, friends. The essence of worship is experiencing Christ as gain. Or to use words that we love to use around our church: it is savoring Christ, treasuring Christ, being satisfied with Christ. These are the inner essence of worship. Because, Paul says, experiencing Christ as gain in death is the way He is exalted in death.

This is where I get the maxim, "God is most glorified in us when we are most satisfied in Him." Christ is magnified in my death, when in my death I am satisfied with Him, when I experience death as gain because I gain Him. Or another way to say it is that the essence of praising Christ is prizing Christ. Christ will be praised in my death, if in my death He is prized above life. The inner essence of worship is prizing Christ. Cherishing Him, treasuring Him, being satisfied with Him.

Now to confirm this, focus with me on the other pair of words. "My expectation is that Christ will . . . be exalted in my *life*" (verse 20 JP). Verse 21: "For to me to *live* is Christ." So the reason Paul gives that Christ is exalted, or worshiped, in his life is that for him "to live is Christ." What does that mean?

Philippians 3:8 gives the answer. There Paul says, "I count all things to be loss in view of the surpassing value of knowing Christ Jesus my Lord, for whom I have suffered the loss of all things, and count them but rubbish in order that I may gain Christ" (NASB).

"To live is Christ" means to count everything as loss in comparison to the value of gaining Christ. Notice the word *gain* turning up here again in 3:8 just as it did in 1:21. "To live is Christ" means experiencing Christ as gain *now*, not just in death.

Paul's point is that life and death, for a Christian, are acts of worship; they exalt Christ, magnify Him, and reveal and express His greatness when they come from an inner experience of treasuring Christ as gain. Christ is praised in death by being prized above life. And Christ is most glorified in life when we are most satisfied in Him even before death.

The authenticating, inner essence of worship is being satisfied with Christ, prizing Christ, cherishing Christ, treasuring Christ. You can see how this definition of the essence of worship is free from Sunday worship services. It encompasses all of life that flows from the heart. But it is tremendously relevant for understanding what worship services should be about. They are about "going hard after God."

When we say that what we do on Sunday morning is to "go hard after God," what we mean is that we are going hard after satisfaction in God, and going hard after God as our prize, and going hard after God as our treasure, our soul-food, our heart-delight, our spirit's pleasure. Or to put Christ in His rightful place—it means that we are going hard after all that God is for us in Jesus Christ, crucified and risen.

Now how might this help us navigate our way through the "worship wars" that bedevil our churches in these days? I mean the struggles about form (contemporary versus historic, worship songs versus hymns, organ versus guitar, dress up versus dress down, stand up versus sit down, band versus orchestra, team versus choir, silence versus conversation, etc.). I think it is of tremendous help. It has kept us together as a church through much discussion and transition.

This definition of worship gives the church an anchor in the storms. It helps immensely to be able to say what it is all about. Why do we do what we do? Answer: We do it either to express or awaken genuine, heartfelt satisfaction in all that God is for us in Christ. We stay riveted to the essence. What is happening in your heart toward the truth and beauty and worth of Jesus? If this is real, the formal details are secondary.

The Word will always be central (this is where we found our definition of worship! 2 Tim. 4:2). The Lord's Supper will remain a permanent ordinance for the worshiping community (1 Cor. 11:23–26). Singing will always be a part of Christian worship (whether in church or home or in the car, Eph. 5:19). But the details of how to put it all together in "worship services" is not laid down for us. Only the essence is radically clear and radically important.

Even though many Christians today esteem tradition perhaps too highly (though tradition is to be esteemed), it was this remarkable inward reality of worship and the resulting freedom that gripped the Reformers, Calvin, Luther, and especially the Puritans. John Calvin expresses the freedom of worship from traditional form like this:

> [The Master] did not will in outward discipline and ceremonies to prescribe in detail what we ought to do (because he foresaw that this depended on the state of the times, and he did not deem one form suitable for all ages). . . . Because he has taught nothing specifically, and because these things are not necessary to salvation, and for the upbuilding of the church ought to be variously accommodated to the customs of each nation and age, it will be fitting (as the advantage of the church will require) to change and abrogate traditional practices and to establish new ones. Indeed, I admit that we ought not to charge into innovation rashly, suddenly, for insufficient cause. But love will best judge what may hurt or edify; and if we let love be our guide, all will be safe.[3]

3. John Calvin, *Institutes of the Christian Religion,* ed. by John T. McNeill (Philadelphia, Pa.: Westminster Press, 1960), 1,208. (*Institutes,* IV, 10, 30).

Luther has his usual abrasive way of expressing the same thing:

> The worship of God . . . should be free at table, in private rooms, downstairs, upstairs, at home, abroad, in all places, by all people, at all times. Whoever tells you anything else is lying as badly as the pope and the devil himself.[4]

The Puritans carried through the simplification and freedom of worship in music and liturgy and architecture. Patrick Collinson summarizes Puritan theory and practice by saying that "the life of the puritan was in one sense a continuous act of worship, pursued under an unremitting and lively sense of God's providential purposes and constantly refreshed by religious activity, personal, domestic and public."[5] One of the reasons Puritans called their churches "meeting houses" and kept them simple was to divert attention from the physical place to the inward, spiritual nature of worship.

The implications for corporate worship of what we have seen in this chapter are many and significant. For example, the pursuit of joy in God is not optional. It is our highest duty (see chapter 7, "Brothers, Consider Christian Hedonism"). Millions of Christians have absorbed a popular ethic that says it is morally defective to seek our happiness, even in God. This is absolutely deadly for authentic worship. To the degree that this ethic flourishes, worship dies because the essence of worship is satisfaction in God.

It will transform your pastoral leadership in worship if you teach your people that the basic attitude of worship on Sunday morning

4. Quoted in *What Luther Says*, vol. III, ed. by Ewald M. Plass (St. Louis, Mo.: Concordia Publishing House, 1959), 1, 546.
5. Quoted in Leland Ryken, *Worldly Saints: The Puritans as They Really Were* (Grand Rapids, Mich.: Zondervan Publishing House, 1986), 116.

is not to come with your hands full to give to God but with your hands empty to receive from God. And what you receive in worship is God, not entertainment. Teach them that they ought to come hungry for God. Come saying, "As a deer pants for flowing springs, so pants my soul for you, O God" (Ps. 42:1). God is mightily honored when a people know that they will die of hunger and thirst unless they have God. Recovering the rightness and indispensability of pursuing our satisfaction in God will go a long way to restoring authenticity and power of worship—whatever the forms.

Another implication of focusing on the essence of worship as satisfaction in God is that worship becomes radically God centered.[6] Nothing makes God more supreme and more central than when a people are utterly persuaded that nothing—not money or prestige or leisure or family or job or health or sports or toys or friends—is going to bring satisfaction to their aching hearts besides God. This conviction breeds a people who passionately long for God on Sunday morning. They are not confused about why they are here. They do not see songs and prayers and sermons as mere traditions or mere duties. They see them as means of getting to God or God getting to them for more of His fullness.

If the focus shifts onto our giving to God, one result I have seen again and again is that, subtly, it is not God that remains at the center but the quality of our giving. Are we singing worthily of the Lord? Are our instrumentalists playing with quality fitting a gift to the Lord? Is the preaching a suitable offering to the Lord? And little by little the focus shifts off the utter indispensability of the Lord Himself onto the quality of our performances. And we even start to define excellence and power in worship in terms of the technical distinction of our artistic acts.

---

6. This and the next six paragraphs are contained in John Piper, *The Dangerous Duty of Delight* (Sisters, Oreg.: Multnomah Publishers, 2001), 57–59 and printed here with permission.

Nothing keeps God at the center of worship like the Biblical conviction that the essence of worship is deep, heartfelt satisfaction in Him and the conviction that the pursuit of that satisfaction is why we are together.

A third implication of focusing on the essence of worship as satisfaction in God is that it protects the primacy of worship by forcing us to come to terms with the fact that worship is an end in itself.

If the inward essence of worship is satisfaction in God, then worship can't be a means to anything else. You simply can't say to God, I want to be satisfied in You so that I can have something else. Because that would mean you are not really satisfied in God but in something else. And that would dishonor God, not worship Him.

But in fact for thousands of people and pastors, I fear, the event of "worship" on Sunday morning is conceived of as a means to accomplish something other than worship. We "worship" to raise money; we "worship" to attract crowds; we "worship" to heal human hurts; we "worship" to recruit workers; we "worship" to improve church morale. We "worship" to give talented musicians an opportunity to fulfill their calling; we "worship" to teach our children the way of righteousness; we "worship" to help marriages stay together; we "worship" to evangelize the lost among us; we "worship" to motivate people for service projects; we "worship" to give our churches a family feeling, etc.

In all of this we bear witness that we are confused about what true worship is. Genuine affections for God are an end in themselves. I cannot say to my wife, "I feel a strong delight in you so that you will make me a nice meal." That is not the way delight works. It terminates on her. It does not have a nice meal in view. I cannot say to my son, "I love playing ball with you so that you will cut the grass." If my heart really delights in playing ball with him, that delight cannot be performed as a means to getting him to do something.

I am not denying that authentic worship may have a hundred good effects on the life of the church. It will—just as true affection in marriage makes everything better. My point is that to the degree that we "do worship" for these reasons, to that degree it ceases to be worship. Keeping satisfaction in God at the center guards us from that tragedy.

Therefore, brothers, focus on the essence of worship, not on the form. Yes, I know that we do not have the luxury of ignoring the forms. I live where you live. So let me close this chapter with something that might be practically helpful at this particular point. When you have spent years preaching and teaching and trying to live the priority of the essence and worship, you may still have to navigate through the storms of controversy. I certainly did. It lasted for about four or five years. At one point of crisis, I formulated what I thought would hold us together. It did. I preached it. I taught it. I tried to live it. And God was merciful to use it to keep us together and bring us into days of relative peace. I will reproduce it here just as I printed it for our people.

What Unites Us in Worship
A Philosophy of Music and Worship
at Bethlehem Baptist Church

1. *God-centeredness.* A high priority on the vertical focus of our Sunday morning service. The ultimate aim is to so experience God that He is glorified in our affections.

2. *Expecting the powerful presence of God.* We do not just direct ourselves toward Him. We earnestly seek His drawing near according to the promise of James 4:8. We believe that in worship God draws near to us in power and makes

Himself known and felt for our good and for the salvation of unbelievers in our midst.

3. *Bible based and Bible saturated.* The content of our singing and praying and welcoming and preaching and poetry will always conform to the truth of Scripture. The content of God's Word woven through all we do in worship and will be the ground of all our appeal to authority.

4. *Head and heart.* Worship aims at kindling and carrying deep, strong, real emotions toward God but does not manipulate people's emotions by failing to appeal to clear thinking about spiritual things based on shareable evidences outside ourselves.

5. *Earnestness and intensity.* Avoid a trite, flippant, superficial, frivolous atmosphere but instead set an example of reverence and passion and wonder.

6. *Authentic communication.* Utterly renounce all sham and deceit and hypocrisy and pretense and affectation and posturing. Avoid the atmosphere of artistic or oratorical performance, but cultivate the atmosphere of a radically personal encounter with God and truth.

7. *The manifestation of God and the common good.* We expect and hope and pray (according to 1 Cor. 12:7) that our focus on the manifesting of God is good for people and that therefore a spirit of love for one another is not incompatible with but necessary to authentic worship.

8. *Undistracting excellence.* We will try to sing and play and pray and preach in such a way that people's attention will not be diverted from the substance by shoddy ministry nor by excessive finesse, elegance, or refinement. Natural,

undistracting excellence will let the truth and beauty of God shine through.

9. *The mingling of historic and contemporary music.* "And he said to them, 'Therefore every scribe who has been trained for the kingdom of heaven is like a master of a house who brings out of his treasure what is new and what is old'" (Matt. 13:52).

> If you live for your private pleasure at the expense of your spouse,
> you are living against yourself and destroying your own highest joy.
> But if you devote yourself with all your heart
> to the holy joy of your spouse,
> you will also be living for your joy
> and making a marriage after the image of Christ and His church.
>
> JOHN PIPER

> A double rule of love that shocks;
> A doctrine in a paradox:
> If you now aim your wife to bless,
> Then love her more and love her less.
>
> JOHN PIPER

29

BROTHERS, LOVE YOUR WIVES

OH, HOW CRUCIAL it is that pastors love their wives. It delights and encourages the church. It models marriage for the other couples. It upholds the honor of the office of elder. It blesses the pastor's children with a haven of love. It displays the mystery of Christ's love for the church. It prevents our prayers from being hindered. It eases the burdens of the ministry. It protects the church from devastating scandal. And it satisfies the soul as we find our joy in God by pursuing it in the joy of the beloved. This is not marginal, brothers. Loving our wives is essential for our ministry. It is ministry.

I know that there is no final guarantee in our love that she will always respond with joy. Tragically some wives forsake Christ and the church and their brokenhearted husbands. Few things are more painful and devastating for family and church. Short of that, some wives struggle with depression or various addictions or temptations of sloth or worldliness or fear or greed. So I do not mean that love will always make everything rosy. That is not the point. The point is that in marriage and ministry this is our calling, just as it was the calling of Christ to love and die for an unclean bride. Loving her like this will bless the church and strengthen our own souls for the wider world of Christ.

So let us ponder the meaning of marriage, and let the apostle Paul put our marriages on the rock-solid foundation of the Word of God.

Paul's theology of marriage starts with the Word of God, the Word of God who is Jesus Christ and the Word of God which is the inspired Old Testament. And since God is not a God of confusion, His Word is coherent. It has unity. So when Paul wants to understand marriage, he looks to the Word of God—Jesus and the Scriptures. When he brings Christ and Scripture together to hear God's Word on marriage, what he hears is a profound mystery with intensely practical implications. Let's explore the mystery and apply the implications to our pastoral lives.

Ephesians 5:31 is a quotation of Genesis 2:24, "Therefore a man shall leave his father and mother and hold fast to his wife, and the two shall become one flesh." Then Paul adds in verse 32, "This mystery is profound, and I am saying that it refers to Christ and the church." Paul knew something about Christ and the church which caused him to see in Genesis 2:24 a mystery in marriage. Let's go back to Genesis 2:24 and look more closely at the context of this verse and its connection with creation.

According to Genesis 2, God created Adam first and put him in the garden alone. Then in verse 18, the Lord said, "It is not good that the man should be alone; I will make him a helper fit for him." I don't think this is an indictment of Adam's fellowship with God; nor is it a hint that the garden was too hard to take care of. The point is that God made man to be a sharer. God created us not to be cul-de-sacs of His bounty but conduits. No man is complete unless he is conducting grace (like electricity) between God and another person. (No unmarried person should conclude that this can happen only in marriage.)[1]

It must be another *person*, not an animal. So in Genesis 2:19–20, God paraded the animals before Adam to show him that animals would never do as a "helper fit for him." Oh, animals help plenty! But only a *person* can be a fellow heir of the grace of life (1 Pet. 1:4–7). Only a person can receive and appreciate and enjoy grace. What man needs is another *person* with whom he can share the love of God. Animals will not do! There is an infinite difference between sharing the northern lights with your beloved and sharing them with your dog.

Therefore, according to verses 21 and 22, "The LORD God caused a deep sleep to fall upon the man, and while he slept [God] took one of [Adam's] ribs and closed up its place with flesh. And the rib that the LORD God had taken from the man he made into a woman and brought her to the man." Having shown the man that no animal would do for his helper, God made another human from man's own flesh and bone to be like him—and yet unlike him. He did not create

1. See John Piper, "For Single Men and Women (and the Rest of Us)" (Wheaton, Ill.: Council on Biblical Manhood & Womanhood, 1992). This is taken from the larger work *Recovering Biblical Manhood and Womanhood: A Response to Evangelical Feminism*, ed. by John Piper and Wayne Grudem (Wheaton, Ill.: Crossway Books, 1991), xvii–xxviii.

another man. He created a woman. And Adam recognized in her the perfect counterpart to himself, utterly different from the animals: "This at last is bone of my bones and flesh of my flesh; she shall be called Woman, because she was taken out of Man" (Gen. 2:23).

By creating a person *like* Adam yet very *unlike* Adam, God provided the possibility of a profound unity that would otherwise have been impossible. A different kind of unity is enjoyed by the joining of diverse counterparts than is enjoyed by joining two things just alike. When we all sing the same melody line it is called "unison," which means "one sound." But when we unite diverse lines of soprano and alto and tenor and bass, we call it harmony, and everyone who has an ear to hear knows that something is touched in us more deeply by great harmony than by unison. So God made a woman and not another man. He created heterosexuality, not homosexuality. God's first institution was marriage, not the fraternity.

Notice the connection between verses 23 and 24, signaled by the word *therefore* in verse 24. "Then the man said, 'This at last is bone of my bones and flesh of my flesh; she shall be called Woman, because she was taken out of Man.' *Therefore* a man shall leave his father and his mother and hold fast to his wife, and they shall become one flesh." In verse 23, the focus is on two things: *objectively,* the fact that woman is part of man's flesh and bone; *subjectively,* the joy Adam has in being presented with the woman. "*At last* this is bone of my bones and flesh of my flesh!" From these two things the writer draws an inference about marriage in verse 24: "*Therefore* a man shall leave his father and his mother and hold fast to his wife, and they shall become one flesh."

In other words, in the beginning God took woman out of man as bone of his bone and flesh of his flesh, and then God presented her back to the man so man could discover *in living fellowship* what it means to be one flesh. Then verse 24 draws out the lesson that marriage is just that: a man *leaving* father and mother because God has given him another, a cleaving to this woman and no other, and discovering the experience of being one flesh. That's what Paul saw when he looked at the Word of God in Scripture.

But Paul knew another Word of God—Jesus Christ. He knew Him deeply and intimately. He had learned from Jesus that the church is Christ's body (Eph. 1:23). By faith a person is joined to Jesus Christ and to other believers so that we "are all one in Christ Jesus" (Gal. 3:28). Believers in Christ are the body of Christ; we are the organism through which He manifests His life and in which His Spirit dwells.

Knowing this about the relationship between Christ and the church, Paul sees a parallel here with marriage. He sees that husband and wife become one flesh (according to Gen. 2:24) and that Christ and the church become one body. So he is willing to say, to the church, for example in 2 Corinthians 11:2, "I feel a divine jealousy for you, for I betrothed you to one husband to present you as a pure virgin to Christ." He pictures Christ as the husband, the church as the bride, and their conversion as an act of betrothal which he had helped bring about. The presentation of the bride to her husband will probably happen at the Second Coming of the Lord, described in Ephesians 5:27 ("that he might present the church to himself in splendor"). So it looks as though Paul uses the relationship of human marriage, learned from Genesis 2, to describe and explain the relationship between Christ and the church.

But when we say it like that, something important is overlooked. After quoting Genesis 2:24 in Ephesians 5:31 (about the man and woman becoming one flesh), Paul says, in verse 32, "This mystery is profound, and I am saying that it refers to Christ and the church." Marriage is a mystery. There is more here than meets the eye. What is it? I think it's this: God didn't create the union of Christ and the church after the pattern of human marriage; just the reverse, He created human marriage on the pattern of Christ's relation to the church. The long-unrevealed mystery of Genesis 2:24 is that the marriage it describes is a parable or symbol of Christ's relation to His people.

God doesn't do things willy-nilly. Everything has purpose and meaning. When God engaged to create man and woman and to ordain the union of marriage, He didn't roll dice or draw straws or flip a coin. He patterned marriage purposefully after the relationship between His Son and the church, which He planned from eternity. And therefore marriage is a mystery; it contains and conceals a meaning far greater than what we see on the outside. What God has joined together in marriage is to be a reflection of the union between the Son of God and His bride the church. Those of us who are married need to ponder again and again how mysterious and wonderful it is that we are granted by God the privilege to image forth stupendous divine realities infinitely bigger and greater than ourselves.

Now what are some of the practical implications of this mystery of marriage? I'll mention the two which seem to dominate the passage in Ephesians. One is that *husbands and wives should consciously copy the relationship God intended for Christ and His church*. The other is that in marriage each partner should pursue his or her own joy in the *joy of* the other; that is, marriage should be a matrix of Christian hedonism (see chapter 7, "Brothers, Consider Christian Hedonism").

First, what pattern did God intend for husbands and wives when He ordained marriage as a mysterious parable or image of the relation between Christ and the church? Paul mentions two things, one to the wife and one to the husband. To the wife he says in 5:22–24:

> Wives, submit to your own husbands, as to the Lord.
> For the husband is the head of the wife even as Christ is
> the head of the church, his body, and is himself its Savior.

Now as the church submits to Christ, so also wives should submit in everything to their husbands.

According to the divine pattern, wives are to take their unique cue from the purpose of the church. As the church submits to Christ, so wives are to submit to their husbands. The church submits to Christ as her head: "The husband is the head of the wife as Christ is the head of the church" (v. 23). Headship implies at least two things: Christ is supplier or Savior, and Christ is authority or leader. "Head" is used two other times in Ephesians. Ephesians 4:15–16 illustrates the head as supplier, and Ephesians 1:20–23 illustrates the head as authority.

First consider Ephesians 4:15–16:

> Speaking the truth in love, we are to grow up in every
> way into him who is the *head*, into Christ, from whom the
> whole body, joined and held together by every joint with
> which it is equipped, when each part is working properly,
> makes the body grow so that it builds itself up in love.

The head is the goal to which we grow and the supply which enables the growth.

Then consider Ephesians 1:20–23:

> God raised him from the dead and made him sit at his
> right hand in the heavenly places, far above every rule and
> authority and power and dominion and above every name
> that is named not only in this age but also in the age to
> come, and he has put all things under his feet and has
> made him the *head over all things* for the church, which is
> his body, the fullness of him who fills all in all (JP).

When God raised Christ from the dead, He made Him head in the sense of giving Him power and authority over all other rule and authority and power and dominion. Therefore, from the context of Ephesians, the headship of the husband implies that as far as possible he should accept the greater responsibility for supplying the needs of his wife (including material needs, but also protection and care) and he should accept greater responsibility for leadership in the family.

Then when it says in verse 24, "As the church submits to Christ, so also wives should submit in everything to their husbands," the basic meaning of submission would be: recognize and honor the greater responsibility of your husband to supply your protection and sustenance; be disposed to yield to his authority in Christ, and be inclined to follow his leadership. The reason I say that submission means a *disposition* to yield and an *inclination* to follow is that the little phrase "as to the Lord" in verse 22 limits the scope of submission.

No wife should replace the authority of Christ with the authority of her husband. She cannot yield or follow her husband into sin. But even where a Christian wife may have to stand with Christ against the sinful will of her husband, she can still have a *spirit* of submission. She can show by her attitude and behavior that she does not like resisting his will and that she longs for him to forsake sin and lead in righteousness so that her disposition to honor him as head can again produce harmony. So in this mysterious parable of marriage, the wife is to take her special cue from God's purpose to the church in its relation to Christ.

Now to the husbands, Paul says, take your special cue from Christ. Verse 25: "Husbands, love your wives, as Christ loved the church and gave himself up for her." If the husband is the head of the wife as verse 23 says, let it be plain to all husbands that this means primarily leading out in the kind of love that is willing to die to give her life. As Jesus says in Luke 22:26, "Let the leader become as one who serves" (JP). The husband who plops himself down in front of the TV and orders his wife around like a slave has abandoned Christ's way of leading. Christ bound Himself with a towel and washed the apostles' feet. If you want to be a Christian husband, copy Jesus.

It is true that verse 21 puts this whole section under the sign of *mutual submission,* "submitting to one another out of reverence for Christ." But it is utterly unwarranted to infer from this verse that the *way* Christ submits Himself to the church and the way the church submits herself to Christ are the same.[2] The church submits to Christ by a disposition to follow His leadership. Christ submits to the church by a disposition to exercise His leadership in humble service to the church. When Christ said, "Let the leader become as one who serves" (Luke 22:26 JP), He did not mean, let the leader cease to be leader. Even while He was on His knees washing their feet, no one doubted who the leader was. Nor should any Christian husband shirk his responsibility under God to provide moral vision and spiritual leadership as the humble servant of his wife and family.

So the first implication of the mystery of marriage as a reflection of Christ's relation to the church is that wives should take their special cue from the church and husbands should take their special cue from Christ. And wherever you find a marriage like that, you find two of the happiest people in the world because their lives conform to the Word of God in Scripture and the Word of God in Jesus Christ.

One final, practical implication of the mystery of marriage: *a husband and wife should pursue their own joy in the joy of each other.* There is scarcely a more hedonistic passage in the Bible than Ephesians 5:25–30. This text makes clear that the reason there is so much misery in marriages is not that husbands and wives are seeking their own pleasure but that they are not seeking it in the

---

2. Note also the context, wherein children are in submission to their parents (Eph. 6:1ff) and slaves are in submission to their masters (Eph. 6:5ff), which rules out the idea that the submission between parties is identical.

pleasure of their spouses. But this text commands us to do just that because Christ does.

First, notice the example of Christ in verses 25–27:

> Husbands, love your wives as Christ loved the church and gave himself up for her, [why did he?] that he might sanctify her, having cleansed her by the washing of water with the word, [why did he cleanse her?] so that he might present the church *to himself* in splendor, without spot or wrinkle or any such thing, that she might be holy and without blemish.

Christ died for the church in order that He might present "to himself" a beautiful bride. He endured the cross for the joy of marriage that was set before Him. But what is the ultimate joy of the church? Is it not to be presented as a bride to the sovereign Christ? So Christ sought His own joy in the joy of the church. Therefore, the example Christ sets for husbands is to seek our joy in the joy of our wives.

Verses 28 and 29 make this application explicit. "In the same way husbands should love their wives as their own bodies. He who loves his wife loves himself. For no man ever hates his own flesh, but nourishes and cherishes it." Paul acknowledges one of the foundation stones of Christian hedonism: "No man ever hates his own flesh." Even those who commit suicide do it to escape misery. By nature we love ourselves, that is, we do what, in the moment, we think will make us happy or reduce our misery.

Paul does not build a dam against the river of this hedonism; he builds a channel for it. He says, "Husbands and wives, recognize that in marriage you have to become one flesh; therefore, if you live for your private pleasure at the expense of your spouse, you are living against yourself and destroying your own highest joy. But if you devote yourself with all your heart to the holy joy of your spouse, you will also be living for your joy and making a marriage after the image of Christ and his church."

When my oldest son was married, he asked me to write a poem to be read at the wedding. I was happy to do it. I include it in closing because it says, as well as I know how, the paradoxical truth that we should love our wives more than we do and less than we might.

Love Her More and Love Her Less
For Karsten Luke Piper
At His Wedding to
Rochelle Ann Orvis
May 29, 1995

The God whom we have loved, and in
Whom we have lived, and who has been
Our Rock these twenty-two good years
With you, now bids us, with sweet tears,
To let you go: "A man shall leave
His father and his mother, cleave
Henceforth unto his wife, and be
One unashaméd flesh and free."
This is the word of God today,
And we are happy to obey.
For God has given you a bride
Who answers every prayer we've cried
For over twenty years, our claim
For you, before we knew her name.

And now you ask that I should write
A poem—a risky thing, in light
Of what you know: that I am more
The preacher than the poet or

The artist. I am honored by
Your bravery, and I comply.
I do not grudge these sweet confines
Of rhyming pairs and metered lines.
They are old friends. They like it when
I bid them help me once again
To gather feelings into form
And keep them durable and warm.

And so we met in recent days,
And made the flood of love and praise
And counsel from a father's heart
To flow within the banks of art.
Here is a portion of the stream,
My son: a sermon poem. It's theme:
A double rule of love that shocks;
A doctrine in a paradox:

If you now aim your wife to bless,
Then love her more and love her less.

If in the coming years, by some
Strange providence of God, you come
To have the riches of this age,
And, painless, stride across the stage
Beside your wife, be sure in health
To love her, love her more than wealth.

And if your life is woven in
A hundred friendships, and you spin
A festal fabric out of all

Your sweet affections, great and small,
Be sure, no matter how it rends,
To love her, love her more than friends.

And if there comes a point when you
Are tired, and pity whispers, "Do
Yourself a favor. Come, be free;
Embrace the comforts here with me."
Know this! Your wife surpasses these:
So love her, love her, more than ease.

And when your marriage bed is pure,
And there is not the slightest lure
Of lust for any but your wife,
And all is ecstasy in life,
A secret all of this protects:
Go love her, love her, more than sex.

And if your taste becomes refined,
And you are moved by what the mind
Of man can make, and dazzled by
His craft, remember that the "why"
Of all this work is in the heart;
So love her, love her more than art.

And if your own should someday be
The craft that critics all agree
Is worthy of a great esteem,
And sales exceed your wildest dream,
Beware the dangers of a name.
And love her, love her more than fame.

And if, to your surprise, not mine,
God calls you by some strange design
To risk your life for some great cause,
Let neither fear nor love give pause,
And when you face the gate of death,
Then love her, love her more than breath.

Yes, love her, love her, more than life;
O, love the woman called your wife.
Go love her as your earthly best.

Beyond this venture not. But, lest
Your love become a fool's facade,
Be sure to love her less than God.

It is not wise or kind to call
An idol by sweet names, and fall,
As in humility, before
A likeness of your God. Adore
Above your best beloved on earth
The God alone who gives her worth.
And she will know in second place
That your great love is also grace,
And that your high affections now
Are flowing freely from a vow
Beneath these promises, first made
To you by God. Nor will they fade
For being rooted by the stream
Of Heaven's Joy, which you esteem
And cherish more than breath and life,
That you may give it to your wife.

The greatest gift you give your wife
Is loving God above her life.
And thus I bid you now to bless:
Go love her more by loving less.

> The tone of the classrooms and teachers
> exerts profound effect on the tone of our pulpits.
> What the teachers are passionate about
> will by and large be the passions of our younger pastors.
> What they neglect
> will likely be neglected in the pulpits.
>
> JOHN PIPER
>
> Let us not merely criticize or commend the seminaries.
> Rather, let us pray for them.
>
> JOHN PIPER

30

BROTHERS, PRAY FOR THE SEMINARIES

WE CANNOT overemphasize the importance of our seminaries in shaping the theology and spirit of the churches and denominations and missionary enterprise. The tone of the classrooms and teachers exerts profound effect on the tone of our pulpits. What the teachers are passionate about will by and large be the passions of our younger pastors. What they neglect will likely be neglected in the pulpits.

When I was choosing a seminary, someone gave me good advice. "A seminary is one thing"—he told me, "faculty. Do not choose a denomination or a library or a location. Choose a great faculty. Everything else is incidental." By "great faculty" he, of course, did not mean mere charismatic personalities. He meant that wonderful combination of passion for God, for truth, for the church, and for the perishing, along with a deep understanding of God and His Word, a high esteem for doctrinal truth and careful interpretation and exposition of the infallible Bible.

I believe his advice was right: choose a seminary for its teachers. Which means that when we pray for our seminaries, we pray especially for the minds and hearts of faculty and those who assess and hire them.

When we stop to think for a while about what to pray, we start to clarify our own concept of ministry. We can't pray without a goal. And we can't have a goal for a seminary faculty unless we have a vision for what kind of pastors we want to see graduate. So the more we try to pray, the more we are forced to define what we value in the pastoral office. And once we clarify this, we begin to ponder what sort of person and pedagogy cultivates these values.

So the will to pray for the seminary presses us on to develop at least a rudimentary pastoral theology and philosophy of theological education. What follows is a baby step in this direction, a rough sketch of what I think we need from our seminaries. My petitions cluster in three groups. Each group echoes a Biblical value at which I think we should aim, and toward which we should pray, in pastoral education.

Under the all-embracing goal of God's glory (first petition), petitions 2–7 echo my goal that we cultivate a contrite and humble sense of human insufficiency. "I am the vine, you are the branches. . . . Apart from me you can do nothing" (John 15:5). "We have this treasure in earthen vessels, so that the surpassing greatness of the power will be of God and not from ourselves" (2 Cor. 4:7 NASB). "Who is sufficient for these things?" (2 Cor. 2:16).

Petitions 8–11 echo my goal that we cultivate a great passion for Christ's all-sufficiency and that, for all our enthusiasm over contemporary trends in ministry, the overwhelming zeal of a pastor's heart be for the changeless fundamentals of the faith. "Whatever things were gain to me, those things I have counted as loss for the sake of Christ. More than that, I count all things to be loss in view of the surpassing value of knowing Christ Jesus my Lord" (Phil. 3:7–8 NASB).

Petitions 12–20 echo my goal that we cultivate strong allegiance to all of Scripture and that what the apostles and prophets preached and taught in Scripture will be esteemed worthy of our careful and faithful exposition to God's people. "Do your best to present yourself to God as one approved, a workman who has no need to be ashamed, rightly handling the word of truth" (2 Tim. 2:15).

You will want to supplement these prayers with the burdens of your own heart for the seminaries you care about most deeply. But these are essential, I think, to breed power and purity in our churches.

I pray:

1. That the supreme, heartfelt, and explicit goal of every faculty member might be to teach and live in such a way that his students come to admire the glory of God with white-hot intensity (1 Cor. 10:31; Matt. 5:16).

2. That, among the many ways this goal can be sought, the whole faculty will seek it by the means suggested in 1 Peter 4:11: Serve "in the strength which God supplies: in order that in everything God may be glorified through Jesus Christ."

3. That the challenge of the ministry might be presented in such a way that the question rises authentically in students' hearts: "Who is sufficient for these things?" (2 Cor. 2:16).

4. That in every course the indispensable and precious enabling of the Holy Spirit will receive significant emphasis in comparison to other means of ministerial success (Gal. 3:5).

5. That teachers will cultivate the pastoral attitude expressed in 1 Corinthians 15:10 and Romans 15:18: "I worked harder than any of them, though it was not I, but the grace of God which is with me. . . . I will not venture to speak of anything except what Christ has accomplished through me to bring the Gentiles to obedience by word and deeds."

6. That the poverty of spirit commended in Matthew 5:3 and the lowliness and meekness commended in Colossians 3:12 and Ephesians 4:2 and 1 Peter 5:5–6 be manifested through the administration, faculty, and student body.

7. That the faculty might impress upon students by precept and example the immense pastoral need to pray without ceasing and to despair of all success without persevering prayer in reliance on God's free mercy (Matt. 7:7–11; Eph. 6:18).

8. That the faculty will help the students feel what an unutterably precious thing it is to be treated mercifully by the holy God, even though we deserve to be punished in hell forever (Matt. 25:46; 18:23–35; Luke 7:42, 47).

9. That, because of our seminary faculties, hundreds of pastors, fifty years from now, will repeat the words of John Newton on their deathbeds: "My memory is nearly gone;

but I remember two things: that I am a great sinner and that Jesus is a great Savior."[1]

10. That the faculty will inspire students to unqualified and exultant joy in the venerable verities of Scripture. "The precepts of the LORD are right, rejoicing the heart" (Ps. 19:8).

11. That every teacher will develop a pedagogical style based on James Denney's maxim: "No man can give the impression that he himself is clever and that Christ is mighty to save."[2]

12. That in the treatment of Scripture there will be no truncated estimation of what is valuable for preaching and for life.

13. That students will develop a respect for and use of the awful warnings of Scripture as well as its precious promises; and that the command to "pursue holiness" (Heb. 12:14 JP) will not be blunted, but empowered, by the assurance of divine enablement. "Now the God of peace . . . equip you in every good thing to do His will, working in us that which is pleasing in His sight, through Jesus Christ, to whom be the glory forever and ever. Amen" (Heb. 13:20–21 NASB).

14. That there might be a strong and evident conviction that the deep and constant study of Scripture is the best way to become wise in dealing with people's problems. "All Scripture is inspired by God and profitable for teaching, for reproof, for correction, for training in righteousness; so that the man of God may be adequate, equipped *for every good work*" (2 Tim. 3:16–17 NASB).

---

1. Quoted in John Whitecross, *The Shorter Catechism Illustrated* (Edinburgh: The Banner of Truth Trust, 1968), 37.

2. Quoted in John Stott, *Between Two Worlds: The Art of Preaching in the Twentieth Century* (Grand Rapids, Mich.: Wm. B. Eerdmans Publishing Co., 1982), 325.

15. That the faculty may not represent the contemporary mood in critical studies which sees "minimal unity, wide-ranging diversity" in the Bible; but that they will pursue the unified "whole counsel of God" and help students see the way it all fits together. "For I did not shrink from declaring to you the whole purpose of God" (Acts 20:27).

16. That *explicit Biblical* insights will permeate all class sessions, even when issues are treated with language and paradigms borrowed from contemporary sciences. That God and His Word will not be taken for granted as the tacit "foundation" that doesn't get talked about or admired.

17. That the faculty will mingle the "severe discipline" of textual analysis with an intense reverence for the truth and beauty of God's Word.

18. That fresh discoveries will be made in the study of Scripture and shared with the church through articles and books.

19. That faculty, deans, and presidents will have wisdom and courage from God to make appointments which promote the fulfillment of these petitions.

20. And that boards and all those charged with leadership will be vigilant over the moral and doctrinal faithfulness of the faculty and exercise whatever discipline is necessary to preserve the *Biblical* faithfulness of all that is taught and done.

Brothers, let us not merely criticize or commend the seminaries. God loves His church and His truth. He ordains to do His work through the intercession of His people. Generations of faithfulness are at stake. Therefore, brothers, let us pray for the seminaries.

NAME INDEX

SUBJECT INDEX

SCRIPTURE INDEX

22:3–4	180	14:22	137, 223
22:26	252, 253	16:1	192
22:31–32	179	16:15, 33	130
		16:31	102
John		16:32	130
3:16	5, 225	17:24–25	40
3:36	115	17:25	39
4	230	19:10	192
4:21–23	231	20:17	192
4:23	229	20:24	185
8:32	164	20:27	84, 102, 110, 266
8:34	48	20:28	84, 109
8:44	114	20:35	51, 143
9:2–3	183		
10:27–28	111	Romans	
11:33–35	175	1:9	231
12:27–28	8	1:17	20, 21
15:5	55, 262	3:1–8	98, 100, 102
15:11	51	3:4	26, 115
16:2	Ix	3:8	224
17:17	60, 164	3:19	115
20:21	196	3:21–22	28
		3:24–26	8
Acts		3:28	132
1:14	60, 62	4:3	25, 27
2:23	140	4:3, 5, 9, 22	31
2:38	127, 130	4:4	25
2:41	60	4:4–5	15, 41
2:42	60, 62	4:5	17, 17–18, 25, 26, 27
2:43, 47	60	4:6	28
4:27–28	140, 180, 184	4:9	27
4:31	60	4:11	28
6:2–4	60	4:22	27
6:3	61, 62	4:25	x
6:4	61	5:3	xiii
10:7	61	5:3–5	223
13:38–39	18	5:6	26
13:42–44	18	5:18	29

DESIRING GOD.ORG

Desiring God Ministries exists to spread a passion for the supremacy of God in all things for the joy of all peoples through Jesus Christ. We have hundreds of resources available for this purpose, most of which are books, sermons, and audio collections by John Piper. Visit our Web site and discover:

- Free access to over twenty years of printed sermons by John Piper
- Free, new downloadable audio sermons posted weekly
- Free articles and reviews
- A comprehensive online store where you may purchase John Piper's books and audio collections, as well as God-centred children's curricula published by DGM
- Information about DGM's international offices and translation work
- Information about the Bethlehem Conference for Pastors

Designed for individuals with no available discretionary funds, DGM has a *whatever-you-can-afford* policy. Contact us at the address or phone number below if you would like more information about this policy.

DESIRING GOD MINISTRIES
PO Box 2901, Minneapolis, Minnesota 55402-2901

Tel: 1-800-346-4700
Fax: 1-612-338-4372

mail@desiringGod.org
www.desiringGod.org

Christian Focus Publications

publishes books for all ages

Our mission statement –

STAYING FAITHFUL
In dependence upon God we seek to impact the world through literature faithful to His infallible Word, the Bible. Our aim is to ensure that the Lord Jesus Christ is presented as the only hope to obtain forgiveness of sin, live a useful life and look forward to heaven with Him.

REACHING OUT
Christ's last command requires us to reach out to our world with His gospel. We seek to help fulfill that by publishing books that point people towards Jesus and help them develop a Christ-like maturity. We aim to equip all levels of readers for life, work, ministry and mission.

Books in our adult range are published in three imprints.

Christian Focus contains popular works including biographies, commentaries, basic doctrine and Christian living. Our children's books are also published in this imprint.

Mentor focuses on books written at a level suitable for Bible College and seminary students, pastors, and other serious readers. The imprint includes commentaries, doctrinal studies, examination of current issues and church history.

Christian Heritage contains classic writings from the past.

Christian Focus Publications, Ltd
Geanies House, Fearn, Ross-shire,
IV20 1TW, Scotland, United Kingdom
www.christianfocus.com